Frozen Teardrop

Frozen Teardrop

The Tragedy and Triumph of
Figure Skating's "Queen of Spin"

LUCINDA RUH

SelectBooks, Inc.
New York

© Copyright 2011 by Lucinda Ruh

All rights reserved. Published in the United States of America. No part of this book may be reproduced or transmitted in any form or by any means, graphic, electronic, or mechanical, including photocopying, recording, taping or by any information storage or retrieval system, without the permission in writing from the publisher.

This edition published by SelectBooks, Inc.

For information address SelectBooks, Inc., New York, New York.

First Edition

ISBN 978-1-59079-213-1

Library of Congress Cataloging-in-Publication Data
Ruh, Lucinda.
Frozen teardrop : the tragedy and triumph of figure skating's "queen of spin" / Lucinda Ruh. -- 1st ed.
p. cm.
Summary: "World figure skating champion Lucinda Ruh, known as the "Queen of Spin" for her creative spinning and her holding of the Guinness world record for the longest spin on ice, tells her story of the harsh realities of the world of competitive figure skating to inspire young people to have the vision and strength to overcome adversity"--Provided by publisher.
ISBN 978-1-59079-213-1 (pbk. : alk. paper)
1. Ruh, Lucinda. 2. Figure skaters--Switzerland--Biography. 3. Women figure skaters--United States--Biography. I. Title.
GV850.R84A3 2011
796.912092--dc22
[B]
                              2011000511

Book design by Kathleen Isaksen

Manufactured in the United States of America
10 9 8 7 6 5 4 3 2 1

I dedicate this book from the depth of my heart to my mother and father who have given me the most precious gift of life, and for truly making me who I am today. I am grateful for their undying and eternal love that can never be surpassed and for their honorable permission to let me tell my story in my way, in hopes of helping others the best way I can. I love you more than ever and for eternity. I give my life to thee.

To my sister to whom I profoundly hope can come to realize that her little sister has always loved her more than she would ever know.

To my Antonio for his ever-growing and ever-lasting love, trust, and respect toward me each and every day. To him, for wiping away my tears as I relived my life and for believing in me.

To all the readers and my fans in whom I have laid my trust so that they may understand the journey of my life.

To God to whom I made a promise that I will make this world a better place in all the little ways I can.

To my fans who, most importantly, have given me the opportunity to spin my way into creations I could accomplish only because of their unwavering support when watching me create my paintings on ice.

Contents

Preface ix

1 Light from the Heavens 1
2 Playground Beneath the Eiffel Tower 14
3 The Three Curses or Blessings? 25
4 Tokyo Alien Girl 40
5 From the Outside Looking In 57
6 Culture Shock 85
7 Misunderstood and Crushed to Pieces 97
8 Chinese Dumplings 109
9 Unknown to Known 127
10 Pains of Error at the Expense of the Innocent 137
11 Beginning of an End 159
12 Broken Wing 169
13 Deadly Frozen 177
14 Terror 186
15 Glitz Within the Terror 196
16 Stars In or Out of Line 210
17 Doctors Galore 218
18 I Know 227
19 Finale and Opening the World to Me 233

Afterword: Being the Mother of Lucinda 239
About the Author 243

Preface

I have lived a privileged life in all the landscapes of my life. I was born into an incredibly loving family and blossomed into a world-class figure skater. I became famous for creating, designing, and performing the fastest and most creative spins in the world on ice, and I am still recognized today by *The Guinness Book of World Records* as the world's longest spinner on ice, and known in the skating community and around the world as the fastest and most creative spinner in the history of ice skating. I am profoundly grateful for the life I have lived and live today, and for everyone who supported me to mold me to become who I am. But much of my story has gone untold and much of my struggle and even my achievements have been kept from the public view. This book is my humble attempt to silence the demons and free the angels. I am hopeful that it will empower others to build on my victories while sparing them my costly mistakes. Most of all, this book is my thank-you to my parents for their undying love for me.

My affinity for loving to spin and loving to feel the freedom of continuous rotation came naturally to me from a very tender age, although a great deal of determination, sacrifice, and unforgiving and unrelenting hard work had to become the main priority in my life for me to be able to reach my ultimate magic on ice. Spinning became my passion, my love, my meditation, and my doorway to internal bliss. It was trance-inducing and provided me with something to focus upon and seek refuge in when other parts of my life became frightening, chaotic, lonely, or confusing. It took me away from the harshness of reality and what became the unwanted riches of my world. It allowed me to soar with the angels, at least for a time, and be whatever I wanted to be—

without those limitations and fears that can overpower and frighten a person of any age. It is known that I have traveled the world and have lived in a multitude of cultures in numerous countries with celebrities and government leaders welcoming me into their lives, but why and how this all surrounded me has eluded the public. It has been a wonderful journey that became more beautiful to me as I entered womanhood, and I'm grateful for all the memories and accolades that came with my experience. I am especially grateful for the friendships and the loyal fan support I continue to receive and that I try my best to honor. Throughout all the places I have lived, trained, toured, and sometimes just wandered, I have never forgotten the people who helped me in my hours of need. I never forgot those who loved me when I had difficulty loving myself, and I never forgot those who faithfully cheered me on while I wrestled with parts of myself they were never permitted to see.

This book, of course, is about more than skating, even though I address my skating development in full detail to honor those expecting a skating story and because skating is so fundamental to who I am and who I have become. Though presented through a skater's perspective, it is first and foremost a book about living, loving, and surviving in a world of increasing diversity and tolerance that, ironically, seems only to perpetuate with greater fervor the prejudices, battles, and mistakes of ages past. A lifetime would seem of little value to me if we learned nothing from it and passed nothing on to others. This book is my attempt to pass on what I have learned.

Frozen Teardrop is my story presented to the world in the hope that others might share in the successes I have known and learn from the mistakes I have made in order to allow others to reach even greater heights of success. It is a book intended for people of all ages, backgrounds, and interests, but it is written especially for the lonely, the lost, the frightened, and the abused who want to heal and have a new opportunity for a better life. Most importantly this is for those who have not realized that they are loved and do not recognize real love. I live to assure you that life is worth living—whatever its challenges, fears, disappointments, and humiliations. It's worth facing. It's worth doing. It's worth honoring. This book is my promise of these things to you. It is worth living as you are, and to be with those who love you with no bottom to their heart.

The image for which I am known is a true one. The spins were real, the skating was real, and all the pageantry, glamour, and celebrity were real. The smiles, sometimes, were not real. Many parts of my life were never exposed or admitted to even in my own mind. Most of my fans never knew what I endured behind the scenes or what I inflicted upon myself in my determination to make others proud of me. From eating too little, exercising too much, isolating myself from nearly everyone and everything, enduring both physical and mental abuse, becoming very sick and debilitated, to finally realizing how much I am loved, I learned the hard way that life is fragile, and that we can cheat our own self when we demand too much from ourselves, from others, and purely from life itself. Very few knew how close to death I came but now all can know how and why I decided to live. It is my hope and prayer that you will also choose to live and live abundantly.

This is a story of becoming a champion in life while achieving your dreams without ever losing your self, your self-worth, or your self-respect.

Acknowledgments

This book and the silk road it has taken me on would not have been possible without those to whom I owe a special heartfelt thank-you, especially to my distinguished agent, Bill Gladstone; my relentless and amazing publicist, Karen Ammond; my creative and dedicated publishers at SelectBooks, Kenzi and Kenichi Sugihara; and to my wonderfully patient and committed editor, Nancy Sugihara.

Last but not least, a profound thank-you to my purely loving mother and father who continually supported me as I put my life on paper, and to my devoted, superman husband who kept on instilling encouragement in me that I could write my story on my own.

1

Light from the Heavens

(TEHRAN, ZURICH)

The past is easy to understand but difficult to accept.

This is a story of my evolution to the present day, a journey of a person living in both glory and despair as I become utterly lost in my circumstances and surroundings. But while in the midst of the chaos, I then found my true self that I had within me all along.

As a child I always felt I had to experience the pain of others in order to deliver them from it. I cannot say exactly why. It is a feeling about the destiny of one's life, one that cannot be explained in words but is written in the heavens above and below, placed so beautifully in all we can and cannot see. Even when in my mother's womb, as she survived the Iranian revolution, I must have felt I had been given the chance to take her misery away from her, and in return, she would call me Lucinda, meaning "light from the heavens."

I want to tell my story with passion and vigor, sensitivity and charm, love, and hope. I very much would like this story to touch the readers' hearts in a way like no other, like an angel brushing a wing on their cheek, and like my spins had done all my young life, to bring a tear mixed with both joy and sadness. This, I believe, is the essence of life. There must be sadness to realize happiness. There must be pain to understand freedom. It is a pity that all the riches of life must be interrupted to be enjoyed.

I am here to help you avoid the most harmful of life's interruptions. I intend to pour my heart out with my story. Since in many ways I will never be able to add anything more beautiful to the world than what my skating has already expressed, all I humbly hope to do is to intensify the beauty in all that I have already spoken.

My story will be the truth I lived and nothing more. It won't be fancy; it won't have a pretty ribbon wrapped around it. If it were to be done this way it would help no one. I will bleed on paper till the white sheet turns red. I will cry on paper till all the ink has vanished and I need to write again. It will be raw and real and might be hard to read or digest at times, but the one thing I promise you is that it will be nothing more than the real life I have led. I thank all those who have made me suffer, for without those I would not know how to express anything in my life. I believe one needs to understand and feel all the joys and all the hurts I endured, to know me to the fullest extent.

Most importantly this is a book for you, the reader. I believe that my life, as I was so fortunate to live and learn from it, was laid out for me for the sole purpose of helping others on this earth to help them know themselves and the lives they lead. I do not mean to take the position of an arrogant teacher in any way, but as I believe there comes a time when the risk to remain tight in the bud is more painful than the courage it takes to blossom, I now intend to write from my soul. The truth will hurt, but never so much as a lie.

This story is one of success and triumph of a soul. It is meant to inspire all to follow their dreams in a way that their soul will not be lost, so that they can learn from my mistakes and from my experiences. This book is to be a road map of sorts to show you the stop signs and red lights in life. It is to present to you that you can only truly win in the end if you have not lost yourself. For if you have lost yourself, then for whom did you win?

I have seen and am now living in the light that glows in glorious measure at the end of the tunnel, so I truly hope you will keep your mind and heart open. I do not want you to be frightened for me, or to pity me, and most of all I do not want you to be angry in any way after reading this book. Let your imagination take you where it wants so that you will discover more about yourself. Just remember I have lived with an overflowing love for life and in no way have I ever lived in hate. I hope this will let you make your own road and let the flowers bloom beside you.

There are three categories of readers: those who read and don't understand; those who read and understand everything that is written; and those who understand what is not written. It would be my honor if you were to be the last two kinds of readers, for I believe that these will best comprehend my life.

I am not writing only in English. I am writing in the universal language of love and a mix of my knowledge of Japanese, Chinese, French, German, and English languages (and these days a little bit of colorful Italian). "You are the product of many languages," I would be told often, a wonderful legacy except when you try to speak all of them at once, but I accept that as my charm. I will write from each culture that I lived and surrounded myself with and, with each stroke of the pen I will create and paint a movement as I have done through my skating. I believe that unlike words, the body never lies when it moves to express itself. So, instead of just writing words, what if I write with my expressions that stem from my heart and then ultimately flow through my fingers? Is that not movement and dance as well? Then my words truly will never lie. I also believe that whether you want to acknowledge it or not the truth has always been and will always be, present.

I have not included other people's names since this story is not about them. It does not mean that they are not important or have not been influential in my life. Quite to the contrary, they have, but I do not wish to speak for them in any way. It is my life I am recounting and I do not want to hurt anyone in the process. Those who have been in and out of my life will know when I speak of them, but please remember I feel no anger against anybody and do not blame them. I love and have forgiven all, since what occurred has been more my fault than anyone else's. I have taken full responsibility for my actions and reactions and I now hope that through my successes and failures I can teach others to achieve their own dreams.

I have worked with and learned from the best possible teachers and choreographers in the world. I have skated and toured with "la crème de la crème" in terms of skaters and productions. I never have nor ever will complain about anything. It was my destiny to live through what I did in the way that I ultimately decided to, and I have never wished or wanted my life to be any other way. My decision to tell my story comes from one simple belief: I believe that a lifetime is not a possession to be hoarded or carelessly discarded but a precious and sacred gift from the universe that allows us to contribute to and radiate from the eternal flow of human evolution. This means, in my estimation, that I am responsible for my choices in this lifetime and I am responsible for making my errors right as far as I am able.

I am also responsible for helping others, especially when my notoriety led them to believe in something that is not entirely true or worthy of emulation. Please understand it is not my intention to speak for any particular religion or philosophical view. I have formed my own belief system through my own experiences and challenges, which I call "Lucindaism." It is my hope that my insight into my life will nudge others to think about their own lives and the ways in which they can find strength in hardship and courage in utter despair and always see the love in all they do.

As I endured the many hardships my life presented to me, including physical and mental abuse, life-depleting illness and injury, cultural challenges and misunderstandings, and being pushed by others into an isolated world of one, I learned to accept these as a sign from a higher power to become my own person. I started to see through the people persecuting me as I came to understand their own suffering and sense of displacement. I sensed a bigger meaning behind the words and actions others presented to me. Eventually I could see that others were rejecting me not because of things I had said or done but because of the feelings of longings, and imperfections within themselves. How could I be angry with anyone for that? I am imperfect as well and I hope to be forgiven for my sins. I served as an inspiration to some and a target for others—depending upon where each individual stood in his or her own unique challenges and degrees of enlightenment.

Please understand, however, that my life never ceased to have a fairy-tale aspect to it as well. Without that magic to offset the darkness, I would not have survived. The magic provided me with an insulated wonderland, which included the unselfish, undying love of my parents and my God-given ability to skate and spin myself into a blissful trance-like meditation. One thing I do know is that it was all worthwhile. My parents did and still do epitomize noble, serene, and unselfish actions which to me are the most radiant pages in the biography of souls.

Spinning allowed me to transcend the limits of physical being and delivered me to a utopia of my own making, allowing every cell of my body to be filled with joy and love and permitted me, for a time, to feel I was truly at home. I would later come to face the harsh reality that I must quickly learn and live with who I am without the escapism that spinning granted. Training from a tender age to become a world-class athlete requires extreme competitiveness and perfectionism—dangerous traits to which I reluctantly became enslaved and had never wanted. It happened gradually, as if by a silent seduction stealing my soul without ever declaring its intentions. The enticements were many, from the thrill of accomplishing great feats to the honor of embodying for others their own unspoken hopes and dreams. Never considering myself an athlete, I envisioned myself an artist, a painter on the ice, coloring the frozen water with the universal language of body and soul as I laid my heart before my audiences. It was an unlikely mixture of terror, sadness, happiness, and elation that together gave life to the paintings I would furiously and sometimes delicately etch onto the glittering frozen canvases.

In contrast to the more abstract and spiritual truths I portrayed on the ice were the more recognizable trappings and glamour of lights, cameras, and action. These were unavoidable parts of the figure-skating world that I tolerated more than I enjoyed. My true desire remained always to express and glorify the sanctity and wonder of life rather than to celebrate my own achievements and accolades. I suppose one would expect me to describe and indulge in the satisfaction of thousands of faithful and loyal fans applauding and cheering as I skated and following me wherever I went, but what truly filled the hole in my heart was the respect and trust I received from individual fans in letters and small gestures of appreciation like tear-filled hugs and smiles on children's faces. The silent fan exposing the expression on his or her face spoke more than a thousand words and to all that I am truly grateful. The more I live and the more I step away from my indulgence of my own skating fame the more I understand and appreciate them. This is not to say that I failed to recognize or appreciate the grandeur and support of cheering masses, but I actually felt unworthy of such magnificent responses and truly unable to receive a gift of such stature.

I feel that to know who I am and where I am going, you must first understand where I came from. I was brought into this world on Friday, the thirteenth of July 1979, on a rainy, thunderous day in the foreign and seemingly spoiled city of Zurich, Switzerland. I describe my city of birth as foreign because my parents had been living abroad for more than a decade despite the fact of their Swiss origin. I call it "spoiled" because life was wondrous and beautiful there. Interestingly, the stormy weather in Zurich was merely a reflection of the tumultuous atmosphere that surrounded my family when I was conceived in Tehran, Iran during the Iranian revolution of the late 1970s.

Born on the thirteenth, I always considered it great luck even though I have had both great luck and great misfortune. Whether misfortune was caused by others or inflicted by myself, I truly can only see the misfortune as fortune, since it awakened aspects of my life to form me into the best I could be. Without the misfortune I would never have understood nor grasped the magnitude of my good fortune laid before me. Every situation was always a blessing. I knew it, felt it, but also knew I needed to see it that way to survive anything that came my way.

My parents, of course, are the beginning to all I have become and the sustaining life presence through all I shall ever be. They have given my sister and me more love and privilege than we ever could have hoped to attain. Our experiences would challenge our strength as individuals and our survival as a family, but we never lost sight of our love and respect for one another. Parents are the gatekeepers of life. It is their love for each other that brings new life into the world and their love and respect for that life allows it to grow into dignified purpose and consequence. My parents fulfilled that role for me with beauty and grace, if not with consistent perfection. I would like to give you a glimpse of the exciting, adventurous, and passionate life my parents lived before I came into the world in order that you might better understand their influences. My father, growing up as the second eldest in a family of three, thrived on his intense interest in academics, animals, history, exotic countries, entrepreneurialism, and finding humor in any situation. He grew up in a time of great tension and uncertainty during the most violent days of World War II close to the northern tip of Lake Zurich that he called home. As Switzerland is a country of four seasons, my father thoroughly thrust himself into the sports the temperatures allowed—the colder months included skiing and skating and as spring arrived, there was swimming, tennis, and all the other activities a young boy might enjoy. Surprisingly, my father took a liking to speedskating. As if through osmosis, his thrill of speed transpired into the racing of cars and ultimately manifested itself in the speed of my own spins. My father is very down to earth, elegant, kind, and masculine, as well as sensitive and quite the gentleman. He is a man of honor and sophistication. It is truly an honor and education to know my father.

My mother to this day has always kept her unshakable faith in God. She had wanted very much to be a nun when she had been growing up, even attending a convent school, when to her dismay (but luckily for me) she was harshly awakened by her father who would not allow such behavior. Surrounded by an incredibly artistic father who repaired musical instruments and a mother who was born to be a mother, my mother flourished in whatever she touched with her creative, independent, and spiritual soul. My mother's unfathomable warmth and love for all things beautiful and eternal carried over in her love for my skating and me. Like my father, she endured in her childhood the perils and burdens of World War II and the sternness of a father who demanded respect at home just as he had earned his respect on the war front. My grandfather never realized his dream of bringing his family to America. I would become the first of his descendants to become an American citizen.

In her early years my mother was a very enthusiastic figure skater, skating all winter long on frozen ponds. She especially loved the thrill of spinning. She very much wanted skating lessons but the cost was simply too great, and so she contented herself by copying the moves of another very talented young skater in the area. In the summers my mother swam in Lake Zurich. She was an all-natural athlete without all the fanfare and support women athletes are afforded today. I am astounded by her extraordinary tenacity and drive fueled by a seemingly endless supply of passion for the things she admires and believes in—always pushing herself to extreme measures as if her aspirations were greater than the compassion she might have owed herself. Throughout my childhood and skating career, my mother used the same approach with me, always pushing me to do better. The push to succeed as a world-class skater took a heavy toll on my body, mind, and soul. I respect and am humbled by her courage and determination and always wished I were as strong as her.

Eventually these world-traveling adventurers would meet and a fast fascination would result in marriage—no small feat considering my mother had broken two engagements before meeting my father. With my father's career well underway and my mother at last prepared to commit to married life, the stage was set for a blissful, adventurous future. Loving their lives as world adventurers, my parents became refined, multi-cultural, multi-lingual world citizens, wanting to offer the same privileges and thrills to their children.

I therefore feel so lucky to have traveled and lived around the world, enabling me to learn five languages—German, French, English, Japanese, and Chinese. As I always expect so much of myself, and millions speak these languages, I feel this is not a trait I need to brag about. I knew I would only feel I accomplished something when I became the only one in the world doing it. That for me was spinning, and I feel it was my thread, and eventually my family's thread that remains throughout our lives.

Because of their unquenchable thirst for being in the middle of excitement and change, it was only fitting that they would enjoy many thrill-seeking adventures together across the world. With luck, they always managed to survive their sometimes perilous sojourns as if destiny were there to prove this was training for travels and tribulations they would later experience with me in my skating career. They could never have imagined, however, the diversity and severity of these challenges yet to come.

After they were married for only a couple of months, my father accepted a promising opportunity in his company that was dependent on their moving to New Zealand. Though my parents enjoyed New Zealand and felt quite welcome there, the stay was short-lived. A mere five months later they moved to the United Kingdom where my sister Michele would be born alongside Mia Farrow's twins, an added joy for my parents who had always supported the arts and surrounded themselves with accomplished performers. They immersed themselves and my sister in British protocol and tradition for four years before returning to Zurich for another three years where my parents and sister would bond as a family.

My father was an impressive business manager, with a reputation that would accompany him through many countries and decades to follow. He always put his devotion to his work first, and therefore promised my mother he would provide anything for her and the children since we would need to sacrifice our lives for his, by moving around the world whenever he needed us to. My mother solidified her own place as wife and mother, a fate she would always honor.

In 1977 my father accepted a new assignment in Tehran, Iran—landing his family smack in the middle of pre-revolutionary uprising just beginning to intensify. The war that had been around Switzerland when they were growing up would prove far less trying than the time they spent in Iran living through their war. My parents loved the Iranian people and found them to be very hospitable as long as one did not interfere with their religious beliefs and political practices that must always be respected when living in a foreign country. Still, events of the day overshadowed what they had hoped would be a peaceful stay.

My father's office building was located beside the American embassy that was bombed during this period when all Americans were asked to leave the country. On one particularly harrowing occasion, some gunmen must have seen my father and his coworkers peering with interest at events in the streets below. They suddenly took aim in my father's direction and fired. A bullet flew just inches above his head as it came crashing through the window glass. My father dropped to the floor and rolled as he had been trained to do during his own military service in the Swiss Army. The situation was obviously very serious and my father began to wonder what additional dangers might lay ahead.

The Iranian revolution is relevant to my story because I was conceived during its most tumultuous times and curfew hours—my conception an amazing development in its own right as my mother had been incapable of conception for over nine years. I hope that I influenced my parents in a very particular way as they hungered for hope in a war-torn land, seemingly without promise or hint of a peaceful resolution. The Iranian revolution, as explained to me, was the overthrow of Iran's then-reigning monarchy followed by the establishment of the Islamic Republic. Historians remember it as a monumental event that made Islamic fundamentalism a significant political force throughout the Middle East. It was, for my parents, my sister, and thousands of Iranians, a very difficult and frightening time.

As they would always teach me to do throughout my own lifetime, my parents made the best of their circumstances in Iran by focusing on the needs of the living rather than drowning in grief for the dead or living in fear of the trials yet to be revealed. They were not indifferent to the atrocities around them, as my mother would later prove. They were simply trying to survive as all must try in times of war. My parents endured threats and personal attacks at home and in the streets of Tehran as they tried to outlast a war against which a family of three can exert little effect. Guns, missiles, and grenades became common inconveniences in their everyday lives as they struggled to find purpose and merit during a revolution to which they also would ultimately surrender.

My parents and my sister were gravely affected by the war and escaped it with only their lives and a few friends in tow. They try not to dwell on those years, but my conception was the event of that period my parents remember with delight, and they named me Lucinda, meaning Light from the Heavens, in testament to how much I meant to them.

My parents had long wanted a second child and had become numb to the reality that it simply would not occur, when suddenly fate intervened. The curfew hours definitely were for a boost to my arrival! You see, there is always a positive in every situation. When my mother did not feel well, my parents, fearing the worst, found a doctor. After the examination the doctor gleefully congratulated my mother, announcing to her that she was, indeed, pregnant. My shocked mother came quickly to her senses to rejoice with my father. The news was understandably accepted with immense joy after facing the medical realities of a seemingly impossible conception due to many factors in my mother's life. And so it seemed, that somehow or another, we always would strive to make life easier for one another. We were one from the beginning and our oneness would grow and be rooted in its own implements.

As the days progressed and the news became truly believed by my parents, they continued to be delighted by the possibility of having another child. In the midst of all their rejoicing it couldn't be denied that those times were very difficult in Iran, especially for a pregnant woman. But my father hoped, as he always did, that eventually things would return to normal and allow us to live in peace without having to leave the country. My father always believed in the best in life and had faith that everything would be all right in the end no matter what had to be endured.

During this time most people could buy food and other daily necessities only through the black market. Many foods were hard to obtain when sold in this way, but during my time in my mother's womb I grew normally despite my mother having no access to animal protein or dairy products, the so-called essentials during a pregnancy. Luckily I was born a very healthy child.

It became extremely difficult for my parents to separate truth from fiction in this land that seemed to be turning upon itself. Electricity was no longer available and the firing of guns could be heard around the clock. My parents and sister slept on the hallway floor to lessen the chance of being shot through the windows. It was a terrifying and desperate time. Yet my parents did what they always did. They held their heads above the water, struggling against the tide, with all the faith God could grant anybody. Near the end of their time in Iran, my parents came home to find written on the walls of their house "Go home dirty Americans!" My parents were not Americans, of course, but they saw no use in arguing the point. Soon after this my parents found their car had been stolen. This left them without an escape route since the airports had long been closed. Many times they had to flee the city to go into hiding in the mountains for a few days and safely returned when things had calmed down.

While many would have given up hope, my parents continued to believe they would survive to see their homeland. Their faith was rewarded when wonderful news came from the Swiss embassy informing them that a Swiss Air Red Cross plane with medical supplies for Tehran would be landing shortly, and there were possibilities for the Swiss still living in Tehran to take that plane back to Switzerland.

There was no hesitation that they wanted to be on that plane when it lifted from Iranian soil. My parents and my sister had forty-eight hours to pack and be ready to flee. The car ride through war stricken Tehran to the airport was terrifying. There were many planes scheduled to take off that day but there was so much chaos on the ground with rounds of gunfire that the plane my family managed to get on was the only one that took off. A sense of relief filled the plane as it soared into the air while everyone clapped and shouted good-bye to Khomeini. Something held my mother back from being overjoyed quite yet, and her intuition was confirmed by the pilot announcing that an emergency landing in Athens would be necessary because of the unwillingness of the ground crew in Tehran to refuel the plane.

My parents and my sister (and I) finally reached Swiss soil in May of 1979. My parents had packed numerous suitcases full of pictures, mementos, and their most prized valuables, but when they arrived in Zurich they were told the luggage had apparently been stolen before the plane even left Iran. After making it safely to Switzerland my parents turned this into an attribute by making themselves believe that the luggage would just have been a hindrance, the loss a tiny matter compared to what they had lived through. Living in the peace and comfort provided by family and friends was awaiting them and they embraced it thoroughly.

The adjustments were many, of course, as they tried to assimilate back into a culture that now seemed so peaceful and too spoiled—quite different from their home in Iran. Having never seen this much candy in Iran, my sister wanted to buy out an entire Swiss candy store, which of course would not be granted. My father's company held a celebration to welcome my parents home, but the sound of the corks popping from the champagne bottles was very traumatic for my mother who was still trying to overcome the sounds of bullets she heard firing in her mind.

These post-traumatic stresses only compounded the stresses of adjusting to a former and now quite foreign way of life, and my father, mother, and my sister Michele would all bear scars—physical and emotional—for many years to come. Those scars would certainly contribute to my formative years, which began shortly after my family's miraculous return to Switzerland—the place of my birth and the land I would always hold close to my heart.

A mere two months after being back in Switzerland, I was to be born. But as with all celebrations and times of rest for the Ruh family, our stay in Zurich soon reached its end when my father received his new work assignment that would take us to France in the fall of 1979. I was only a couple of months old at the time and Paris would prove to be a wonderful beginning for me and a wonderful place to learn and develop as a little girl. My father's work responsibilities increased and I would see less of him while my mother and I grew ever more interdependent in the struggle to keep up with the activities of my sister Michele. I have many wonderful memories of Paris and I appreciate them in light of the struggles and hardships my parents and grandparents endured in those war-torn terrains so many years ago. I am grateful for the courage, the vision, and the determination that kept them going in seemingly impossible circumstances against seemingly impossible odds.

I am grateful for their managing to see beauty in the midst of ugliness, hope in the midst of despair, and love in the throes of prejudice and hatred that could—and did—break the hearts and minds and lives of so many. Why was it my family's fate and destiny to survive when so many others perished in places where my family could easily have been? It is destiny, it is fate, and it is the engrained personality of the soul in the human being. I'm grateful they endeavored to endure and I'm grateful they lived and longed to give life to me. I sometimes still wonder who draws the lines between hatred and love and who keeps us from going too far in either direction. Is there a line at all? Who decides who lives and who dies and who fails or prospers? These are the questions that burden the thoughtful mind and these are the enigmas that would form and fashion me.

Some may wonder why my parents chose to live all over the world and why my sister and I were always encouraged to follow our own bliss in life. My whole family believes that our decisions were based on a love for adventure and on their deep interest in humankind, human evolution, and other cultures. People like us who take the challenge to live this way, keep evolving through our travels and tend to lose our sense of belonging by detaching ourselves from any one particular place. You learn to start over frequently and leave everything behind. It is also very true that having an interest in a new culture and even developing a love for it does not necessarily diminish one's love or respect for people of previous cultures. When any of us are asked which culture we like best, we all insist that we were at the right moment in the right place. It is truthful but also the only way we can think about it, as we have to learn to quickly adapt and make the new country our home. There is not much choice.

Leaving anything or anyone was always difficult for my mother. It is understandable since she devoted all her time and effort and passion to make a place comfortable, first for her children and husband, and then for herself. Then, when it would come time to leave, everything had to be dropped and left behind except for the memories carried in her heart.

I do not wonder about the friends I would have made and the family members I could have known more closely had I remained in Zurich my entire life. My life would surely have turned out differently in many ways and on many levels but that does not interest me in the least. The life I lived is the one my soul and I were presented and it was glorious and exciting. A life lived abroad is different from all other lifestyle choices. I never see anything as good or bad; it just is.

My parents' words ring true when they speak of the lessons we learned living abroad and the effect it had upon my sister and me. When living abroad, our needs, interests, and experiences were so different from those of loved ones that we had left behind. They no longer spoke the same language or related easily to us, who went abroad. This does not mean the love for family and friends is lost or the memories of past places are forgotten. But one's baseline is lost when moving from place to place and the new nuances keep coming without constants against which to compare them. The effect on one's mindset can be substantial. People and places change in one's absence—just as they would change if one were present—but those changes can make loved ones seem almost like strangers when experienced apart rather than together.

We always became a part of the cultures we lived in, and each change made to accommodate a culture is a change within one's self. This describes how we always approached the various cultures. We always lived within the culture rather than outside of it. Many nationalities keep to their own people, when living in a foreign place but we did the opposite. I must be frank, too. There are not that many Swiss people to make a Swiss town as compared to the number of Chinese, nor is there that passion for our culture ingrained in us as it is in Italians! So we did not have any group to confine us. My parents always encouraged us to learn and take in all the beauty and wonder a new culture had to offer.

Even today they continue to sustain their excitement and interest to see, learn, and experience something new every day. They have no fear. They keep evolving. They remember and will always love the people and places of their past, but they never stop embracing the newness and wonder of the people and places they encounter today. They have always lived in the present. I believe I am wiser and richer for having lived in so many different places although I became fragmented and broken for the very same reason. Skating would become my refuge and spinning my doorway to the universe beyond all these burdens—leaving me one day to wonder how the madness in the beauty and the beauty in the madness engulfed my life and me.

2

Playground Beneath the Eiffel Tower

(PARIS)

The Eiffel Tower reaches boldly to the Heavens, while strongly rooted in the Earth just as we must aspire to do.

A vivid and colorful imagination has always flowed freely within me. I like to believe the purest forms of love—love of life, love of learning and love for others—have always dwelt safely within me as well. It is ironic that I would one day be known for my physical dexterity and flair when I have always been quite introverted when circumstances allowed me to be. Quiet solitude remains to this day a very inviting and comfortable place for me. As a child I would escape from reality by letting my mind wander to pastures far beyond my actual existence, creating my own world of stories and adventures to indulge in. Some say it is the mark of genius to live in such a way while others claim it is the root of insanity. I claim neither, and I prefer never to judge and I no longer wish to be judged. My real life led me from the war-stricken deserts of Iran to the clean and picturesque living of Switzerland and then to (OOH LALA) the charm and romance of Paris! How far I had traveled in my first five months of life! My young soul was exposed to a wide variety of cultures, traditions and passions—- contributing to my thinking and actions then and now.

Paris afforded me an incredible foundation of idealism, freedom, and community, all of which would remain central to my true identity and most cherished aspirations. Paris was a magnificent city filled with hope, romance, and the promise of eternal youth and love, manifested explicitly in the fast and independent lifestyle so many Parisians lived. The French language is recognized as one of the most delicious languages in the world, yet to foreigners it can sometimes seem a bit too ornate and disorderly—minor concerns when compared to the romantic emotions with which French is typically spoken!

As a quiet family of humble demeanor unaccustomed to such boldness in speech and gesture, my parents and sister were shocked at first by this extravagant language and place. Just a few months after settling in Paris in 1980 my father would again leave to pursue his business ventures across Africa, leaving my mother, my sister, and me to take care of ourselves. My mother would one day lament that she never wanted to be both mother and father or later on best friend and coach and so on for my sister and me. She would have liked to be truly only our mother but future circumstances would leave her no choice. Despite missing my father during his absences, our days in Paris were filled with enriching trips to the world-famous museums and landmarks for which Paris is known—the Eiffel Tower and the Arc de Triomphe were two of my favorites.

My sister, as the avid athlete of the family during our time in Paris, was extremely passionate about figure skating, and nothing ever stopped my mother from delivering her to the skating rink each morning and night for her training. Since I was just a baby my mother carried me along to the rink in my crib, keeping me covered in hand-made gorgeous blankets and feeding me whenever she could. Skating was my sister's love long before it would become my own and I am certain her interest eventually fueled my own passions toward it. In my very early years I apparently cared nothing about figure skating.

I literally learned to eat, drink, walk, and speak at this Parisian skating rink, where according to my mother the other mothers occasionally politely reminded her that she had another child besides the child on the ice—an observation suggesting that I might need more individualized attention. True or not, I am certain my mother intended to neglect no one. If she is guilty of anything, she was guilty of trying to please too many people and trying to be all things to two daughters at once in a land where everything was foreign to her and both of her children proved to be quite demanding.

At the age of two and a half I started attending nursery school and I absolutely loved it. I had been learning Swiss-German at home and now going to a French school I added a second language to my vocabulary—or to my complexity, as some might see it. The school dean told my parents that everything I attempted I seemed to quickly master. It was a wonderful report for my mother and father to hear but it undoubtedly created extraordinary hopes and expectations within them and for myself regarding my ultimate potential in life. I do recall my French school providing a wonderful learning environment for my classmates and me. Our days were filled with endless creativity and wonderful French songs, plays, and musical performances. We spent hours at a time simply drawing and painting, our instructors encouraging us to express our inner selves through the richness of color and shape.

These wonderful arts and crafts experiences channeled my emotions into meticulous little creations that I proudly brought home to my mother, insisting that my artistry be displayed for all to see. My mother always obliged and faithfully gave me more glowing reviews than my artwork at the time probably deserved—as many mothers do for their children. She was always there for my sister and me in these simple but critical ways in the early years. Time, stress, her own life history, and many of my own life choices would one day make of her someone I could barely recognize, but she always—always—did mean to do her best and to love and provide for both of her daughters. This I would know throughout my life regardless of circumstance and regardless of her impact upon me. My mother faithfully accompanied us to and from school and tried diligently to help us use our free time in productive pursuits that were of our own choosing. My sister's school ended much later than mine, so while waiting for my sister, we went to the park to play, surrounded by culture left and right.

I would remember throughout my life the grandness of scale and the intricacy of design represented by the famous Parisian monuments. They affected me profoundly in my early years, though I clearly could not verbalize my feelings. The Eiffel Tower would always remain for me a statue of tremendous strength and promise, a simple but incredible beauty of shape and size rendered, as if magically, from the cold harshness of steel. I would often find this paradoxical mixture of beauty and harshness useful to me in dealing with my own sometimes perplexing realities. I saw the Eiffel Tower every day since we lived very close to it and it also seemed to show up en route to every place we went. I would stare at it with soft inspired eyes making a mental imprint of it in my mind as I walked or played beneath it. The top of the tower was especially intriguing to me. It would be visible one day and might disappear the next, leaving me to wonder what was really going on up there. It looked to me like the tip of an iceberg or the twirl of whipped cream on an ice cream sundae.

The tower represented for me a person standing firmly and proudly with his head gazing high into the sky, his arms and hands clasped formally behind his back. Maybe, I thought, this is the best way to stand in life—strong and confident with our feet deeply grounded in the earth below, but always keeping the imagination and mystery within my head. I wanted to never lose the magic. Yet within any magic, such as what I would later create on the ice with my spins, I learned the hard way that just creating magic is not enough. There is a price for it and there needs to be rules. While creating my magic, I sadly had no rules for myself or for my sanity.

There also was a beautiful public garden very near to our home that was a secret and magical wonderland for me. I played there for hours at a time without ever losing interest in the glorious flowers and trees and the always amazing little insects walking or flying busily about. I went on donkey rides there every week. My senses were completely awake and engaged during play times and I especially enjoyed the puppet shows performed in the open air. My mother and I saw these shows at least twice a week and they were my absolute favorite. I had the time of my life watching these amazing little puppets—for once something smaller than I was—moving about in unimaginable ways, reciting enchanting stories and clever observations. I laughed in absolute joy while sitting on the rickety little chairs thoughtfully provided on the perfectly manicured lawn. It was a magical time for me and I never wanted the stories to end.

It was wonderful as a child to watch these puppets move, dance, and speak without ever understanding how it all worked. We were allowed to believe it was real just as I would one day lead audiences to believe my own fairy-tale was real. My own fairy-tale was of course real in a sense, but I always left out the troubles and the traumas endured behind the scenes, just as those magnificent puppeteers had done for me. I suppose distinguishing realities would always prove a significant challenge for me since my childhood seemed always to be an intoxicating mixture of both harsh reality and made-to-order euphoria—especially in later years when realities would become more complicated and the puppeteers less benevolent and altruistic.

Throughout our time in Paris the following of my sister's activities was the first priority since she was the eldest. She was so talented in many areas of life. She was extremely intelligent and at times stubborn, yet she had a kindness of heart and soul that radiated throughout the whole family. At that time she was my hero in many respects but I don't think she ever felt quite the same love toward me. She would take responsibility of babysitting me during my toddler years but she was still a young child herself and so rather uncomfortably, she would clumsily drop me or allow my head to bump against a wall. I think she felt I stole the show from her, first from my birth and then with my success on the ice, but this was never my intention or desire. In telling my story, I hope she can see that many things were not as she envisioned them and I always loved and admired her in a myriad of ways. I suppose it is always difficult for a child to accept a new sister or brother after being the only child for so many years. Other stresses, inherent in so many of our life circumstances and choices, seemed only to compound the awkwardness between us.

My sister attended many summer and winter skating camps in France and neighboring countries and since my mother accompanied her, I went too. I would skate a little as well, but every time my mother entered the rink with me in tow I cried and screamed as if I did not want to enter such a foreboding place. And so I mostly played outside in the sunshine with all the other young siblings of the future figure-skating champions. The moment I entered the building I entered another world apart from reality. The smell of gasoline from the Zamboni machine mixed with the smell of frozen ice, the sounds of blades on ice while teachers shouted their criticisms or occasional praise could be heard over the all-too-repetitive classical music—all combined into a surrealistic pseudo-world I could barely tolerate as a child.

The moment I returned to the outside world I would enter into the bright light of day and savor the warmth of the sun and the strange awareness of skates lying dormant in my hands as opposed to being laced around my tiny, aching feet. It is truly a life like no other to be thrown from one world into another—back and forth, day in and day out for years and years on end. It seemed to me like transitioning from a horrible place filled with witches and frozen in time to a place with beautifully decorated gardens and magical gnomes. When given my preference, my sister skated inside the frozen buildings as I sat on sun-drenched patches of grass peering through the tall fogged windows— content with the sunshine, the flowers, and whatever little creatures I could manage to rescue.

I loved ballet during my years in Paris. At two years old I begged my mother to buy me a pink ballet tutu and little ballet slippers. She bought them for me and I danced and pranced about the house, telling stories with my movements and transforming characters into fairy-tales. With the costume on I felt I could become whatever I wanted to be and the movements made my mother smile. I always enjoyed those times when I could make my mother happy since she seemed so burdened by the responsibility of raising my sister and me. I suspect she was still quite affected by her terrifying years in Tehran.

Things were easier when my father was home. I felt my mother relax as if she were finally able to focus on being the mother she so longed to be. My father would take us for long bike rides in the beautiful parks surrounding our home and it brought great magic to the family and a sense of togetherness. The family was most balanced when we were all together holding hands as if giving one another the warmth extending from our hearts and encouraging one another to endure whatever challenges might lie before us.

The days my father left for a business trip abroad would be quietly and intelligently covered by my mother keeping us busy. She took my sister to school and ice skating and took me on excursions to smell the flowers so that we would not have to undergo the sadness and pain of our father leaving us yet again. While I am sure my sister and I knew he would always return, in our childish hearts and minds the actual event of his departure caused much anxiety and fear of abandonment. My mother always smiled through it all, never showing us a tear or sadness of any kind. My mother had become so strong outwardly and yet I would always fear her courage was only on the outside as I could sense she was carrying an enormous emotional burden.

The departures were secret but the times of my father's return were always celebrated conspicuously. On one such occasion when I was nine months old my father returned from Paris to find us all waiting at the airport. My mother wanted to surprise him with my newly acquired walking ability. She let me go and I walked proudly to my father, wearing a smile from ear to ear, my arms outstretched and the rest of me ready to fall into his arms. My father, as he walked those long steps from the baggage claim area to where we were waiting patiently for him, couldn't contain his excitement at seeing his daughter growing up before him and his eyes welled up with tears. Though we missed my father very much during his absences, he made up for every day he had missed with us by giving his all. He truly was present and he was a present to us.

My mother was ever-present, of course, never wanting to let go of her angels in a foreign land. Until I was about four or five years old I ate very little. I did not want to eat or drink anything but my mother's milk. I held onto my mother as the only constant thing in my life. I was holding on to my safety.

Therefore, I was still breast fed through all our years in France, and although the hours at school were magnificent and filled with laughter and friendship, I always had trouble letting go of my mother. Fear would consume me whenever we said goodbye. Parting at the schoolyard gates was torturous for me and must have been that way for my mother as well since I cried relentlessly, fearing again that I would be abandoned and left alone. What overwhelmed me was that I feared for my mother so much. I felt I needed to be always there to save her from what was bad in everything and everyone. I felt I had to take care of her and that this was my main responsibility as a child.

Some frightful things did happen in Paris to add to my prevalent fear of being hurt by others. One was the horrible experience of returning to my parents' car to find the windows shattered and the smell of thieves all around us. Our car was broken into several times after that. We felt violated, as if some unknown predator intended to get us in one way or another. I feared someone out there was following us and watching our every step—a feeling reminiscent to my parents of their experience in Tehran years before. As if violations of this sort were not enough to terrorize and demoralize my mother, my sister and me, even our home would become subject to unwelcome intruders.

I remember vividly how one beautiful Parisian day my mother, my sister, and I were returning home from the ice rink playfully talking and laughing, only to come to a full stop as if time and life itself suddenly halted. We found the door to our home broken down with pieces of wood scattered all across the floor. My mother and sister rushed into the house to find every drawer turned upside down with clothes thrown all about and everything else seemed in shambles. I stood motionless, not quite sure how to process the magnitude of the incident as I felt streams of tears running down my cheeks. Home to me was my life. It felt like my life had been taken and spun around as if it were no more than a child's toy to be played with and callously tossed aside. All of my parents' jewelry, precious family heirlooms, silverware, and most of our clothes were stolen.

For days after the incident we had to sleep in our home with no door because it had been gunned down. For weeks afterward I was in a daze and too terrified to sleep in peace. I refused to wear any of the clothes that had been overturned because I believed the viciousness and anger-filled fingers of the thieves would live in whatever they touched. Parisian police, indifferent and quite accustomed to such occurrences, showed up and wrote some meaningless sentences describing the incident, concluded that nothing could be done, and wished us a great day. My parents tolerated their indifference to the best of their ability, hiding and repressing their feelings until some future time when they might feel better prepared to experience such a devastating blow.

As the weeks passed I began to feel frightened about being alone and not being able to hold my mother's hand and have her right beside me. I vividly remember the many steps to be safe that my mother took before she and my father went out for an evening—whether for a business dinner when my mother accompanied my father or for some other occasion. Although these evenings did not often occur, I would experience a terror of my mother and father leaving. I knew it would be one of those evenings when I recognized the distinct smell and sound of the hairspray my mother used before she and my father went out. It wouldn't be the sweet perfume or the high-society sounds of her heels hitting the wooden floor. It would be that nasty chemical spraying from a can that would trigger my fear. When I awakened in the morning, my parents would magically appear again, but shutting my eyes for sleep without them there affected me for years afterward.

My family celebrated holidays elaborately during our Paris years with Christmas and birthdays being the biggest celebrations of all. Our house at Christmas was filled with beautiful holiday music, and at the center of our living room was always a strong and luscious evergreen tree with gifts and real candles and flowers placed beautifully upon the branches—each location having a specific purpose and meaning. My mother did the decorating with artistic flair, and my father acted out conversations with Santa Claus, bearing the gifts allegedly just delivered on Santa's sleigh on Christmas Eve.

Throughout our time in Paris my birthdays were filled with parties with my friends, beautifully carved cakes, entertainment by magicians and other professional entertainers, and rooms filled with balloons—still to this day my all-time favorite toy. It was truly special and completely mystifying how all of this seemed to come out of nowhere as if brought by an angel during the hours of dreams in my sleep. As if at the strike of a wand I would open my eyes to the new day. It does seem like a life in a fairy-tale. In many ways it was, and that is why I have said that these years were essential for my survival and me. I found myself fortunate in later years to have these blissful memories etched deeply into my heart and soul so that I might rely upon these glorious, dream-filled days and nights to know that this was truly how I needed to see my life. I knew that this was the real Ruh family.

Because my sister was nine years older than me we actually spent little time together in Paris. We were always present in the same places but there was always a void between us I never seemed able to fill. I was just learning to walk and talk when she was already accomplishing great things in school and sports. Our lives tended to remain separate as her undying love for ice skating kept her busy training hours on the ice with her international friends. When I tagged along, I looked up at her with love in my heart and awe in my eyes. She always represented to me someone I knew I would never be able to catch up with. I saw in her the essence of what was before me—my example to follow and my idol to emulate. I do owe her credit for the success of my own life on ice. Without her passion for twirling and gliding I would never have laced up my own skates and never would have ventured onto that endless sea of frozen water.

I would like to write passionately here about the glorious beginnings to my own skating career, but glorious is not how I remember it and, in truth, glorious is not how it would become.

My mother and I spent grueling days and nights accompanying my sister to that less than spectacular, and less than delightful, Parisian rink where I learned to eat, drink, walk and talk, and do all the things a young child would normally do in the privacy of a home or amid the relative comforts of family and friends. It seemed only fitting that I should experience the sensation of skating, having lived at the rink my short but full life; and so, with curiosity, fear, and no doubt a little bit of flair, I boldly embarked upon the new experience. I would be four years old when my feet first touched the ice, and I remember it not from a photograph or a video, but from an ephemeral dream that is part memory and part recollection by others through the years.

What I do know is that on that otherwise uneventful day, my mother carefully helped me lace my little skates around my tiny frail ankles. With a helmet strapped to my tiny but ever-calculating head, we ventured together out onto the ice. I clenched my mother's hand tightly in my own as I moved one foot in front of the other and made my way—slowly but surely—round and round the borders of the rink. The older girls swished boldly past me.

My long curly hair blew in the wind as my little knees struggled to find their own place and momentum somewhere between my skates and the rest of me. I wish I could recall the exact thoughts and feelings of that moment but I cannot. I surely felt elation for having crossed over to this long-mysterious and forever-daunting frozen plane. I surely made my laps in utter concentration upon body and ice with occasional curiosity about my mother's thoughts and the thoughts of the older skaters whose ranks I had now joined.

I was but a speck upon the ice and I probably made little impact on the lives or even the day of the other skaters at the rink. It was, however, a major event for me—not because of unforeseen victories and accolades to come, but because I had crossed over from one world to another. I had accomplished the transition from spectator to ice performer, at least in my mind, and though many falls and decades of training lay ahead of me, I was no longer just a little girl watching through fogged windows. I was now an active participant in this strange frozen world and perhaps one step closer to earning my sister's admiration.

As always I am certain I was dressed like a doll—and surely not much taller than one—since my mother always dressed me in beautiful one-of-a-kind embroidered smock dresses with bows, headbands, and braids in my hair. My mother was majestic and elegant and she dressed her children the same way. No one else dressed like us and other kids were visibly envious of how we were presented. It was both how we were dressed and how my mother and father taught us to wear our clothes. It was not necessarily the brands we wore, but the way we carried ourselves.

To this day I am meticulous about my appearance and how I present myself, and I have my parents to eternally thank for their noble ways. How little I knew about this world I had entered and how innocently I celebrated this quietly monumental beginning. I had no idea how very much of my life would be spent on ice and how significant the toll would be on my family and me.

It is important to note in these early, formative years that despite their inclination toward spoiling us lavishly as if no other world existed beyond the borders of our own family's love and happiness, my parents did, very sternly, teach and show my sister and me the basic and most important aspects of manners, etiquette, and ambition. They always said we were to be champions in life and champions in our souls. It mattered not what we did, but how we did it. They always insisted on us taking responsibility for our actions. We were taught to always respect our elders and never to speak back in any way. We were afforded luxuries and nannies and maids, but we were, without question, always brought back down to earth and in no way allowed to demonstrate any spoiled behavior. We were taught the basics of right and wrong and we were prepared for life in the outside world, however imbalanced that world would turn out to be.

My mother and father strived diligently throughout our childhood years and well beyond to provide my sister and me with all the things young girls could possibly want and need. We were spoiled in many respects. Yet we knew we had to walk a fine line to keep the privileges coming, since my mother was very strict and my father expected great accomplishments from us. Although the struggles of circumstance would sometimes blind us to how privileged we actually were, we always knew in our hearts and minds that our parents loved us and sought only the best for us.

Beginning in these early years my mother and father taught me, as they would exemplify throughout my life, that honesty, honor, heartfelt love, and respect were the ideals to live by. They taught me from their hearts and souls that the only way to understand their masterful teachings was through the lives we were to lead. I was always grateful to my parents and my head would forever be bowed in their presence. I would take these values to heart. I would make for myself a prison of body and mind to have my sole intention be to make the best of myself both on and off the ice. In the process I prayed I would make my parents proud and earn their respect.

3

The Three Curses or Blessings?

(TOKYO)

Hear no evil, see no evil, and speak no evil. A blessing or a curse?

A new journey in any context is always a step to widen your horizons. It breaks you free from ties and bridges and it allows you to erase all your history, presenting you with a clean slate on which you can rewrite your identity. Yet a new journey can also bring incredible struggles and trials that no one could fathom nor expect. I am meticulous about everything I care and am passionate about. I want to describe the details of my life as if they are sparks from a shooting star, painting every movement I make to match what I feel inside. This must have been a huge task for my mother to deal with in my childhood. If something did not match what I was conceptualizing inside I would erupt with crying fits. It was as if I wanted the outside world to match my fairy-tale world exactly as I saw and felt it in every little detail. This is how I would skate as well. I gave every little detail in life a chance to let it take a breath of air.

After my first four intense and inspiring years in charming Paris, with many growing aspirations and my mind opening up to more ideas than it actually could process, I was filled to full capacity. With my sister also blossoming from her years there, it seemed like it was time to move on and my father had news for us. His trips before, mainly to Africa, had also now taken him farther than we had envisioned—including the distant land of Asia—and his news would reflect his travels. He announced to us that he had accepted an even bigger opportunity within his company with a position overlooking the whole Asian region. It was an opportunity too good to pass by, and we were all to move to Tokyo, Japan in 1984.

My mother was without hesitation, excited by the challenge. She had always had a deep affinity for Asian culture, but until now had no reason to cultivate it. This news brought life to her heart. My sister was also thrilled, thinking in her teenage mind that it was very cool. She readily accepted the change with the one condition that she would be able to continue her skating and practice every day with a coach. I was only four years old. I just wanted to be with my family. Naturally I went along, as ultimately I would always do.

We would not take a direct flight from Paris to Tokyo as my parents wanted to show us the world and had the great fortune to be able to do this. My father planned our trip so that we would fly from Paris to New York City, take a helicopter ride around Manhattan, and stay a little while to enjoy American culture while seeing Broadway shows and trying on the high-fashion attire of the fashion city of the world. Then we'd fly to Disney World in Florida where we would celebrate my 4th birthday. After that we would lift off to Maui to tan under the sun and swim with the dolphins before finally jetting off to Tokyo with Japan Airways. We traveled first class on the Asian airline because my father wanted to give us a feel for Asian culture even if it were 25,000 feet in the air before being engulfed by it upon arrival.

On the flight leaving from Paris to New York City many tears streamed down my mother's face. Leaving was not what she was best at doing and the flight attendants were very concerned about my mother as they tried to calm her down. But as we arrived in New York my mother was once again all smiles. The helicopter ride over the sights of Manhattan was a feast to the eyes and the few days we spent there were filled with culture trips in this totally diverse culture to exhibits reflecting the personalities of the American people. A feeling of freedom filled the streets. It gave me a sense of what I would always look for in my life from then on.

Disney World was unique and filled all my childhood expectations of a fantasyland. I loved Mickey Mouse and Winnie-the-Pooh. I was elated to wake up on my birthday to a stuffed American mouse (taller than me, by the way) on the table filled with other gifts and candles burning delightfully everywhere. I entered the room with my hands folded in prayer since I felt like I was in a church surrounded by angels and was thankful for this magical moment. The week of fantasy was highlighted by my favorite ride, the submarine. I feel it takes very little to make me truly happy. Being able to see the fish underwater from the little round window of the ship made my heart beat with joy and my sister and I really enjoyed the experience together. Then of course Peter Pan enhanced my enthusiasm about being in Never-Never land! However, I must admit my sister was much more courageous when going on all the roller coaster rides. I preferred watching from below with ponderous eyes as the speed and velocity of these rides both amazed and frightened me. Plus I was way too small.

When we were at the airport ready to leave Orlando for Maui, I suddenly realized I had left my American souvenir, my Mickey Mouse, in the hotel room. My father made a plan to send a taxi to retrieve it at the hotel, return with it to the airport, and instruct the airline to mail it to us in Hawaii—even though my father didn't really believe that I would ever see my Mickey Mouse again. Maui was beautiful and my swimming evolved to near perfection. I loved being like a fish in the water, carefree and able to dance and succumb to my own world where nothing could be heard, nothing could be said to me, and no one could catch me My own world was where I often retreated. After a few days of sun and water, to our pleasant surprise, I returned to our hotel to find my Mickey Mouse waiting on my bed! My father was completely impressed by the promise the American people had kept, and of course I jumped for joy.

My parents always seemed to make everything happen magically without telling me how it was accomplished. It was truly wonderful how somehow my mother and father always made everything better. The week was wonderful, yet I am sure my father and mother must have been preparing mentally for what was to come in our new destination of Tokyo. It seemed as if this vacation was our refuge before an incredible and out-of-this world experience in the very different and foreign island of Japan, which was silently waiting for our arrival, like a lion waiting to pounce on its prey.

Since I was just under five years old when I moved to Japan in the summer of 1984 it is unlikely I can really remember much of what was going on within me, much less around me at that age, yet while remembering in the normal sense of the word might not be possible, I believe every cell has a memory. Certainly the body and mind and heart do remember, and events after any event can trigger those memories within us.

I must say lots of memories have been triggered! We are so innocent, so pure, so alive, yet so completely in our own universe at that age. But I think when we are children we see and feel everything, and even though adults act in ways that seem all too confusing to us, we as kids try so hard to be perfect for them. It is quite frightening to know that every little experience could change a life in a totally different direction at any given time. Every circumstance has an effect not only on that person but also on those around them, and effectively every single other person in this world. Yet isn't it ironic that what we least remember can form you in the most incredible ways? Or so I truly believe.

When we arrived in Tokyo, Japan, my parents were determined to make it a wonderful new home for all of us, knowing that this transition might be the most extreme and trying of all, but we actually didn't even have a physical home to go to at first. In a way a HOME for me was more of an emotional state of being wherever my parents were because I moved places so many times, so I felt at home, but our actual physical home became an incredibly beautiful hotel. Since it was a hotel, I think that in my mind the long vacation had not ended. I didn't really realize we were going to live in Japan rather than returning to my home in Paris.

Coming from the influence of Paris where children seem to be more of a nuisance than a celebration, Tokyo was pleasantly the polar opposite. The staff at the hotel was incredibly courteous, gentle, and respectful. They treated me like a doll and treated the whole family like royalty, giving us gifts and showering us with compliments. (If they were just this way on the surface and it was not truly genuine is another matter, and if they were bickering behind our backs, at least we had no notion of that at the time.) All of the staff members became our family. Another difference from baguette to sushi was the cleanliness of the place. You could have eaten from the sparkling marble floor any time of the day.

Every morning after awakening I would prance around the lobby in my smocked dresses and marvel at the flowers in the huge vases that were larger than life, with every single stem and petal facing exactly in an artistically correct direction, glistening in the morning light. They often changed the arrangement and it was such a nice surprise to see what was on display that day. The fragrance of the various flowers filled the lobby with wonderful perfumes and the pitter-patter of the Japanese women's traditional getas on the floor gave the day a rhythm to follow and dance to. The hotel staff wore their traditional costume but once they were out on the street the normal and monotonous clothes of the West hung loosely on their thin-boned Japanese frames.

It was a joyous, fairy-tale time as I lived the life of a princess. Not many foreigners were living in Japan in the 1980s and especially not little kids with blond, curly, long hair bouncing around. To them we were like aliens (they actually called foreigners living in Japan "aliens") or Barbies landing from another planet. When they constantly wanted to touch my hair and look into my blue eyes it sometimes made me feel awkward, like something was wrong with me, or as if they wanted to have a little piece of me. Unfortunately I would always feel judged by them.

I was always a child of nature, liking to tend to the bees and birds. I will never forget the wonderful stone and tree garden that engulfed the area outside of the hotel. Here, too, it seemed every stone, plant, and tree had been planted with thought and meditation in mind. I would feel guilty if something moved due to my existence. Yes, guilt was a huge emotion that would reinforce itself as I lived in Japan, feeling guilty perhaps of my own existence. The pond was filled with golden carp, a lucky fish in Japan signifying good fortune in all areas of life. I would bring the left over bread from our meals here and feed the carp every morning and evening and say a prayer or two. They were my friends and my mother and sister accompanied me many a times as we played hide and seek throughout the garden. We stayed there for three months and our stay there was the best playtime ever.

During this time my dad went off every day to his new office and my mother, my sister, and I explored the hotel grounds. Slowly my mother ventured with us outside into the big and rumbling city of Tokyo. As our stay became longer and longer I started to realize that we were not leaving this place. I unfortunately became very sad. Paris has the Eiffel Tower and Tokyo has the Tokyo Tower, and for years every time we would pass by this Japanese tower I would cover my eyes and cry and scream, "I do not want to see this tower. I want to see the Eiffel Tower." I was struggling inside and longed for Paris and my friends and life there but I had to get used to my new surroundings.

On the other hand, this was in the mid-1980s, so it was the bubble time of the economy here and everything was flourishing. There was an abundance of anything you would want in the world, plus all the new and interesting foods and products and accessories that I had never seen before while living in Europe. It was all at your fingertips. For any kid it was like being in Disney Land materialistically, but emotionally I was deprived. On top of all the new surroundings we were becoming accustomed to the language, which was intriguing and completely incomprehensible to us. A secretary from the office came with us most of the time to help by translating for us, from Japanese to English and back and forth, but to me it was still all gibberish since at that time I did not speak any English either. My mother, having lived all around the world, already had her method of starting over and getting accustomed to a new culture, language, and land and I never ever heard her even once complain about anything. My mother was and still is very courageous and I wish even now I had half her courage.

It was still the summer holiday when we arrived in Tokyo. School had not started yet but would soon, and my parents were visiting the various top private schools around the area to see where my sister and I were to attend. My sister who was born in England had always attended English-speaking schools while so far I had only attended a French-speaking kindergarten. Therefore my mother and father wanted to put my sister in the international school and me in the French-speaking school. That would have been wonderful since my parents wanted to keep as much as they could as similar as possible while everything else around us had changed to the utmost extreme.

But, unfortunately, something else we definitely had to get used to and overcome our fear of was the ongoing movement of the land. This was a new word for us: earthquakes. They were terrifying and one of our first experiences happened within the first month of moving to Tokyo. We were in the hotel and suddenly everything started to shake and a rumbling noise became louder and louder. The windows were shaking and books and clothes started flying of the shelves. The alarm in the hotel went off and instructions were heard over the loudspeaker. My mother quickly handed us helmets that every hotel room was conveniently equipped with. She took my sister's and my hand and off we ran down the exit staircase.

My mother kept a calm face, as she knew she was my sister's and my only support. After a couple of hours of being kept in the lobby to make sure all was safe, with all of us quite traumatized from our first time experiencing this, we slowly all treaded back to our rooms. Following like sheep was the correct way; no emotion was to be showed. That was to be learned in Japan. To be respected you needed to speak no words, show no tears, and voice no screams. Silence, although with trembling hearts, was necessary to keep face. I was holding my mother's hand so all would be good.

There was no discussion afterward about it, other than saying this is what needs to be done when this happens. I truly wonder how scared my mother was, if at all, because she never showed it. I wanted to follow suit and be just like my mother. We were told that the helmets were placed everywhere so that people could use them in time of earthquakes. In our school we were told where they were kept, right in the beginning, and many, many earthquake drills were done throughout the year. Later in our home we would have a separate container near our beds with helmets inside, as well as some food and water to be taken with us in case of a serious earthquake. We would always be on high alert for earthquakes and throughout the thirteen years there were many more serious ones we lived through.

Since the two different schools we were supposed to attend were about a long, one-hour drive apart, my mother decided after this incident that she would put both of us in the same school. Then in case of an emergency my sister would be able to take care of me. Again, I had no choice except to follow my older sister. I wasn't asked or talked to about any of this. I would go where I was guided, and it was really necessary for my own safety. This comes with living in foreign countries. Our parents needed to make the decisions and we needed to follow, because as kids we already had so much to contend with by never being in the same place for very long and not being familiar with our surroundings or people that our parents did not want to burden us with one more thing on our plate.

Not having any familiar faces or places around you that you see all the time can be very scary to a child. It really has had a profound effect on me. So in one way it was wonderful of my parents that none of this was ever discussed so that we as children could be sheltered and feelings like this could be overlooked. They provided everything to me and in the best possible way and in the most beautiful wrapping. All I had to do was to play when I was young and to produce when older. So I.S.S.H, International School of the Sacred Heart, it would be, and we would start right away while still living in the hotel.

I.S.S.H was the most prestigious private school in Japan. Even the Crown Princess of Japan, Empress Michiko, had attended it. The classes went from kindergarten all the way to the university level. It was an all-girl English-speaking Catholic school with classic uniforms. My sister would enter the eighth grade and I would enter my first year of kindergarten there. However, in Paris I had already gone to kindergarten and the plan was that after the summer I was to skip two years and enter first grade at four years old because I was advanced. I was so thrilled since I was done with the cutting, drawing, and singing. My brain was working overtime and I was very ready for the advanced learning. Even when I was older I loved to think ahead, and at seven years old I said to my mother, "I am not content with the books in the school library. I think further than the library."

So you can imagine my parents' and my reaction and disappointment when my new school in Tokyo informed us that they would not budge on their policies, saying I had to do another two full years of kindergarten before being allowed into first grade. My parents were very angry but the nuns were adamant and so was the Japanese culture weighing on them. Nothing could be done.

I started kindergarten in September and during the next two years my French, bubbly, confident, and I must admit, a little cheeky, personality came through. In those two years of kindergarten there were frequent episodes where I had to wait in front of the dean's office to be later scolded for no reason that made sense to me. My mother would be called in to meet with the dean as well but it never was big enough to be taken really seriously. It was for things like my picking flowers when and where I shouldn't have been, or throwing my shoe out of the kindergarten gate so that I could climb over and get it. Even when another girl started a fight I always seemed to be the one to get blamed. It was my way of rebelling and wanting freedom since I was so bored with what they were teaching me in kindergarten. I wanted to learn and to explore and I felt they were holding me back. But what I did learn during this time was the English language.

In October of 1984 we moved into our new home. This was the most beautiful and huge apartment I had ever seen. My mother always wanted the family to live right in the middle of the city so that we would be near to the embassies, hospitals, schools, and my father's work in case of any emergency. My mother was always on alert and thinking for everyone. I think this mentality and the strength my mother needed for the whole family put a lot of strain on her and she became very tough on us. I am also sure, although it might be hard for her to admit, that my mother was scared.

The new home was wonderful. It was big and spacious and I was totally elated when our furniture had arrived from Paris. My parents were adamant that when we moved around the world for my father's job, the furniture would always come with us to keep some things consistent for the children. It was the best idea because it made me feel so much at home. Each piece of furniture was filled with wonderful memories.

During this time I continued with my ballet and skating and now started piano classes as well. Since school was not enriching my curious mind, my mother organized after-school classes for me that taught the Japanese language, Japanese arts and crafts, and various other subjects to keep my mind intrigued. We used to have these classes in our new home and have some of my best friends from school join as well. Or we would explore in the parks and catch tadpoles or play with my turtles I had as pets. I loved reptiles and bugs and refused to kill any living organism.

And yes, there was ice-skating. It was there, and boy-oh-boy, in a different way than it was in Paris. For my sister, of course, going to the ice rink was one of the first things she did upon arriving in Tokyo. She absolutely loved ice skating, I think more than I did then or ever would. My parents found the best skating rink in Tokyo and there my sister began lessons from a Japanese lady coach. She was the second-best teacher at the rink and my parents took her because she spoke English quite well and was a good fit for my sister.

I started with group lessons cornered off to one side of the rink while all the older skaters swished by. I would look at them in awe, wanting private lessons as well and wanting to skate on their side of the ice. I detested the group lessons and showed it. I actually never liked doing anything in groups. I liked to be alone, in my own world with my own thoughts. I didn't like to be told what to do and having everyone else doing the same thing as me. I refused to go to the group lessons, but still wanted to skate, so my mother had me start private lessons with the lady coach. My sister went every morning and afternoon before and after school. I went just in the afternoon, as I was only four and my plate was already full with once-a-week skating lessons, three-times-a-week ballet lessons, once-a-week piano lessons, and of course skating on my own as well as attending school, so my parents didn't want to push me more.

My sister and I were the only foreigners at the ice rink and so the teasing began. They used to joke about my sister's long legs, about our blond hair, our freckles, and anything you could imagine. We were outcasts and although I was so young and did not understand the language, body language can express all that is needed to understand. Kids know more than they can say and unconsciously I started to get more and more insecure about myself. As years progressed it would get worse, and the kind of French self-confidence and bubbly characteristics I previously had would soon be frozen in time like the water I skated on.

By the time I was eight years old I was in second grade and absolutely loved school. I could sit in my room for hours studying and reading and making experiments or being out in nature playing with God's creations. But there wasn't too much time for that since I had now had picked up cello to add to the piano and my skating, and ballet became more and more serious. At age seven I had received a scholarship to the Royal Ballet of London and spent a summer at the school to see if it was to my liking. On returning to Tokyo my mother told me that I had a very serious and important decision to make that would impact and change the course of my whole life with this one turn of fate. I had to choose to pursue either ballet, skating, piano, or cello, because I could not succeed in anything properly if I were to do them all. There just wasn't enough time in a day, and I was excelling at them all so it was time to devote my energy and talents into one avenue.

I was always told, however, that school and academics came first. If I received grade letter A's in school I would then be allowed the rest. I was only eight and I felt the weight of this decision-making tremendously and it was torture to be told that this decision would affect my whole life. On the other hand, how wonderful it was to have the luxury of choice. However, I had never really chosen anything in my life until this big dilemma and I was confused. Ironically for me, it really boiled down to ballet or skating, although just lately I found notes that my mother had written that I had said I liked cello much better than any other art form I had been doing. Nevertheless, maybe skating and ballet had seemed grander to me, or somehow I was trying to follow what my older sister was doing, and so I seemed to have narrowed it down to those two. I knew that if I chose ballet I would have to leave home at age eleven to go to the boarding school of The Royal Ballet in London, and if the choice was ice skating, I would be able to stay with my family.

I didn't know anything about either lifestyle, but already I knew they would both require serious work. But what did I really know when I was that young? It felt like I was being thrown two wrapped gifts at the same time. I had no idea of the contents of the gifts so how could I know which I wanted more to therefore catch first and let the other fall to the ground? It was a one-shot decision with no turning back. I would never be able to unwrap the other gift. I did not want to choose. I wanted both.

What did I love more, what did I want to do for years and years to come, which world did I want to spend hours and days of my life in, and what did I want to become? I had no time to decide. Both arts have short-lived lives. It was now or never. For months it was the only thing on my mind. My mother started to put ballet and skating stickers on my belongings and write notes on my lunch napkins that she would support me on whatever path I chose, and I used to tear up thinking I had to give up one or the other. I seldom have favorites in life, so it was a very hard decision for me. I didn't feel one was better or worse than the other for me, I didn't love one more than the other, nor did I hate one more than the other. I took life, and still take life, as it comes. I always flow with the tide and that may be good or bad. It is who I am and I don't think I need to defend myself on that point, but this made me not quite understand why I had to decide at that time. In my child's brain, I wanted to just see what would evolve in my life. But that's not how an athlete's or an artist's life goes. You have to devote everything you have to it from a very young age or else it will be too late to succeed. Or so, that is what we all believed.

Even now I like most things and I am not fussy. I just accept things as they are. I detested then and now the need to make decisions. Choices are important but likes and dislikes seem like spoiled decisions to me. Maybe it came from always being told what to do and not having the chance to choose or maybe it is just my personality in that I never wanted something to be my fault, so I wanted to let others decide for me. I did not want the responsibility for my parents' disappointment.

Finally a couple of months later while in the car after school, I told my mother I had decided to put all my energy into skating, if that was all right with her. I wanted to please my mother and hoped the decision was the right one for her, too. I thought that if my choice was to skate I still could do ballet to help the skating. But if I chose ballet I wouldn't need to skate. I didn't want to lose anything so I felt this was the only way I could keep both. I also liked the idea of being alone on the ice, doing what I wanted and dressing as I liked. In ballet everyone had to look, dress, and do all the exercises the same way. With skating I could invent and create, to be as unique as I wanted. I could just be me, or so I thought then. I would glide and feel the wind on my face. I could change anything I wanted in the last minute.

My choice was based on the simple and pure emotion and fact that all I wanted was to keep doing it all. It is truly fascinating to me that when I watch videos of former Olympic skating champions who competed at that time, they said on camera that they wanted to be Olympic champions when they grew up. I never, ever, not even once, had that thought in my mind. I guess I never wanted to be an Olympic champion, but what I did want to be was an artist, and somehow in my child's mind, an angel, good to all. I always wanted to look after everyone, to take care of people in need and those feeling lost. I felt that was always my mission, and it is what I later on hoped to do when I spun on ice.

When I chose skating, my schedule changed. Ballet three times a week became once a week, skating once a week became every day, and finally cello and piano were each reduced to once a week. I did however continue with my cello and piano recitals and ballet performances, and now serious skating competitions were starting. I was a very busy child and did not have time for friends or social activities. I don't ever remember going on a sleep over or playing much with my friends after school. I had work to do. It wasn't that I was working to be a champion. It was just that I was excelling at everything so quickly that my parents believed strongly in me and expected so much from me. They wanted to see where my abilities led me.

The mentality was to use the talents you have. You are already lucky enough to have them so it would be a disgrace and shame to God not to work on them. Nothing in my family was every done half way. It was always all or nothing. I was so busy I wouldn't see my father much as he was also traveling nonstop across Asia, and I would be able to spend time with him only on the weekends when we weren't at the ice rink. My sister, who was so much older, was on a completely different schedule, so really all my memories of this time are of my mother and me.

My Japanese skating coach's way of teaching me was foreign and uncomfortable to me after my instruction in Paris. She did teach me in English, but I was just learning the language so it was a little hard for me to always comprehend what she wanted from me. Everything was so different. In France there was communication between the coach and student, and since I was so little there would also be a lot of giggling. But here in Japan, oh, no. Such emotions were not allowed. The training was strict and overbearing and condescending. There was to be no talking, no having fun, and definitely no smiling. Those were the rules.

Skating was and still is a very expensive sport. Very famous Japanese families such as the soy sauce Kikkoman family and the Seibu train and hotel family surrounded me and they were treated with more respect than I was. Since my coach was teaching these families she was to train them with more care, and so my lessons were put to the side and my parents felt I was not taken care of properly.

After a short while I started to not enjoy her lessons, or really the lack of lessons, and my parents decided to switch me to the top coach at the rink at that time. He was the best there was in Japan. My parents were told he would never accept me as his student because I was coming to him from the lady coach who was his rival. My parents decided to try anyway, and surprisingly the coach agreed to take me on. He said I was very talented but since he was too busy at the moment to take care of such a little thing as me, I would have to prove to him that I was worthy of his instruction. I would have to come in every day and work hard on the ice on my own for six months before he would start giving me a twenty-minute lesson once a week. I was seven years old! Now, is that dedication and beautiful respect demanded from a student by the coach or is that just plain absurd?

Anyway, my parents had started to learn the three monkeys of hear no evil, speak no evil, and see no evil, and the offer was accepted. No arguments, no discussion, just accept or leave. So for six months I skated every day after school for hours on end with my mother correcting, supporting, guiding, and helping me in any way she could. It was extremely hard to watch all the other kids get lessons while I could not, but I bit my lip. I trusted my mother and all I knew was to follow her lead. We were alone in this. Skaters didn't talk to each other much and it was to be a lonely sport. But deep inside of me I knew as long as I was with my mother everything would be good. She would protect me from all danger.

Perhaps because all of us in my family were a product of many languages my mother always translated everything back to German, her first language, in order to truly understand the nuance of a word. Nonetheless there were many words my mother forbade me to use, including all the swear-words, of course. One word in particular when translated into German sounded terrible. It was the word "want." Therefore, I was never allowed to say "I want ..." Instead I had to say "I wish ..." It was incredibly hard, especially in school later on because if I said "I wish a cookie" my classmates would simply reply, "You can wish all day long, but you will not get any." But I always did what my mother told me or I would feel incredibly guilty and would have to tell my mother what I did since I could not lie. So I lived in my world of wishes, never wants. I just wished everything. It translated in my mentality to be everything I would have to overcome. It did not give me strength but it gave me my own fairy tale world that I loved to live in. Even just recently as I was reacting to a situation I said with a giggle, "I wish to swear!" I was told that this was quite cute!

Here the three curses and/or blessings of see no, hear no, and speak no evil really started taking charge of my life and of how my mother started disciplining me. No matter what, I was not to stand up for myself. I was told to cover my eyes, ears, and mouth, just give one thousand percent, and to do as I was told and be quiet. We were in a foreign country and especially at the ice rink, since it was Japanese turf, it had to be done their way or we had to get out. It's only understandable that my mother followed the rules when she knew that if we did not follow the Japanese culture I would definitely not get any lessons. That fear overrode all else, overrode all humanity, and overrode all sense of self and human preservation and self-respect. It overrode my mother's own sense of self and her beliefs. It was almost like we were slaves to the Japanese culture and our teacher.

But my mother was certain we would rise above the challenge because she saw my talent on the ice. For that talent, all must be done. She gave away her self-respect and put all of her trust into the coach's methods. I was not taught to fight for my rights or beliefs. Instead I was to just show how good I was by results whether in school or on the ice. Show double, or triple the success of what others were doing. Work and produce more than anyone else, but do not talk, do not fight, do not express your opinion or emotions. Saving face was the way to go. Just do this, no matter what the sacrifice is.

I was working and working wherever I was and I was excelling at it all. I was doing things on the ice no one else was doing and I stood out not only for my blond hair but also for my swift executions of all the tricks. I was creating and inventing moves and positions never done before. I loved doing that. I was the ballerina on ice. I could do that for hours, but strict repetition, or not necessarily repeating, but doing everything the same way over and over, was not my thing. I changed everyday what and how I did things. That was my freedom. I was winning all the competitions I entered. I was an A student.

As everything seemed to progress on the outside everything was falling apart on the inside. I was becoming shy and embarrassed. I was becoming afraid of people, of authority, and circumstances. I was most afraid not to please my mother, to fail. I was afraid that with all she was putting into me I wasn't living up to her expectations. Conversations started to become only about skating and I do not remember talking to my mother much about anything else. My mother had all the responsibility on her shoulders since there was no other support. Therefore she became very strict with me about my skating and I was so afraid to make mistakes. I wanted so badly to make my mother proud of me.

"Sorry" is a very common word in Japan and used so frequently in their language that you find yourself and everyone around you apologizing for everything. "Sorry" became every second word I voiced and felt. I was sorry for coming into a room, sorry for disturbing anyone, sorry for my existence. Sorry for eating or breathing too loudly. Sorry for this, sorry for that. I started to feel I was a nuisance to everybody.

At school, however, I felt accepted since it was filled with foreigners, but my real life was not there. My life was on the ice and there no matter how much I tried to fit in and act like the other Japanese kids, to eat like them, and even to pick up the language and speak like them, I was thrown to the side. I would get the last lessons of the day or no lesson at all if there was no more time. I would get laughed at for what I was wearing when it was different from theirs. I was told to go home where I came from. They said I had no right as an outsider to take away time from the Japanese coach. They laughed at my long eyelashes so much that I started picking them out until I had no more left. I would never be accepted as a Japanese person but to me at that time as a little kid I didn't look at outside appearances, so I didn't understand. I just felt hurt by the situation and I couldn't speak out because I didn't know how, so I expressed it with my skating.

I was supposed to be a happy child, not sad. I was supposed to be the sunshine of my mother's life. I could not show her my weakness. All I wanted was to have friends and be one of them but that to my great disappointment would never happen. The more success I had on the ice the worse the bullying got. And so it all began. Without realizing it, my teardrops froze and my life took a dangerous turn and to become frozen over time.

4

Tokyo Alien Girl

(TOKYO)

A Barbie or an Alien?

What is age? Is it identified by a number, or the amount of wisdom, or depth of understanding a person has? Is it how you look or how you act or just the number you tell people? Can't a person be older or younger than his age? Don't we grow sometimes in one dimension or in one direction and not the other? Don't we stay childish in some areas and mature in other realms, and in the end doesn't the life in your years count more than the years in your life?

I feel respecting someone else comes first and foremost after respecting yourself, but certainly has nothing to do with age. All humans should respect each other. But in Japan age is the most sacred attribute a person can attain and anyone even a day older than you is to be respected and is to be bowed to. It is not by their wisdom or by their actions that they demand respect but by their time of birth, their time of appearance on this earth, as if that gives them the right to look down upon all others after them. You are not to cross someone older than you. This is huge in their culture and therefore the suicide rate is extremely high due to the bullying inflicted by the older kids or adults on younger children who can't bear it. If an older kid than I at the rink dropped something, I would have to pick it up for them or be bullied the rest of the day. It was like treading on eggshells all the time. It was like being of service to the older kids. If an older kid was preparing for a jump but I had the right of way I would still have to get out of the way and let the other do the jump.

On top of this, teachers are incredibly respected in Japan and they are considered always right. They can do no wrong and you are never to speak to a coach unless spoken to. My coach was the top teacher at the rink, and this plus his age gave him enormous authority. We were told that it was a huge honor to be taught by him and we owed our life to him. My life and respect was all laid before my coach. When we entered the ice rink all the coaches would be lined up and we would have to go to each and every coach to say either good morning, good afternoon, or good evening according to the time of day it was. Then when the session was over we would have to go to each one again and say good-bye and thank-you. If this was not done, you were scolded and would be shunned. My coach's order was my command. Or you would be thrown out. What a disgrace and shame that would be, not only for me but also for my mother. We would not have been able to face any of them again. So the pressure of all these rules was extreme, and whatever my coach told my mother and me, it needed to be done or we were told to not dare show our faces there again.

I honestly do not know much about my Japanese coach. I could not figure him out and the longer I was there the less he showed me of himself. He was a coach who taught me. He was not there to be understood by me. He was not there for me to become friends with. He was to remain an enigma and in that way we could respect him. My coach did not speak to me much. He would teach me with few words, few actions, and with a stern face glowing with an expression that I was to fear him. This way it was thought the best would come from his students. The idea was to break them down so that they produce. But whatever happened to building them back up? The building back up part came with getting another lesson the next day that showed you were worthy and good enough to have his time for one more lesson. That was success enough. If you won a medal no words of praise were uttered. The medal was to signify good work but it represented that more work was needed. Plus, it was to be believed in my home as well that we should never be too happy; otherwise bad things would happen to us. Was it just plain fear? Fear always takes away love and where there is no love there is no joy and no true success.

Coaches would lash out at their other skaters with physical and mental abuse but since I was a foreigner they were too afraid to hit me. I was never touched, but my coach did scream at me and showed his anger at me in different ways, such as not giving me lessons for days on end and not speaking or looking at me. Coaches would punish their students by making them walk around the circumference of the ice rink barefoot for the remainder of the session. This could be for an hour or more. They would hit them until they bled. They would scream and parents would just watch. Parents would continue the abuse off the ice hitting their kids with the skate guards, bare hands, or whatever else they had.

There was one boy from another coach who was hit so much he couldn't walk straight anymore and was trembling nonstop. There was a little cafe by the rink and they would pull him in there and beat him like crazy. The memory of his screams and cries still make me sick to my stomach to this day. They made the music louder to drown the noise. Coaches wouldn't hit the older students as much as the younger ones. But it started with skaters who were around nine years old. Why would they lash out? Well, it could be because the skater fell, made a mistake, or the coach just thought they weren't trying hard enough.

As years progressed my skating training became extreme. But at that time everyone was doing what I did so it didn't seem like a big deal. Being in Japan, an island far away with no contact with other skating worlds or methods, my mother without questioning followed the other mothers and the protocol presented. In the beginning we lived quite close to the ice rink but we moved into a home even closer to the rink so that it would be easier for my sister and me to train. How ironic, that a few months after we had moved, the rink closed and we then had to skate at an ice rink even further away, going all the way to Shin-Yokohama, which was quite far away from Tokyo.

This was to later recur and recur: Whenever we disrupted the family for some drastic change just for the sake of skating, the actual object we were trying to get closer to would just get further away from us. It's as if you always only lose what you cling to. It was so true, but we were too close to the problem to see what was happening. We were too close to see and there was no one else we could turn to for help. All we could do was blame ourselves about doing something wrong and yet keep on trying and trying to do everything possible.

Every day from the age of about nine I woke up around 4:45 a.m., my mother around 3:30 a.m. Everything was on a tight schedule and I had to hurry all day long with no time to stop or think. Time was of the essence. My mother and I were out the door by 5:00 a.m. I would have to run for about ten minutes as my mother drove behind me. Then I would jump into the car and eat my breakfast my mother made me on route to the ice rink. My mother cooked amazingly well and I never ate fast food. My mother made sure I always had the best quality homemade food. Breakfasts were always my favorite meal. She would prepare a whole basket full of food like I was going on a picnic. It was a heavy basket! I had salad, soup, fruit, bread with honey, and always a little protein, eggs or meat. Lunches at school were so delicious that all my friends were jealous. My mother made every meal a celebration, colorful and scrumptious. I loved to eat it all and I ate so much! The smells and the presentation were so thoughtful and wonderful.

As we neared the ice rink she would drop me off ten minutes away from the rink so I could run the rest of the way and warm up. I was on the ice by 6:00 a.m. and skated until about 7:10 a.m. I would always have to end the practice on a good note with a perfect jump, but time was crucial. I would run off the ice and would hop back in the car with my skates on since there was no time to put them off at the rink. The route to school that was about one hour away, took always much longer during the morning and afternoon rush hour. In the car I would change into my school clothes and finish my homework. School was from 8:30 a.m. to 3:30 p.m. I was late a lot of the times but the school knew the reason and although upset, couldn't do much about it since I was an A student.

Sometimes my mother forgot socks or shoes and I would end up putting on hers and walking into school with high heels that were way too big for me, that I wore until my mother could go home to get my shoes and bring them to me! After school my mother picked me up and brought me back to the ice rink. In the car I would recount every little detail to my mother of the day at school and all the tests I did and got back and all my grades. I would then have a snack and have a nap since I would be exhausted. I then skated again from 5:30 to 7:00 p.m. Then I'd have an hour break to eat dinner and do homework and off-ice training and skate again for another hour before leaving the rink to return home.

On the car ride home my mother told me how my practices went and then usually I did more homework before I was again dropped off ten minutes away from home so I could run the rest of the way. We would get home around 10:00 p.m. and be in bed by around 11:00. The day was run on our adrenaline and it was exciting as we went from one thing to another nonstop. Sometimes when time permitted, or on the weekends when I was done with my homework, I had time to enjoy the car rides. I would stare out the window and just drift off into another world. I loved doing that and I would do it often. I made up tons of stories in my head. My mother would ask me what I thought about as I daydreamed, and I never could give a straight answer. my thoughts were stories that I made up, happening so fast, one after another, alive and descriptive. I saw them clearly in my head like visions. I would see another person in the car next to us and a whole book of his life came into my head. I had a huge imagination. Agatha Christie books were my favorite at this time and the way the minds of the characters worked fascinated me. I devoured their personalities and ways of thinking. Their intelligence was clearly arousing to me.

Being on the ice was exciting. I learned new things every day and there was a competition at the rink about who did what better. All eyes were on everyone. It was challenging and taught me discipline and dedication. I would fall hundreds of times a day and when finally I could succeed at something for the first time there was a celebration. But this had to be quickly forgotten since much more was to be learned and achieved. I miss that time even today. Sometimes we would take some other skaters back with us and drop them off at their home after the evening practice. My mother was the only mother to do that in our thirteen years there. Most skaters after their skating practice would go to a night school called juku, until the wee hours of the morning. So I had it easy, my mother would say.

Saturdays I would train all morning on the ice from about 6:00 a.m. to noon. Then I'd do off-ice training for a couple of hours and ballet class for another two hours before collapsing into bed in the evening. My parents bought me a video player and in the car once I finished my homework I watched other skaters' performances diligently to learn and visualize myself doing it like them. Every minute counted and was not to be wasted and every minute was a chance to learn something new. I was on the road and path of privileged education and knowledge.

Sunday mornings I had dance class for a couple of hours and then my favorite part, a wonderful lunch with my parents. I would be spoiled with a slice of pizza, and believe it or not that was the highlight of the day. The wonderful experience of biting into the juicy flavors of pizza was a paradise that would be lost all too soon as I became older and there was no time for such luxuries of taste, nor would it be allowed in my strict diet thereafter.

Filling the rest of the day was homework, studying, and tutors, one coming after the other in history, English, and then math and the sciences. I loved math and it was one of the subjects I could totally indulge myself in and my teacher was awesome. He was like an uncle to me and he took great care of me emotionally and mathematically. He would teach me for almost eight hours straight and it would go by like a minute. Solving problems was my Sunday desert. He was a mathematical genius and had a genuine heart of gold.

Even though he has now passed on to a better realm he often visits me in my dreams and I hear his voice often calling me "good job, kid."

Off-ice training included a range of exercises such as running, lifting weights, plyometrics, and trampoline training as well as other specific exercises our skating coach gave us to do. Swimming exercises were a big part of my off-ice training that my mother invented for me. During the summers we were members of an exclusive swim club and in between my morning and afternoon practices I trained in the pool. Lengths were to be done under the water to improve my stamina and laps were to be done consecutively for around forty-five minutes. It was an Olympic-size pool and I had to swim one full length all under water. It took a while for me to able to do it, but either from the pressure of the water or from my mother watching intently above, it was more about how it MUST be done sooner rather than later, and when accomplished it had to be repeated several times. The feeling of suffocation from being under water with no air to breathe in was a feeling I would have to control throughout my skating career. My mother and I had our training routine down pat and nothing could be left out or we would feel I was lazy. We were a great team.

The off-ice coaches were part of the team too. They came to the ice rink and all the skaters would train together. We had a route where we ran about forty-five minutes. All the other skaters would cheat by taking a short cut but I just never could bring myself to do that with them. I would go off on my own and do the whole route as told every single time. But every time I came to the finish line I was still in first place because I would make sure that I ran twice as fast to catch up with them. But not once was I given a pat on the shoulder or told I did well. It would disappoint me so much. I could never figure out what I had done wrong or not good enough to be unable to please my coaches. I always felt so bad that no matter how much I did, it never seemed good enough.

Not once in my whole skating life did I cheat or not do what my coaches or my mother said. I usually did more than was asked of me, and I think this hurt me more than I could have imagined. I thought I was doing well, yet it led me to be injured, and later destroyed me for the sport. But what did I know? Everyone was always pushing me to do even more so I just gave everything I had. I was becoming mentally and physically so tired.

I had several ballet teachers. One of my first came to our home to teach me. She started coming when I was about five years old. I was so frightened of her. She was from Paris and was incredibly tough, viciously strict, and never smiled. She was mean to me, calling me a pig and other names; I'm not quite sure why. However, I was not flexible at all when I was young, and I do not think I ever would have been if it weren't for her. People look at my skating performances and think I was naturally flexible but this could not be farther from the truth. I looked forward to ballet classes because of the bar exercises, dancing to the music, being a little kid, and expressing my emotions, but she would not let me do any of that until I became flexible. So for almost two hours once a week for almost two years we would be in my parents' bedroom on the floor with her sitting on top of me, in all possible positions to force my body to become flexible while I cried nonstop in pain.

The other days it would be my mother sitting on me. I guess it worked and I did not get injured from it, so she must have had a method to her madness, but oh boy, was it painful. I hated these classes and I used to cry before she came but I knew it had to be done to be a good skater. If my mother said it was all right then it was. I trusted whatever my mother said. Also it has to be understood that kids will do whatever they are told to do. They look up to authority and want to be directed so I knew I was making my mother proud by doing what she said.

Although the training was tough, my mother made sure she made me happy every day. The little things she did for me were huge and I loved being with my mother. I cannot stress enough how my mother was everything to me. No matter how tough anything was, being with her and feeling how much she loved me was the best. I wanted to be the perfect child for her. I would have died for her.

For some reason I never felt then or now the need to talk much, and going to Japan and with the stress of skating I started speaking even less and less. Maybe there was less and less time to speak or maybe to me it felt like there was not much use in talking since what I said didn't count. I also now spoke four different languages but still didn't feel I could really express my emotions in any of them. I felt I could only express my emotions on the ice with my movements where no one could say I was wrong, at least for that moment. That would change, especially now that I am putting all my emotions on paper. It seems after all the years that I kept all my words bottled up inside of me, I now finally have a chance to be heard. Before my words were seen with my skating; now they are to be heard.

My mother never, ever, missed a practice and she was my constant protection and tree trunk of support. If she did have to go to my school for a meeting or for a company dinner with my father I would lash out at her in tears. I was starting to fear not being with my mother and not having her with me twenty-four hours a day. I started to need her like never before. I felt so lost and so incapable of taking care of myself without her. I felt I had nobody but my mother and without her I was nothing. I was nonexistent and I was only complete with my mother by my side. I was only complete when I had my mother telling me what to do, what to wear, what to say. I remember sometimes my father asked me a question and my mother would reply for me. It was as if I was my mother's puppet. My mother did not realize it at that time and I, not knowing anything different, wanted to live for my mother.

I remember so vividly thinking that if my mother died I would definitely not be able to survive. There would be nothing for me to do without my mother. This is how close and yet how isolated we had become. It was to bring much tragedy in both our lives in the years to come but at that time we were oblivious. We were so busy trying to be perfect for each other to attain a goal that even to this day I am puzzled as to what our goal was—other than to be the best you could be at everything you touch, and nothing could disrupt the energy of that.

My coach conducted a skating camp every summer for a week and only my coach's students were allowed to attend. It was always in Karuizawa, which was a couple of hours drive from Tokyo and we all went by bus together. The first time I attended I was eight years old. I had never slept anywhere without my family, not even a sleepover at a friend's house, never had tied my own skates or had done my own hair, so the first few times I went to this camp all I did was cry and cry for days. It was a mess and the other girls would unwillingly have to help me with my hair and skates and they made fun of me for it.

At that time we didn't have cell phones and at the camp house there was a coin telephone. I would lock myself in the cupboard next to the phone with the phone cord pulled through the crack of the door and have a jar filled with coins next to me. For at least two hours I was on the phone with my mother, crying, huddled in a fetal position, feeling like I was going to die and never see my mother again. It was torture being away from my mother. It felt like someone had pulled my heart and my lungs out and I couldn't breathe. I could not bear not seeing my mother's face every day and I could not bear my mother not seeing me skate and train. I could not endure the pain I felt when I was on the ice and did not see my mother's silhouette from the big, never-ending frozen pond. I felt I was taking away my mother's joy by not being with her and by not letting her see me skate, which I thought she so much loved, enjoyed, and needed. I felt guilty that I was away from my mother by leaving her and going to camp. It was terrible. I was so convinced that I was to make her happy in this world and in this life and that I was the one to make her smile. It was my responsibility and I couldn't forgive myself if I couldn't do this.

On top of that the training session was always the first week of August and my mother's birthday is on the third of August. For years to come I would not be able to be with her on her special day, and it tore me to shreds. I never could forgive myself for doing that to her. I might have been feeling this way because unconsciously as kids we take upon ourselves other people's hurt and pain. Her hurt and pain could have been all in my imagination, but to me at that time her feeling of this was so real. I could touch it, smell it, and feel it. It was living inside of me and there was no way of letting it go.

Years later when I was bedridden and my whole life had seemed to collapse for me, these memories would become alive again and I would relive every single detail of them. However, I did change as I grew older as I started to enjoy the camps more and more. For me it was a change from my daily life and home in Tokyo. The food was home-made Japanese style, and my favorite was Japanese curry and the onigiri rice balls. Since it all was not what my mother cooked it enticed my taste buds. The onsen, hot steam baths, were soothing and sleeping on bunk beds gave me great joy. Also we were in the wilderness, so the bugs and little creatures were my friends. I was known to be the one to call when someone saw a bug and I would save it from its death by bringing it out of the camp house.

The training was fun without parents present and it gave us a little bit of freedom, but I always reported to my mother how my practices went and made sure the reports would be stellar. We still painted those figures on the ice as we worked on demonstrating the language of skating, which was then called Compulsory Figures. I loved this practice. I would be lost in my own world and let my blade follow my paintings on the ice, one on top of another over and over for hours. Again and again we would trace figure eights and loops to ultimate perfection. We would draw our circles with our compasses making sure each skater had enough place on the sheet of ice. Each drawing was like a mathematical equation and as I was a thinker on ice, I was incredibly sad to see this practice later being thrown away by the skating union. This practice was like a meditation and a foundation for beautiful skating that is truly lost in present day skating.

At camp, when part of a group, I was jubilant that here I would have my little but precious social time. Evenings we would do the small hand-held fireworks and enjoy barbecues. My coach and his wife were more relaxed then and it was nice to see that they also had a more humane side to them. But I do have a sad memory of an occasion when I watched my coach washing his face one morning. He looked down at me, since I was so tiny, and in anger said, "You see, I even wash my face with intensity. You do not do anything with intensity!" Those words stung in my heart.

I did have one good friend growing up who lived by our new house down the block. He was of Japanese and American descent and like me working day in and day out for the love of an art. He was the same age as me and we met in kindergarten. He was a violinist and while I was feverishly practicing on the ice he was magically making music with his little hands on the tiniest violin I ever saw. He would attend my competitions and I would attend his recitals, I, in sparkly glistening costumes and he, in his tuxedo. We were friends for many years to come and his mother and my mother would emotionally tear up about the harshness of our arts in their both similar and different ways. When we had time we would build gingerbread houses together at Christmas time, or play on the block as all kids did, but we treaded carefully since he was not to damage his hands or me my feet. We were well aware of the consequences if we were to foolishly ruin our careers, or so we already saw our then meek accomplishments as a life-long job.

When we were very young and schedules were not so harsh, we both loved the bell that rang throughout the city at 5:00 p.m. every day. It signified it was time to go home. I had that song etched in my brain and when I left Japan I missed it terribly. It felt homey to know that for a few minutes everyone in the whole city was hearing the same tune at the same time. It gave a sense of unity. It is funny how the little things like these make such a magical impact on a person's life. I would even miss the plastic bags that foods from a grocery store were put in to take home. The noise they made and the feel they had on my fingers were unique to Japan. Oddly these were the things I would miss most about Japan.

My family always took wonderful trips together. This is when we could really all enjoy each other. I loved them and looked forward to them so much. Thailand, Hong Kong, and all the beautiful parts of Japan were frequently visited. The school summer holidays were three months long, so we always had a long vacation trip planned to go back to Europe, including Switzerland and neighboring countries to visit family and friends and then maybe visit a new place or an island on the way back. But with my training getting so serious and my level improving rather quickly on the ice my coach did not want me to be off the ice for longer than a few days, so our family summer trip when I was nine years old in 1988 would be the last.

My sister in the meantime had stopped skating at age sixteen to focus on her studies and she was not enjoying Japan. She graduated from high school with the International Baccalaureate in 1988 and would start University in Switzerland right after the summer. Her wish for her graduation gift was to ride the famous Trans-Siberian Railway. We took a train that included the Trans-Mongolian route to go from Beijing all the way through Mongolia and Russia right to Moscow. Her wish was granted. I was so excited and this was to be my most cherished vacation journey ever.

My skating coach was definitely not pleased that I would be gone for so long, but I am so happy that my parents stepped up to the plate, kept the family time together as a priority, and for this one last wonderful and magical trip they took initiative. We promised my coach that I would take my skates with me and skate when in Europe. We would be back by the middle of August and I had a competition right away, so my mother and I knew that the competition result would be the proof of how loyal we were to him and to his teachings.

That would mean off-ice exercises every day on the train, and skating every day once we were off the train. My mother read a quote from a famous ballet dancer and repeated it so often that we believed in it and lived by it, and it became ingrained in us: "An artist will feel it in their body when they have not trained for a day, the people around them will notice after two days, and the whole world will see it after three days." So that meant I could not stop training for more than a day. It was all right for me to feel it, but once other people saw your weakness they would pounce on you. That was the fear we lived in. But at that time it was an exciting fear.

We flew to Beijing from Tokyo and spent a couple of days there. My father who had already travelled all over the region was accustomed to Beijing. An employee from the office helped my dad with translation as he showed us all around the city. It was fascinating, and my sister and I enjoyed all the nuances and the different festivals and foods. Our parents took us to many different concerts and Chinese performances. The Great Wall was impressive but I remember more the bugs and beetles on the ground as we were walking the Great Wall since they seemed to captivate me much more than a wall of war.

Turtles were and still are my favorite pet and so it was to my great surprise that as my family and I were waiting on the platform to board the Trans Siberian train, the secretary from the office presented me with a pet turtle in a glass jar. I was so thrilled and elated that this turtle was to be my friend during this trip. As we boarded and said our goodbyes, and as the train started to build with speed, we explored the whole train and especially our room. It was a moderate room, the biggest my father could get, with four beds, two on each side, one on top of the other and a table in the middle. I placed my turtle right in the middle and called my new friend, Xie Xie, meaning thank-you in Mandarin.

My father had talked about how the train's wheels on the tracks would make the repetitive sounds of "chuchu-chuchu, chuchu-chuchu," and for months leading up to the trip that was what I would tell all my friends at school and what I was so excited about. My father always brought lightness to a situation and I loved not having to worry about anything with him. I wish my father had been more present as I was training on the ice so that he could have watered the fire burning inside my mother from all the responsibilities she had. My father also talked about how we could just look out the window to see the ever-changing landscapes as we went from China to Russia and that enticed me and I had high expectations.

The train trip lasted for ten days and there was no shower, only a small bathroom where my mother washed me every morning and scrubbed me down. The food cart was as interesting as when we were in China. It was bustling and noisy and all kinds of ethnic Chinese food were served. As we entered Russia the food cart was more subdued and all we got to eat was borscht. We played cards, played chess together, looked out the window for hours together, and talked together, It was the beauty of this experience that you didn't have to do anything to feel the love in the family and the inseparable devotion we had for each other. This time would be etched in my memory forever. It was the chosen glances and words we spoke with that made the trip the most memorable ever. As promised, I did my exercises diligently everyday as well as my ballet-bar work, and I worked on my flexibility with my mother helping me on the bed and on the floor in the hallway.

There were a couple of interesting incidents during the trip. Often the train would unexpectedly come to a stop at any time of the day, but frequently in the middle of the night and police would raid the trains, coming into all the rooms, checking our passports on a search rampage. It was rather terrifying for me because I had no idea why police were on the train and what they were searching for. Later on my parents told me they were looking for drugs and illegal transport of goods. A lot of the people would stuff drugs into Russian nesting dolls (Babushka or Matryushka dolls). One interesting incident in particular that I will always remember happened during the middle of the trip. I was sleeping soundly and suddenly awakened by my father's voice telling us to quickly get up and put some clothes on and get off the train. The train had come to a halt and it was about two in the morning.

Not knowing what was going on, we got off. It was pouring with rain and it was pitch dark and we had no idea where we were. We didn't really make friends with others on the train but we saw familiar faces also waiting outside, huddled under a broken roof under umbrellas. We stayed close to another family we had become acquainted with. We waited and waited while not being told what was going on. We must have waited at least two hours. It was getting cold but my sister and I kept each other company. My parents thought something had happened to the train or police had found something suspicious. But to our relief we suddenly saw that the train was lifted and that the train wheels were being changed. How captivating it was for me as a child to watch what was going on in the middle of nowhere with no light and in pouring rain.

Once my father understood what was happening, he explained to me that we were on the border of Mongolia and Russia and the tracks were different in each country. They would become wider as we entered into Russia, so they had to change the upper carriage on to a new undercarriage to fit the new tracks. It took another couple of hours but it was truly interesting to watch them work on it and to know how things worked back then. I feel lucky to have had such unforgettable experiences.

The ten days went by way too quickly and the sight of the Lake Baikal, the deepest, clearest, and oldest (25 million years old) lake in the world, made the trip top the charts. I was in heaven. On arriving in Moscow we had much more to experience. It was an astonishing sight to our eyes going from the characteristics of the Chinese people when we left to the colorful personalities of the Russians when we arrived. Both were very poor at that time so it was like the same people inside, but just camouflaged in different attire on the outside. We scrambled through the markets on arrival and people wanted to sell us all sorts of products. We got a taxi and went to the hotel. At that time Russia was still Communist and our hotels were wired. All our conversations and telephone communications were listened to. Since this freaked me out, I did not dare to utter a word in the room or on the phone. Having not had a bath for ten days, my mother filled the bathtub with water and I got first priority to sit in the tub for a while. It felt luxurious even though the amenities of the hotel were scarce and bare.

At that time my mother and I especially admired the woman skater of the Russian Olympic champion pair skaters. I used to copy a lot of her moves and expressions and many people commented about how I was skating just like her. You truly become who you look up to the most. My parents knew that they were training at the Moscow athletic government training center, and they promised me we would go there where I could skate and meet them. I couldn't contain my excitement. I don't know how my parents managed for me to skate at the same rink where the Russians champions were since at that time it was government owned with very strict quarters, but again they always made things possible. At the rink I was up and ready with my skates laced up and I stepped onto the ice. I was warming up ready to show them all the moves I could do and to show off of my skating. But to my disappointment they did not come. We learned that they were away at a training camp near the sea of Russia.

I was too happy to be truly sad about this, because for me to be able to etch a painting on the same frozen water as they had skated meant nothing could dampen my mood. Nobody else was there and I soaked in their wonderful past energy and prayed I would be as good as them some day. I was however a little relieved, too, not to have the pressure to show the woman skater my skating. Whenever I was on the ice I felt tons of pressure from my mother and ultimately myself. Little did I know I would be skating in shows with the Russian skater later on in my life.

With my turtle still in tow, being in Moscow and our next stop in St. Petersburg gave us lots of memories. One such memory is when we were stranded in the outskirts of the city trying to get back to the hotel but no taxi wanted our Swiss money. Another is the meal we ravished in a restaurant in the most beautiful dome-like hall where people brought their own liquor and own flowers to place in the stained glass vases filled with water placed in the middle of the table. After about eight days we were off to Switzerland. I remember the vast difference encountered coming all the way from Beijing. Switzerland was like another planet after what we experienced on this particular vacation, expressed with luxuriant green forests and spotlessly clean sidewalks as if money grew on trees here and even the cows seemed to be living a spoiled life. It was beautiful and it overflowed the eyes and soul after the depth and truth we had seen.

We stayed in the mountains and I skated every day. My turtle lived in the bathtub and the maids were terrified of it! My sister and I played a lot together and visited the ponds and rivers and rolled in the grass. It was as if my sister was saying goodbye to me but I did not know this. One day my sister and I were sitting on a towel in the garden and we placed my turtle in the middle of us so it could have some fresh air as we read our books. After only a few minutes of reading I looked up and saw my turtle had vanished. We panicked and started calling out its name as if it would run in turtle terms, or slowly walk in human terms, back to us! We searched and searched. But the grass was vast and green and the turtle was green, so it was an impossible feat. There was a river nearby and we went up and down it asking our neighbors if they had seen a turtle walk by! They must have thought we were nuts! This was all to no avail and my Xie Xie was gone. I was so afraid to tell my mother, but after scolding us for not looking after my pet properly she comforted me as I wept. For days after this we kept on looking. I still to this day hope it is alive and hopefully found a better home in the Swiss wilderness.

After a couple of weeks it was time for my parents and me to go back to Tokyo. I did not know this at the time but my sister was actually to stay in Switzerland and not return with us to Japan. She was to complete a skating test and then head off to University. She would live with my aunt near the university she was to attend. I am not sure if I was not told this, or I was too young to quite comprehend, or I was too engulfed in my own world, but nevertheless I remember being somewhere in the Swiss alps and my parents and me hugging my sister and crying profusely, then getting into the car and asking my mother and father why my sister wasn't coming with us. I started feeling like my heart was being torn apart.

Then I remember so vividly being in the back seat of the car, my mother and father in front crying and my looking through the rear view window to wave at my sister. I still see her today standing on top of the hill wearing blue and white sweatpants and sweatshirt as our car slowly inched away from her down the hill. She looked to me like little girl, so lost and scared, and I still to this day feel the rip in my heart. I asked my mother and father if I would ever see her again and they reassured me that of course I would. But I did not see it that way. I felt she was taken away from me and I was so scared and worried that I never would see her again.

My sister and I, although I haven't mentioned her that often, have a special bond and there is no denying it. What drew us apart was the fact that we had so many years difference in age that our experiences and our lives were on two different paths. They never crossed. My sister let me believe in my visions like Santa Claus and the tooth fairy for the longest time, and most importantly she was a great example of determination, confidence and dedication. She let me keep my innocence no matter how much she longed for it too. Our destiny of our sisterhood had yet to evolve and hopefully would one day.

Back in Tokyo it was all business. School would start soon again and training was back in full force. Competitions were nearing and I had the first one come right up as if to smack me in the face. I, understandably after such a long holiday, did not do my very best, but I won, and I felt proud. My coach did not agree with us and was not pleased. We had let him down and his opinion mattered more than ours. Well, I guessed the only resolution was more work.

My mother and I always carefully and delicately chose the music choices I skated to for each competitive season. When I was in school my mother would be in the music store for hours and surprise me with all the choices in the car on route to the rink. I loved this time and the excitement surrounding all the decisions to be made for my skating. It was wonderful as a child to have everyone running for you to provide you with all that is needed.

On the other hand, I knew I had to produce or there was no providing for me, and that is a huge toll and much responsibility to put on the child. It's a full time job. After presenting our music choices to my coach they were rudely torn apart by my coach's wife, the choreographer of the team. She chose what she wanted and saw fit for me, and remarked that our choices were too advanced for me and I was not good enough for them. It hurt my mother and me, but again we did not have much say in anything and we accepted it. However, the costumes that I wore were entirely always my mother's and my design. We would listen to my new program music for hours on end in the car and we would come up with a design. I must say I had always the most remarkable costumes and definitely one of a kind.

At ages eleven and twelve my most distinctive skating years would start. This would take my mother and me on roller coaster rides far scarier than you could imagine, and to distant places with trials and tribulations mentally and physically. Now, looking back, I tend to think that there was no way these times could have been possible to survive. Skating had now become not only my dream but my mother's as well, since skating is not a sport in which you can leave a child alone. It is not a sport a young child can get to alone. It is not a sport a young child can even practice on her or his own. There is no other way to succeed in this sport other than to have a whole team of people surrounding the skater who must also believe, want, and live that same dream.

And so the child feels that skating never belongs only to her. It belongs to all those involved, and for that she must work for not only herself but for all of them. Therefore we never fathomed what would come and even if we had, we would have not believed it. As it did unfold we did we not realize how serious and dangerous a world we were in until we lost it all. We definitely did not follow a path and we were leaving a trail and praying for it not to be followed.

5

From the Outside Looking In

(TOKYO)

Or is it a clouded window?
What you have in your mind, discard, but what is given in your fate, accept.

How much is too much? How much is too little? Where is the balance? Is balance even a requirement in a sport that relies only on being extreme? Extreme with training, with mental and physical strength, with eating habits, and with patience and tolerance for all things. At least that's the way I had to do it, or maybe that is because I did something so intense instead of just taking the middle road and winning the gold. The gold medalist does stand in the middle of the podium, right? Does that signify anything? The champion has balanced both the right and left side and has come out on top. Maybe that is why I never became an Olympic gold medalist. I am not trying to downplay the medalist in any way shape or form. It is an amazing achievement, but I am just saying I know a lot of Olympic gold medalists and their training regimen was astonishingly much less harsh then mine.

Sometimes doing too much of something actually gives you an opposite effect. I don't see how I could have achieved my spinning by having balance in my life, as the training for it was to the tenth degree and every day I needed to spin faster and longer and more. It was a huge toll on my body, mentally and physically. I had to create such a vacuum around me so that I could create my spins. But isn't it odd that spinning is all about attaining balance on ice, yet I had none. Spinning for me did not just happen naturally, but it was a whole technique I had come up with. No one ever taught me how to spin. My mother helped me the most and my Japanese coach insisted I work on the basic spins, but as for the technique, I just figured it out myself. I knew I had to go faster to make my mother happy so there was no choice except to make it happen. I had to find a way and I don't think I really skated for me anymore. I wasn't in the equation. I would, however, have to pay the heavy price.

I did love school. I stood out here academically and artistically and as everyone always picks on the one that stands out, there was some trouble from other parents. But other than that school was wonderful for me and I could have stayed there all day. I truly loved studying. I loved tests and learning something new every day. I was curious about life. I received many awards for having the most A's in school. I was the lead actress in plays and would always have the main roles in dance class. We had fitness tests and I would always come in first.

I even dressed a little differently. We had uniforms but instead of a plain white shirt my mother would have me wear frilly white shirts with details. They were beautiful. Everyone remembers that about me. Yet I loved the Japanese school uniforms even more. They exuded such charm and innocence yet were flirty at the same time, and so on national school day I dressed up in a Japanese school outfit! I loved their backpacks and made sure my mother got me one too, but the American style textbooks were way too big compared to the little Japanese ones and nothing would ever fit in it! I would always have my hair in braids, or a French twist, or a ponytail, but my hair would never be let down. Ever! No matter what, I always strived to be the best, and following my father's advice I made sure that I was the only one to do what I was doing.

Festivals were great in Tokyo. Two of my favorites were the family festival at school and the New Year's celebration in the city. They both brought charm and excitement to me. The ringing in of the New Year was especially beautiful with all the Japanese lanterns burning lights of hope and faith and the festival at school was a day of fun with no responsibility. There was a Swiss stand and it felt like a little piece of my home would light a candle of joy in my heart. I have so wonderful memories of my school. It was heaven on earth and for me, the best school in the whole world.

I had so much love from my mother and father and I lived a beautiful life filled with everything I could have wanted—beautiful home, beautiful clothes, everything the best that both money and no money could buy. I was surrounded by luxury. But, and I cannot stress enough the "BUT," I was not spoiled in a negative sense nor was I a spoiled brat at all. Things came with consequences. Even though skating destroyed so much in my life it also taught me so much. Maybe skating is what grounded me and taught me to work and to appreciate every luxury. I cannot think what my life would have been without skating because how can I be so arrogant to even think that I could know what it would have been. How could I be so arrogant to take such luxury to decide to change an incredible aspect of my life?

And maybe skating did save my life, by awakening me to see and feel things I would have otherwise never touched. Without skating I might have been that spoiled brat. In sorrow we discover things that really matter; we discover ourselves. Without sorrow there is no joy. Without water there are no trees. Without the rain we would not see the rainbow. Without the struggle we would never get to the top of the mountain and without the depths of the ocean we would not have the horizon. Only when we can lose sight of the shore will we have the courage to reach the other side. I feel skating and everything that came with it was my lesson and was the biggest lesson of all. Without it life might have been too easy and you never know how I might have taken advantage of it. Yes, I am thankful for skating, for what it gave, what it took, and ultimately what it presented me with.

At around twelve years old I began to participate in serious competitions and was winning them even outside of Japan. There was one competition I had in Switzerland where we met another Swiss girl who was skating in the exhibition. She was much older than I and was the Swiss champion at that time. Her spins were incredible, the fastest and most innovative back then. My mother loved her spins. She told my coach right away she just wanted me to stop skating then and there and to throw my skates away! She thought I would never have better spins than that! In fact, I would, but this girl had more going on than her spins. I remember seeing her in the restroom as she was scratching away at her scalp and nervously picking her skin on her fingers until she bled from every which place. The stress had caught up to her and my mother told me she hoped I would never get to that stage. Little did we know.

I was starting to have to travel to Switzerland a lot because as a Swiss citizen I was to compete internationally for them and had to pass their skating tests on top of the Japanese ones that I was already doing. I was up for the challenge and incredibly excited. It felt prestigious to be able to be in this sport. I was also going to start competing in the Swiss National Figure Skating Championships starting with the Junior level and then proceeding on to the Senior level. I would never become a Japanese citizen and so therefore I would never be able to compete for Japan, but the federation there loved me. I was the only skater that was so artistic and the only one in Japan who did such creative spins, especially the Biellmann spin.

In Japan whether in sports or in school, students are taught to copy, not to create, and although I was in their system I had been taught by my parents and at my international school to be creative. I was a different species from them and they were evaluating me non-stop. Therefore the federation wanted and allowed me to compete "out of competition" at the Japanese regional, sectional, and national levels. The Japanese federation wanted me to be present in order to push their own skaters to do what I was doing, and for me it was great practice. "Out of competition" meant that I would not take a spot away from any of the Japanese skaters. So even if I placed first, the second girl would actually be first.

The other skaters despised me for entering with them. Even the skaters my mother used to kindly give a lift home after evening practice, would bully me in the car saying I was a disgrace and it was so terrible of me to even be in Japan. They said I had taken away everything good from them and on and on they would talk. By now my Japanese was great and I understood everything. My mother, although understanding a little, didn't quite get all the nuances and I didn't say anything to her about what they told me. I just sat there and let the other skaters talk. It was their way of venting and as much as I tried to push away the hurt, it affected me internally very much. I wished I did not understand their language.

Maybe to some people it would become the drive do better but I am not that type of personality. Everyone deals with a situation differently, usually to the best of his or her ability, and for me it closed and shut me down. I am too sensitive, an over-analyzer, and being a fighter was not my thing. I would hide like a turtle. It must have been hard on my mother as well. She was the only foreigner at the rink and no other mothers dared talk to her in public for fear of losing face. They feared it would destroy their social status by talking to a so-called Alien. My mother was very alone, and not having my father around either to help out, she must have been going through a lot of anger and pain inside of her as well. Remember, it was only the two of us in our world.

Competitions were so exciting in Japan. There was all the preparing my mother and I did together, the rituals and superstitions, and I always couldn't wait to show the world what I could do. Whatever number I drew to skate, would be the number of times I would repeat all my exercises until the competition was over. My mother always did my hair in the most wonderful updos and I would be the only one with that style. I would show it off proudly. We also prayed together for good results and that I would skate my most possible best.

My mother especially, being a great believer in God, made sure that prayer was always incredibly important and poignant in my life from the time I was born. Whenever possible, Mass would be attended, and each morning, evening, and before a meal our prayers were always said. My evening prayers would always last at least ten minutes as I made them up myself, always somehow praying for everyone else but me, wishing for world peace and the happiness of my family. While I attended a Catholic school I would pass through the rites of Baptism, first Communion, and then Confirmation with much devotion to the higher power. To this day, prayer and God are always my constant vision. I am thankful for this and realize how important it truly is in one's life. Without it I would not have survived.

My mother always made sure I did not just get on the ice and do a program. I would need to tell a story and paint a picture on the ice, and my whole look from head to toe matched my music and story that I was telling. I was an actress and I absolutely loved it. It was like a world I went to and sold my emotions nakedly on the ice.

Before I went on the ice my mother gave me sheets of math questions that I would have to do in my head. There were always about one hundred of them, and as she corrected them, both her focus and mine would be on how many I got wrong, not how many I got right. I needed, not even wanted, but needed, to always be perfect. I would be totally disappointed in me if I got any wrong because then that would mean I might not skate well. The purpose was to get me to focus and concentrate and it did work wonders. Being in the zone was an amazing place to be and it made me skate perfectly.

My mother always did everything for me and she never did something for herself. Watching me skate was filling her cup of joy. After the competitions, the minute I stepped off the ice, I would be flooded with gifts from all the other skaters that overflowed in my tiny arms according to their custom. But there was always a gesture dance of refusing the gifts a couple of times to show your appreciation before accepting it. Timing in Japan was everything, in speech and in actions. Gift giving is a beautiful and necessary form of communication with rules of its own in Japan. It brings so much joy to the person who receives the numerous gifts, but they are never to be opened in presence of the giver, to save face just in case the receiver is disappointed. I remember coming back from international competitions with my suitcase filled with souvenirs that I would happily give out to all those that you were required to give to on returning home. There were rules of who needed to be given these gifts and they would be followed thoroughly.

At age twelve I won my first Swiss Junior National title. It qualified me and gave me the exciting honor to skate for Switzerland at the Junior World Championships. I later on competed at four more Junior Worlds, and after winning the Swiss Senior Nationals I went on to five Senior World Championships. The season would be filled with competitions all around the world as I also did the Grand Prix Circuits and European Figure Skating Championships. I had competitions in many different countries and I was so fortunate to be traveling the globe. I was going to exotic and far-away places that only my classmates could imagine. They hardly saw me anymore. I was more absent than ever, yet still getting all A's. I always said it was much more informative, challenging, and brain stimulating than any history class I could have taken. I would see and be immersed in many different cultures. It was an amazing life to lead. Even all the various airports were enthralling. I was becoming a world citizen.

Exercise was very prominent in my life and my mother and I had a fear that if I didn't do it constantly I would forget how to skate. I was terrified of that. So even during layovers at airports, and during the flight itself, I was never allowed to sit and rest. With my running shoes on I would run around in the airports for my jog, and in the plane I would do sit-ups and my mother would stretch me on the floors in the gangways on a towel we always had with us. It was so exciting to be at such a high level in my sport and to train so hard at it to see how good I could get. I do not want to make this book, however, about how I prepared for a competition, or how I was nervous before getting on the ice, or how I just wanted to have fun out there (or so other skaters say, not me).

In this book I do not intend to explain and write about the moments leading up to the jumps, recount how many jumps and spins I did, what I felt when the marks came up, placements, figures and numbers, and so forth. I think this will bore the reader and I know too many books are out there with all this repetitive nonsense. It would be much simpler to write about this and tell you what I placed when and where, and what jump I landed or didn't. But who I am and who I have become is not about that. To me, the results never did and never will impress me. That is why, perhaps, I never wanted to be an Olympic gold medalist.

To me it is the life one has led, the thoughts one has thought, and the actions one has taken that intrigue me the most. The psychological nature of a human being fascinates me. You are reading this book because destiny has led you to it and I am here to express to people about the humble little slice of life that I know about through my experiences. Not a skating life but a human life. That is what I feel I must do.

Living in Japan I never could travel with my teammates to the competition because they were flying from Switzerland and I was far, far away in Tokyo. The Swiss federation would do a despicable thing when paying for the trip for my coach and me. If the competition venue was closer to Switzerland than Japan, they would pay for our flight to join the team from Switzerland, but if the competition was closer to Japan, they would pay only for our flight from Japan to the competition location. It was rude and unforgivable and was just added to a list of things they would later do to me.

My mother always came with my coach and me to competitions. I was too young to be myself and I needed my mother so very much. I loved having my mother with me. She was my best teacher, supporter, tree trunk of life, my savior and most of all my best friend, all intertwined with being my mother. She knew she had to be all of these for me, as I had no one else. For my very first World Junior Championships skating competitions we did, however, travel with the Japanese team and it was a great experience. We stopped in Vienna for a bit to train before going to Budapest in Hungary for the competition. I placed sixth overall, and although I was happy with my result the Swiss were not.

It was very hard for me because I was living in Japan, yet wasn't Japanese, and skating for Switzerland, yet wasn't really Swiss either, because I had lived there only four months of my life and they did not see me as a typical Swiss. By now, I really didn't know where home was. I was always a fish out of water, the odd one out. People used to tell me "You're so spoiled," but little did they know of all the turmoil I was going through. No one could have guessed it by just looking at my life at that time as I was good at hiding my emotions and putting a smile on my face. But I didn't speak. I didn't ever voice anything out loud because I was too scared.

The Swiss tragically never saw me as a Swiss. In their thinking I didn't have their views, I didn't have a Swiss coach, I didn't speak just like them, and so forth. As for me, I thought, "Just watch me skate. Judge me on that, not on where I live or whom I speak to." I wanted them so badly to be proud of me, their skater. But skating doesn't happen that way. It is a very political sport and a skater can't just skate well. They need the whole village, the whole country to back them up so judges can be bribed and marks can be tweaked. You alone cannot win anything. Pure skating alone will not win anything. That is the sadness of the sport and the part that I detested most.

The Swiss delegates were not able to see my skating on a regular basis due to my training in Tokyo. They expected that when I did go to competition, nothing was good enough other than winning the gold medal. As a result I was a big failure to them in their eyes and I felt it. Not having support from my own people, or my own coach who was more my dictator, or my own federation who were mere trial judges, was hard to deal with as a child. Once again, it was just my mother and I who were trying to figure everything out.

From when I was little, spinning and artistry was always my forte and that's what set me apart from anybody else, and really that's the only thing I wanted to do. I however, from the very beginning, always mentioned that I would never be a show skater. I loved skating for me, but just for a little while, not forever. I wanted to skate, but I would become doubtful of it as I grew older. I became too scared to skate anymore. The responsibility and consequences were too heavy on my shoulders. It was like a snowball rolling downhill that became bigger and bigger, that we couldn't stop until it would smash into an obstacle so large it would break into pieces.

Most importantly skating seemed not pure anymore and became tainted with politics. Competition skating was too harsh on my heart and soul, and later on, show skating sold something that was too sacred for me: Spinning. Spinning had been my glorious meditation and I felt I could no longer do that for the judge's marks or for money. I felt it was a disgrace and a dishonor for me to do to my God-given talent. I became ashamed of myself for spinning in that way and in that arena. I could not see how happy I was making people with my glorious spins, while I was so trapped in my own pain.

How did my spinning start?, you may ask. Well, when I was about eight years old my father told me to find something special, something that no one else could do and that I would be the only one in the world to do it. He said that this is what would make him proud of me. He never said that it would make me win a gold medal, or it would make me a champion. But for him to say that this would make him proud of me, made me want to do it even more. As kids all we really want is for our parents to be proud of us. He had come home one time from a trip to Switzerland and had seen a Swiss skater spin and told me that I would not only have to spin like her, but even better than her. I felt from the time I was little that spinning would now be my thing. I would spin faster than anyone else, longer than anyone else, and in positions that I would create, and that only I could do. Spinning was to me the thing that would make me a champion in my father's eyes. That became all I wanted.

On the other hand, believe it or not, jumping wasn't a problem for me either. I was very tiny, even the tiniest among the Japanese kids my age, and I never missed a jump in competition and rarely in practice. But, as I became afraid of the intense pressures put on me as I started to do triples, my body and I began to fall apart. The fear broke my confidence in jumping. It was not my height that was the problem then. I didn't really start growing until I was in my mid-twenties. This was due to the hard training I was under and my not resting or sleeping enough so my body didn't have time to grow in any direction. At age nineteen I was five foot five and by the age of twenty-seven I was five foot nine. My growth plates in my spine were still open at age of twenty-five! Even my feet that had been so cramped in my too small skates (since my Japanese coach had always said the boot needs to be very fitted) grew two sizes once I stopped skating!

I didn't see my father much, yet I felt his presence strongly. He used to bring the most wonderful gifts back to us from all of his travels. I collected turtle figurines and he would make sure I had one from every country he visited. I loved the days when he returned and was so excited to see him. It would be like Christmas on those days. My father and I didn't need to talk much and we knew what the other was thinking. Even if he wasn't physically present, his wishes and his love were strongly felt. My father must have had so much courage to do what he did. He too must have suffered from being away from the family so frequently. I didn't talk to my sister much and the only real daily contact I had was with my mother. Looking back at that time I can see now that it was getting very intense and dangerous. At that time, however, neither my mother nor I realized anything.

I wasn't going to go through puberty in my teens and actually did not until I was twenty-six years old! While I was young, I was actually happy about it. First of all, I didn't really know what it was, since my mother never spoke to me about it, and I wasn't around kids my age enough to be talking about going through it or about cute boys or about anything girlish at all. In whatever ways the other kids my age were developing mentally and physically, I was not. I didn't know how to communicate with other kids, didn't know how to socialize or talk about normal things, and I didn't know how to have a good time and laugh and party. I was at a standstill, but I sure could skate better than anyone else.

My physical change and growth as a human spirit and soul were frozen and nothing was done about it. Either we didn't see what was happening or we just turned a blind eye for the sake of my skating, convincing ourselves that this was the normal way to do things. I didn't think I was missing out on anything when I didn't even know other things existed. Nothing seemed to be a problem because no one else made an issue out of my circumstance. I was so isolated in my mother's and my own world. We were in the bubble we had created. We both unfortunately didn't have enough courage to pop out of it for fear that our life, as we knew it, would collapse.

While I was around Japanese women who are for the most part more flat-chested than Europeans or Americans, nothing seemed to be a problem with my not developing. In school we had to wear white shirts with our uniform and I remember starting to see the other kids wearing bras under their shirts. I was so proud that I didn't have to wear one yet, because you can understand that in sports (well, I speak for skating) it's a nuisance to have breasts or hips or butts. We want to be flat-chested and skinny so that we can skate faster and jump higher and rotate quicker. Because of this anything will be done to delay puberty. Puberty is especially hard for a girl athlete in a sport like figure skating that ends when women are so young.

I remember overhearing other Japanese skaters saying that they did not want to get breasts because then they wouldn't be able to jump. They were laughing and teasing another girl who had developed a little. They said they bandaged their breasts tightly like the older generation used to do with their feet to keep them small, as a sign of beauty. That really struck me, and so then and there I decided I also wouldn't get breasts. I would wear tight tops and would stay skinny enough not to get them, and if I noticed them growing that meant I was gaining weight and I would have to get rid of them.

I never told anyone what was going inside of my head but a lot was turning and turning inside of it. Plus, I thought, what is the use of telling anyone? Everyone is doing it and my mother is doing everything possible for me to skate so I must take responsibility into my own hands and do everything possible for me to keep this body as it is and skate well and train hard. She was doing her job; I must do mine.

Injuries were a huge part of my skating life. I wasn't being trained in a proper or smart fashion by my coaches, and wasn't getting any physical care such as massages, and so the end result was that I was being injured. I was in pain every day from the age of eleven. I was so tired every day as well. Whenever my mother asked me how I was, I would say, "I am so tired of being so tired." And we would laugh at the expression. That was the only way I could express it. But for us that meant I was working hard and it was a good sign.

The first serious injury I had was when I was eight. I broke my chin open on a spin and had to be rushed to the hospital to get stitches. Then I had a serious ankle injury when I could hardly walk, a broken toe from the trampoline class, and to top it off, a serious stress fracture in my spine when I was twelve, which had me off the ice for just a little while before guilt set in and I returned to training. Concussions from falls were ongoing too. This was just the start and many more injuries were to destroy my body. From the age of around eleven years I don't remember skating without pain.

My mother never, ever missed bringing me to a practice. We were at the rink no matter what, even if I was sick, or had a fever, suffering a concussion from falling on my head, or even if there was a flood or a monsoon. Even one time when my mother had surgery, the next morning she pushed herself to drive me to the rink at five in the morning. Half way there she was so dizzy that she couldn't drive me further. She ridiculously apologized profusely, as if what she had wanted to do was even remotely possible. She had to drive back home and, not wanting me to miss a day of skating, she dropped me off at the train station so I could get to the ice rink. Even when we once were victims of a car accident she stayed behind but arranged to get me a car so that I could get to the rink. Her dedication and strength was absolutely remarkable and incredible. She would and still does just drop everything, to do anything for me.

Still to this day I marvel how and where she got that strength. It could only be the deepness of how much she loves me as love conquers all. My mother is truly incredible. Sometimes we were the only ones at the rink. Not even my coach would be there because no one but my mother bravely drove through any kind of weather and circumstance to get me there. There was no way I would miss my skating practice, not even if hell froze over, not even if the sky collapsed, maybe not even if I lost a leg. It was done from the mentality that skating will cure anything. As long as I was at the rink and could skate, I was okay.

But it didn't come from me and I don't think it even came from what my mother believed in. It came from exterior pressures. For me, I was so young that all I wanted was for someone to tell me what to do. I wanted to be guided. By that time I had already chosen to skate so there was to be no more discussion if I still wanted to skate. That would be absurd. If I chose it I must always want it. Also, if I had a bad practice, my mother said, "Oh go to your room and paint." It was something I loved to do, but at those times it would feel like a worthless thing to do.

Everything became less important than skating. Everything became of lesser value than skating. Everything else was put down because skating was elevated, high up on the list of being worthy. I even wanted to do ice dancing but at that time ice dancing was regarded as the failure of single skaters. But since when did what other people think and what society ranks high become so important in life? I think my mother didn't realize what made her think this way. She thought that she had the responsibility to produce a great child, a responsibility to my coach, to my father, and to herself. She thought her obligation was to get me to wherever I needed to go, well-prepared, dressed and fed, and then I should be great. Pleasing my teachers was our first priority. Then, for me, it was pleasing my mother and father. I was not important to myself. I felt guilty that so much was done for me so I thought the least I could do was skate and be an A student. Even if I answered one question wrong on my tests, I would feel so unworthy.

Sometimes on the car rides from school to the rink I wished for a lot of traffic so I could nap longer, or for my ballet teacher to be stuck in traffic so I would not be able to have my lesson. I was so exhausted but I knew if I said something I would sound too easy on myself and my mother might erupt. I never wanted to make my mother upset. I was to become very frightened of her.

As I have said earlier, coaches hit the skaters but my coach never touched me. He only would continually complain to my mother that she did not prepare me enough to perform for him. He instructed her to bring me to the rink on a silver plate, saying it was her responsibility that I skate perfectly every single time. Unknown to me, he put all the stress on my mother. I was about ten years old when, because of pressure from my coach, or for some other reason, my mother decided she needed to physically punish me in order to make me a better skater.

My mother started to routinely scream at me and hit me. This sentence is so hard for me to write because I still would like to be in denial that it happened. I know my mother never meant for anything bad to happen to me and

I love her so much. I want so much to protect my mother. But without telling this, my story cannot be written truthfully and in no way do I blame my mother for any of this.

I became terrified and was truly petrified of my mother. My mother told me that I was always hit because I did not fight enough on the ice. How ironic that I was taught to follow the three monkeys, but now in this circumstance I needed to fight for my success or I was to be hit. The ice rink became a frozen prison for me. There seemed to be no way out and if I did get out for a while, it would also be a hell outside of the prison. At least when I was in the middle of the ice I couldn't hear anybody. When doing my jumps or spins I didn't want them to end because when they did, I was required to hear my coach complain and criticize me, and when I went off the ice it would be my mother's turn. That's why I liked to spin and was able to spin for so long. At least for that period of time I couldn't be touched or spoken to. It was my piece of heaven in the prison.

I've wondered at times if others would like to be the best spinner in the world if they knew my mental and physical torment. But everything happens for a reason and I truly believe that without the sorrow I wouldn't have been such a good spinner. I am blessed with a gift among the curses. Others might have relied on drugs or escaping from home to relieve their pain. My spinning was my drug, and although it might seem like it isn't as dangerous as drugs it might as well have been as dangerous because it made invisible what was happening to me. It was my escape when, even though I longed to rest, I dreaded getting off the ice because then the time of torture would start and I wouldn't be able to rest either mentally or physically.

I should explain that I am writing about my emotions at that time but without the knowledge that I have now of what was going on in my life then. It is only clear to me now that I have healed and become my own person. All the time I was skating and going through this I had no clue whatsoever of what was happening. I had reactions when events occurred but my mother and I were blind to the reality of the situation. We never once thought there was anything wrong. That is what can happen when you are experiencing something like this. You continue to live for your goal that overrides all else. Only later in my life, when I had no choice but to look at the past and understand the heavy consequences of the affects of skating on my body, were my mother and I able to unwrap the blanket in which we had so tightly covered ourselves and reunite in ways we never had before.

At that time I was confused and completely stressed out. Being overweight was not the issue for me since I was over-trained and too skinny. Everyone thought I was anorexic but I ate a lot. I just was doing more than my body could handle. I didn't know about bulimia or anything of that sort at that time, and if other skaters were going to extremes about eating, I was oblivious to it until I went to America later on.

The issues and my mother's frustration were always because of my skating and mostly because of my jumps, nothing else. Jumps did not come that easily to me as I grew older, maybe because I was not correctly taught technically, maybe because they were hard for me to do, or maybe because when I started missing them I was hit. That consequence terrified me so much that fear would overpower me and I would make more mistakes, and so it was like a catch twenty-two.

But I truly could not understand why I was being hit. If I had not given it everything I had or if I had been lazy and spoiled about it I would have then understood. But I was someone who tried so hard and never gave up. Yet I was condemned for the things I was trying the hardest to do, and I felt misunderstood. I was working so hard, but I was told that wasn't good enough. I wished I could have clicked my red shoes and magically made my jumps happen, but all I could do was give it everything I had.

It was all so confusing and hurtful, especially for me to have my own mother to do this to me. I think when someone outside the family like a coach abuses you, you can distance yourself from it, but when it's your own flesh and blood it is more emotionally hurtful. Even more than the physical pain it caused, I just couldn't come to an understanding of why she was doing it to me when I thought I had done everything for my mother. The only support I had, the only person I trusted, was hurting me the most. But since I trusted her so much I believed I was wrong. I had to be wrong. There is no possible way that my mother could be wrong. She was doing it out of love, for certain, and therefore I must accept it since I deserved it. So I worked and worked harder and harder, longer and longer.

The hitting me was getting more intense every year as I entered middle and then high school and would only get worse. The fear of my mother hitting me started to overpower the pain of the actual beatings. I remember when I was about twelve, that before one of my skating tests my mother lashed out severely at me. I can't tell you why, because to this day, I don't know why. But I was hit and screamed at and spat at. I never, ever, fought back. A few hours later

I was on the ice with my sparkly costume and smiles on my face and passed the test with flying colors.

My mother thought she saw that after hitting me I skated better. Sometimes this was true. Maybe the adrenaline would rush through me, or from so much fear I would skate faster, or maybe God gave me a gift to skate well so I wouldn't be hit again that day. So maybe she was correct that it did work. But a reprieve from the hitting definitely didn't last long because the same thing would happen day after day.

The evening car rides home from the ice rink became a torture. I would be happy to have another skater with us since their bullying me was better than having my mother hitting me. When I had no such luck, I was instructed to sit in the front passenger seat, although I always begged to sit in the back so that I could rest and so that my mother's hand could not reach me. But my mother would order me upfront and my mother, while driving, would hit me with her right arm and hand across my face, chest, and legs during most of the trip home. When I was let out to run the rest of the way home, I cried as I ran.

I was so afraid to open the front door upon reaching home. I was scared and sad because I wanted so much to be able to understand why my mother was so angry with me. I wanted to be able to take it all away from her and be her sunshine. I loved it when my mother laughed and smiled. I would go straight to my room since my mother would tell me I needed to go to sleep. Doors were never closed in my family's home and falling asleep frightened me even more because I wasn't sure when my mother would pounce back in the room and wake me up and start it all over again.

This happened often, and one time in particular I remember well. It was one of those terrible evenings, and I had fallen asleep while crying softly so my mother wouldn't hear. At around 2:00 a.m. my mother suddenly came into my room and pulled me out of bed while screaming and hitting me. She demanded I go for a run since I didn't work hard enough that day. So in my pajamas she threw me out the door and I had to go on a run.

It's amazing that I just didn't sit outside somewhere and cry and wait for some time to pass. I actually ran. I ran for at least an hour all around my neighborhood with my pajamas and sneakers on, crying the whole time. I wished I could run longer. There was also this feeling inside of me that I wished something really bad would happen to me so that all this torture would stop and she would feel sorry. I felt bad for thinking it, but did not know another way of stopping this whole thing. No matter how much I tried and worked I just did not seem to be able to do what my mother wanted.

I was so afraid to come back home but, on the other hand, I wanted to see my mother because I still had this little candle of light and hope burning inside of me that she might actually be proud of me and say, "wow, good job, good run," hug me tight, and smile and apologize. I longed for her to apologize, and I had hoped that the run would have made her anger go away and that she would be smiling upon my return. I think God gave me the strength to keep that hope alive all though my years with my mother. Otherwise I don't think I could have survived the torture inflicted on me no matter how well it was meant. What I just could not swallow was that my mother would do this to her child for the sake of a sport. For skating? I could not believe she would put skating before me, her child. This was very hard to accept as a child.

Strangely, when my mother hit me I would look into her eyes and it was as if another human being had entered her and it was not my mother hitting me. Either I was trying not to really see my mother in fear of it hurting me even more, or maybe some other spirit really did enter her and engulf her to do these things. This made it possible to take on the beatings. I felt that I would succumb to being her punching bag; that much I could do for her. I felt she had so much anger and frustration with the whole situation that I was the only person she could take it out on. I was the only one who would just take it and not fight back or say anything. Also, I was the cause of the frustration. Without skating, or me, there would be no problem. I was the stimulator of this and I didn't know how to fix it.

Later on in my life, when I graduated from high school, my training schedules changed and dinners were at home together, and this period was incredibly frightening and scarring for me. These times were excruciating. Dinners became hostile environments and sometimes for hours I would be hit nonstop while I cried and screamed. To my astonishment not once did neighbors or anyone else say anything. I once entered a competition all black and blue from the beatings and really too tired to even care how I would skate. I was nineteen by then and hope started to fade.

Maybe the reason I could endure this for years to come was that when I awoke in the morning, my mother would be all smiles ready to start the day full of energy and determination in her eyes to make me happy. She would act as if nothing had happened and nothing was ever said about it. I swallowed my hurt and followed the lead, believing that my mother had realized what she had done and wouldn't do it again. When that did not happen, I would just pray and pray for the day not to come to a close for fear of it. On the ice I became very petrified to make mistakes, as I knew the consequences.

As I grew older holidays and birthdays were the worst because my mother asked that I give not material gifts but gifts of execution on the ice for her. I would want so much to always give her the best gift ever. It didn't matter what holiday it was; for me it was always her holiday as well. Even on my birthday I believe a mother remembers the event more than the child, and so I wanted to make her as happy as she had been when giving birth to me. The least I could do was to give her a gift. My mother didn't want a gift money could buy. She wanted a gift that was the hardest for me to give, because that would mean the most.

But sometimes the practices went on for hours because in one way or another I couldn't achieve what my mother wanted from me for her, or what I wanted to give her. I would get so angry with myself and hate myself for not being able to do it. I would have fits and start shaking and crying, have panic attacks, and then of course it all would get worse. I had to recuperate and then try again and again. I would not be able to leave the ice if I didn't do what was wanted, not only because of the consequences from my mother, but also because throughout the day I would then have a huge guilt that I couldn't give my mother the one thing she wanted. She gave me everything, so why couldn't I do the same?

I started tearing out all my eyebrows and eyelashes again, due to anxiety, and started picking my skin until I bled. My fingers were covered in blood all the time. My mother used to tell me stop picking, but the reason I picked was never addressed, so no matter how much I wanted to stop I couldn't. I didn't know why I was feeling so anxious. I just felt I wanted to change everything about me because I couldn't change the real unknown reason that we were all too afraid to face. I cut all my hair off when I was seventeen out of the anger deep inside me. I trembled all the time and even the slightest noise like a door closing, or a drawer shutting, or a person coming into a room would make me jump. The reason for all my behavior and symptoms was never, ever discussed. We just continued as we were. Work, work, work, was the motto. People lost limbs in the war and still continued to walk, so what I was going through was nothing.

My father didn't know about any of this and neither did my sister. I wasn't able to tell my father because I hardly saw him, and if I tried telling him over the phone my mother would get angrier with me. My mother never wanted my father to know of any problems because she never wanted to put any pressure on him and always wanted him to feel that all was well. She wanted to be the best possible for my father. My sister and I were not close enough for me to feel that I could turn to her. Most importantly, I didn't feel anyone needed to know, because I was wrong, and I deserved this treatment, that this is what needed to be done. At that time it didn't seem wrong to any of us. My mother never once hit me in front of other people so no one at the rink knew about it either. I didn't see a reason to tell my coach, since coaches were doing the same thing by hitting their students.

I thought I was only getting what I deserved, since my mother was ultimately just trying every way to make my coach happy after he said she needed to prepare me better. She had thought innocently that hitting me would solve the problem. My mother had given the coach her word to do her part to make me the best for him, and her word was to be kept. This is what the relationship between my mother and me had become. How truly sad.

When I was about fifteen years old my father had to leave Japan to return to his post in Switzerland. Usually the company had us stay in one country not more than three years, but by this time we had already been here for more than ten. This was because my father was bringing so much profit to the company and because not every family with little children could adapt as well as we had to a continent like Asia. They had kept us there as long as possible. Without asking or telling me so as to not hurt me, my parents decided that my mother and I would not follow my father. The family would separate and my mother and I would stay in Tokyo to finish my school and continue skating with my Japanese coach.

I felt the decision was primarily made because of my skating and the winter Olympic Games to be in Nagano, Japan in 1998. They thought staying in Japan would only be to my advantage. At that time I did not know that my father was going back to Switzerland. They just mentioned to me that he would be traveling more and more to Europe and I would see less of him. They did not want me to panic or worry about anything other than my skating. Their world revolved around my skating and me.

My father traveling more to Europe did not seem to me a big deal because by then I was used to my father not being around. No one realized that the little I could have seen of my father had we all stayed together would have made a difference in what was yet to happen to me. Even for my mother, if she had known that my father was at least present and that she could talk to him, it would have helped her stay more grounded and supported. For him to be now completely gone and so far away tore the family further apart and crushed my mother and me. Furthermore, living in Japan, which is a male chauvinist nation, two foreign women on their own would not make it very far.

The Olympics was nearing and there were big problems for me to contend with. Switzerland was accepting me less and less since they didn't like the fact that I lived far away, nor did they think Japan was appropriate for me. They didn't like the fact that while I was getting much acclaim for my spins being the best in the world, my jumps were suffering, and skating was a jumping sport.

The Swiss had a unique way of dealing with all of this. They would deliberately put me in second place at nationals almost every year so that I wouldn't be able to go to the European championships. Since the rules were that only one Swiss girl who placed first could be sent to these championships, they wanted to send another skater of their choice in the hope of having her as a European champion. On the international stage I was always the best Swiss skater at that time, so it was puzzling for people to never see me at the European skating championships. But it always bit the Swiss delegation in the back, since the girls chosen to be sent to the European championships instead of me did not even once qualify in the top twenty-four. So they then would always come back running to me to ask if I would like to go to the world's championships. It was ridiculous, but I went to five World Senior Skating Championships and only one European championship. That's not how it should be done, but the Swiss are a different breed, and to this day I shall never understand what their motives have been in their relationship with me.

Thinking back I really had no one to back me up in any situation. I would have loved to see their faces if my coach or someone had confronted them and said, "Sorry she is not available for the World Figure Skating Championships, either!" But my mother and I were too alone and too scared of every conflict, and we were brainwashed to just be quiet and accepting and hope that justice would be served later on by God, if we were so lucky.

My Japanese coach started to complain to my mother that he felt I had hit a wall and if I couldn't figure out why and how to get over it he didn't know what else he could do for me. He mentioned that I was so different from Japanese people that he couldn't fully understand my body and its rhythm. My mother would tirelessly try to make me get over this wall with the only method she knew, which was beatings and screaming. But I didn't know how to get over it either, since my coach was also not giving me constructive help.

Nothing was helping and everyone was probably only making the situation worse. He also had given me for a short time some extra care by helping me with off-ice training. But one day his wife mentioned to us that he was starting to get too tired, that he would need to pace himself, and would not be able to help me anymore. She said he needed to survive to go to the 1998 Olympics and I couldn't tire him out.

So it's safe to say that thanks to me, it is now 2010 and he is still coaching and going to the Olympics. I am truly glad I gave myself up so that I did not tire him out so much! Even all the off-ice coaches that the skaters had suddenly started ignoring me and turning their backs on me. Everyone told me that they were all too tired to coach me. Everything started to crumble. They were all tired of having a foreigner in their space. It was a space reserved for only them and I was an intruder they wanted to get rid of as fast as they could. In the end I do not think it was my Japanese coach's method of teaching but the whole culture around us that broke the team. When my Japanese coach gave in to his wife's wishes, he had no power to stand up for anything he believed in. He was a crumbled man himself.

My coach's daughter had been going to Canada a lot for training, and one summer she suggested we go with her to have some new costumes made for me. Although Canada was as foreign to me as Japan had been in the beginning, it felt great to get off the island and see how others were training and learn about their environment. On our return to Japan my situation with my coach got worse and he became even more distant and cold. At competitions he taught me with such anger for no reason that I was frozen in time and skated terribly. I was in constant fear. He lied to my mother about various things. He didn't want to be seen with my mother and me, especially when I wasn't skating too well and he felt ashamed to be with us. We felt incredibly hurt since my parents had done so much for this coach. We had taken him around the world. I was his first student with whom he could travel and attend competitions in wonderful places. We took him on mini-vacations after the competitions and spoiled him with gifts and my parents spent all their money on him. Every single time after a competition I wrote him a thank-you card with a poem I made for him. We had opened up the world for him and this is how he treated us. He must not be a coach to treat a student in this way. That is not the way of a teacher.

I had to attend a prestigious show for the World Economic Forum in Davos, Switzerland at the very beginning of the year of 1996. The same man who had designed my new skating costumes the year before was also there to skate and conveniently he also mentioned that he was a skating coach. He really fell in love with my skating and my personality as his prospective student. Enthralled with the potential he saw within me, he invited me to move to his rink in Toronto, saying he would take care of me and coach me to become a star. A month later I once again saw him at the World Championships in Canada where he was there again to show his own paintings at an art exhibition that was part of the competition. He was truly a man of many arts.

He first invited my mother and me to his estate in the mountains in Mexico and we excitedly accepted the invitation. Our stay in his lavish, charming, extravagant home was enticing and wonderful as we frolicked by his pool, ran through the parks nearby, and had alluring conversations till late in the night. He was educated and intelligent and we never had a dull moment with him. We would awaken every morning to be once again enthralled by his energy, aptitude, and humor. It drew us nearer and nearer to the decision to move to Canada to have him train me. I felt a very close connection to him and felt it was destiny to have him be my new coach.

On returning to Japan my parents and I decided it was time for a drastic change and Canada it would be. We sprang on the possibility of feeling worthy and having someone so willing to help and so confident that he would make me a star. We were not used to that after being at the mercy of others for so long, so it was unfortunately falsely refreshing. Much more leg work of trying out other training facilities and coaches should have been done but "would have" and "could have" are the worst words in the English vocabulary since they bring nothing to the table. Everyone recommended to us that we should leave Japan, and I was looking forward very much to a change and to the new Canadian coach who gave me hope. It was what my parents knew at that time and they were trying to do their best with all that they had. All they wanted was to make me happy. By sixteen I had also finished high school in an accelerated program and I graduated with flying colors.

Our expectations were high for Canada and all that was promised to us, but it ultimately presented us with a devastating challenge and lessons for a lifetime that were learned the hard way. It would not only be a culture shock to us but also the beginning of a downward spiral that went on for a very long time. We would be swimming upstream for years to come.

From the February, 2001 issue of *Paper* magazine *(Photograph by Nigel Barker)*

My mother and father, always the fashionistas, in Capri, Italy, 1966
(Photo courtesy of Lucinda Ruh)

My mother and me in Paris, *(Photo courtesy of Lucinda Ruh)*

My skating life begins in Paris, France, closing a show in 1982 *(Photo courtesy of Lucinda Ruh)*

Having so much fun at four years old *(Photo courtesy of Lucinda Ruh)*

Four years old and already loving to spin *(Photo courtesy of Lucinda Ruh)*

Enjoying a vacation with my family as we traveled all over the world *(Photo courtesy of Lucinda Ruh)*

Picture of me doing the Biellmann spin at only nine years old!
(Photo courtesy of Lucinda Ruh)

Gliding with the angels on the Philippe Candeloro French Tour in 2003
(Photo courtesy of Gerrard Vandystadt)

6

Culture Shock

(TORONTO)

None are so blind like those who refuse to see.

$\mathcal{I}$ started to have a recurring dream where my eyes were always tightly shut. I would desperately try and try again to open them but would not be able to. The problem in the dream was that since I could not open my eyes, I could not see anything. I would wake up scared but relieved that at least I could see. For years I had this dream, but once I came to understand it, never again. At that time, my eyes were shut in the dream, as they were closed shut in my waking life. I had been refusing to see for a very long time.

Starting all over again and again can be exciting, daunting, and thrilling. It can be all these emotions rolled into one like a sushi roll that tastes oh, so good, that all you want is more and more. The different flavors melt in your mouth and give you an orgasmic feeling. But when you start taking the pieces apart and eat them separately your reaction is not the same and after one or two bites you have had enough. That is what can be so self-destructive about the need to start over. If you could take each emotion and dissect it separately and really feel each one on its own it wouldn't be that marvelous, but all together, wow, it is!

Starting over can be a cover up for what is really going on in your life. It can be done as a need to get out of circumstances because of regret and anger, or sometimes from wanting to cut the strings by leaving, disappearing, and throwing everything up in the air. Starting fresh is much easier than dealing with troubling issues. And who says we can't give ourselves a break by taking a road that might be easier for us in hopes that it will give us more happiness? Starting over can have incredible benefits and incredible downfalls. For my family, starting over frequently was necessary because of my father's work, but later it became my need.

The jolt and excitement it gave me when I could just drop everything, not see the faces of those who hurt me so much, and start over again became ingrained in me. It came from feeling so much pain and hurt with other people that I couldn't bear the fact of being around them. Picking up and leaving was my way of dealing with it. Wanting to start over was much more exciting than dealing with the present situation. It happened again and again over the next ten years, until I had to face my fear, hopes, dreams, my true spirit, and heal my demons.

In June of 1997 I remember so intensely boarding the bus that took us to the airport in Tokyo with my mother by my side and tears rolling down our faces. I was so scared of what was to come. We were leaping full force into the invisible, as if we were jumping over craters of the earth hoping someone was on the other side to catch us. We looked at my father, who had come to help us with the move, waving at us as we waved back. He looked so sad and helpless, yet so kind and as if he just wanted to give my mother and me the world. I wanted us to jump off the bus right then and there to stay with my father. But skating pulled me back again since I felt skating had to come first, although I wished family could have. I wished either my father could have gone with us to Canada too or we could have gone home to Switzerland with him. I had hoped deep inside of me that he would say, "Don't go to Canada. Come back to Switzerland with me. We will find a coach there and it will be all right."

I wanted so much for my parents to take initiative and pull me back since I was too afraid to do this myself. I didn't want to say that this was what I wanted because I thought I would be blamed for not wanting to put my skating first. And I really did want to do everything for skating, but I felt I was losing myself in the midst of the chaos. At that time I just wanted family time. But my parents thought they were making me happy by moving anywhere in the world for the right coach. We knew we had to leave Japan since it was holding back both my personal development and my skating but why could we not go to Switzerland? Japan had changed my personality into a shy, reserved, and scared girl and it held back my artistry since any artistry of a different kind was shunned.

Little did we know at that time that just being a family again and going back "home" might have cured all these problems. But we pushed on. We saw that going back to Switzerland would mean giving up, and giving up was not the Swiss or Japanese thing to do. We hoped that I would be more accepted in Canada and treated more as one of them. We hoped I would get the attention I needed to skate my best. We hoped I would get my confidence back.

The bus and plane trips to the other side of the world were torture and it felt like my heart was being ripped apart. In one way, I just wanted everything to stop. However, I wanted to be strong for my mother and make her feel that I was so happy and grateful that this was all being done for me. But this was very superficial. I could in no way tell my mother my true emotions. That would be too selfish of me. It would tear my mother apart and I could never allow myself to hurt her.

I was confused but I was also excited for a whole new life. I was sixteen but I was more like a twelve year old since I had been so sheltered from the outside world. I stuffed away my emotions as I had done since arriving in Japan and that's where they would remain for more years to come. There was so much stacked away in there that every time I put more emotions away I felt it in my stomach and heart. I would feel like I was suffocating, sick to my stomach and trembling. My emotions began to show up physically. But there was no way I could not follow through with the plan. My responsibility was too big now. There was no turning back for me in my situation. How could I disappoint my mother? That would be the death of me.

Upon arriving in Toronto, to our surprise my new coach greeted us at the airport and gave us a great welcome. We felt appreciated but this would be quite short-lived. Again, our place to stay was a hotel until we found our new home. Our first stop was to go to see the ice rink and unfortunately, to add to my mother's angst, my new coach mentioned that there would be no ice for another two weeks! That infuriated my mother since she was used to my never, ever taking more than one day off. In Japan I used to go from airport to school to the ice rink and back and forth without wasting any time.

Ice rinks and ice time were always our first destination when we arrived somewhere. I remember my mother always saying, "Look, here is the ice rink. Don't you want to go see the ice rink?" I really did not care to when I already was breathing, eating, living, and dreaming skating, but my parents would be so excited. I'll see it later, I thought. For me the big white buildings with ice inside symbolized much more to me than just an ice rink. The moment I entered it seemed like I had a great big mountain on my shoulder. There was so much emotion attached to it and more would be added in the next few years—fear, anger, hurt, excitement, happiness, love for spinning, and being artistic all rolled into one. Another great sushi roll I was addicted to.

Skating was becoming a chore for me. It was work, a job, and I desperately needed a break from it but neither my parents nor I really understood my feelings. We were blind. But it wasn't all filled with despair. When on the ice and spinning and doing my programs, expressing myself and being excited about the training that led up to a competition, were wonderful. The adrenaline rushed through my body and gave me great energy and determination. The constant training or rather addiction to it was enticing. It was exciting! Having constant goals and being able to train for them was amazing.

The spinning is what really did it for me. I felt I could morph myself into all sorts of positions and creations. It was my playtime and I would do it for hours and hours while it silently and unknowingly was killing my body. I really loved training as well, more than the competitions. I was addicted to over training. It felt great to push and push myself beyond my limits. It felt great to be in pain and have my bruises to show that I worked.

I had finished high school and attending university never crossed my mind. Skating was the only thing in my head. I lived for skating. I loved to study and when I was younger I wanted to be a scientist or an architect but skating had entirely engulfed every other aspect of my life and my parents never discussed my attending a university with me. It was as if there was no other choice but to skate since I was so successful at it, and my parents and even I thought we knew that's all I wanted. Here, strangely and awkwardly for the first time in my life, I had a little more time to relax in between the training times. I went with my mother to the supermarket, or to window shop with a stroll in the city, which was almost a first for me. I really had trouble picking out what I wanted to buy since I never had to do that. Everything had been presented to me on a silver platter. My mother always wanted me not to have to do any chores other than school and skating. Here my mother didn't like the fact that I had free time. It made her feel she wasn't doing enough for me and wasn't used to having me with her doing all those chores.

For me, too, it was a huge change. I wasn't feeling useful, and felt like I wasn't being productive enough all day even though I had a heavy schedule of skating and off-ice training. The level I was at was more intense than ever. When not training there really was only time to eat and sleep and then rest a little, which again I was not used to doing at all. I missed studying and I missed being super, super busy. Resting for me was so awkward. It was uncomfortable. It brought up more feelings that I was so trying to repress. What was I supposed to do? Just lay there? I was so accustomed to rushing everywhere and not having enough time that when I did have time for myself I had no idea what to do with it and my emotions were just getting in the way.

So I figured I would just train more. I would do sit-ups while watching television, vowing to myself I would never really just rest. I would feel too guilty to just lie there and read a book. I would do exercises all day. Now that was really not a good idea and I ended up inflicting bad things upon myself. I would in fact train so much that I became so injured that I would require even more time to rest, making me even more anxious and sad. It was a never-ending vicious cycle. But in the end, you really do get what you want. The injuries were voicing for my body what I wasn't speaking in words. It and I wanted rest.

Everything was so different in Toronto when compared to Japan, that it took my mother and me a while to adjust. Some ordinary foods tasted different, especially essentials like milk and water, and my taste buds rejected them in the beginning. The streets, people, culture, and way of doing things were very different from what we were used to and we had a hard time getting accustomed. It was amusing because in Japan taxi doors opened and closed automatically, and so when we wanted a taxi in Toronto we would stupidly wait for the door to open. Or else we forgot to close the door when leaving until we were shouted at for our mistake and would suddenly remember we had to manually close it.

People were not as gracious and courteous as in Japan. Compared to Japan, of course, it was dirtier and the Canadian fashions seemed odd to us. We really felt like aliens this time, whereas in Japan we were considered aliens but felt more like one of them. Here we fit in more on the outside but on the inside we couldn't have felt more disparate. The training, especially, with the new coach seemed completely absurd to me. Here there were very few skaters on the ice at one time. In Tokyo when I had skated during public sessions in the afternoons there would be sometimes fifty people on the ice. In the freestyle sessions there were usually about thirty people and no one would ever get in anyone's way. We all knew where everyone went as well as their patterns so everything worked like clockwork as all else did in Japan. In Japan we had mothers of the skaters play our music and there was a list of those who wanted to do their programs. In military fashion music was played according to the list. The order was never changed and you would have to wait your turn. The list the next day would start off where it ended the day before. You had only one chance and if there wasn't enough time you had to wait until the next day to do your program.

Now in Canada there were perhaps only ten people on the ice and everyone seemed to be in everyone's way. You had to play your own music and you could repeat and repeat sections of the programs. Everyone seemed to be pushing for their rights and want their way. Here skaters had water and tissue paper on skating boards that they frequently went to. In Japan we also had tissue paper because the ice rinks are cold and our noses ran a lot, but in Japan it was forbidden to take a tissue during a lesson. We would be allowed only one tissue a session. If the coach or your mother saw you taking more than one you would be yelled at. Even when we did take a tissue we couldn't just stand there and blow our noses. You would take it while you were skating by the boards and blow your nose while continuing to skate and then throw it conveniently in the garbage can placed off the ice. In Canada, the skater stayed in one place and blew and blew and blew till you thought their whole nose would come off!

Oh, and the skaters actually smiled and talked to each other and they even talked to their coaches! Wow, it seemed like everyone was just playing and it was some sort of a game. My mother and I definitely didn't like it and we thought we were being taken advantage of. How could skaters be having fun on the ice? It wasn't playtime. It was working on the ice. No resting, no talking, no smiling. That was skating. What was happening? We missed the dedication, the beautiful respect skaters had for coaches, the determination and the order in which all was done in Tokyo.

We moved into an apartment a few months into our stay in Toronto. I hated staying at hotels since they did not feel like my home and this just added to the fact that I was not HOME. But I see now that my aggravation about not getting a home more quickly was only the natural emotion of a girl feeling lost. But this was definitely the wrong reaction to our situation because we had to move again only a few months after moving to our new apartment. This would happen quite often to us. As it had happened in Japan when we had moved closer to the rink and it closed down, again in Canada as soon as we tried to cling to what we wanted we would lose it.

I befriended a young man who was an admirer of mine. We met at the ice rink. We were both seventeen years old and he was handicapped, but oddly enough it seemed to disturb him more than me. He would sit with my mother and watch me skate for hours. He would join me when I ate lunch in between my skating sessions and he later sometimes came over to our new home. He took me out to the movies, a first for me since I was so used to doing things only with my mother that even just going to the movies without her gave me anxiety. I feared for my mother, that something would happen to her when I was gone.

I felt I was responsible for my mother to my father, since it was because of me that they were apart, and it would be my fault if anything happened to her. It was a huge undertaking for me and I felt the pressure nonstop. The young man and I had a great friendship, not anything else, although he might have liked more. But although I was seventeen I was so sheltered that I wasn't even thinking of relationships with boys. I had gone to an all-girls' school all my life and had never had interaction with boys except at the ice rink where there was only time for skating. I was so very shy around them.

My friend also managed to hurt me very much. Although he was quite handicapped physically, mentally he was as sharp as anyone and very determined. He somehow managed to play tennis, swim, and even drive a car that was made especially for him. He was remarkable and I looked up to him. I made sure that I treated him just like I would anybody else, and I think because he was not used to that he loved it. But he also then took great advantage of this and would be very mean to me with hurtful words, actions, doing things behind my back and complaining to my mother about things I never did. He used my mother as his crutch. I realized it came from his frustration from his disabilities and his feelings that he never would be considered normal, or in his mind have a chance to really date me so I always forgave him. But alas it makes me think that wouldn't it be so nice if we all just could love ourselves so much that we could just be who we are and not have to hide under so many blankets of denial? I wished that for him.

My skating was not proceeding as we had thought it would. I loved, however, finally being allowed to be more artistic and expressing my emotions from the heart through my new programs. A couple of new opportunities opened up to me as well, such as skating with a Canadian skating star in a television movie he made. I was skating with more freedom. My coach was a person of intensity in whatever he did, mixing it with humor and passion, but he could be extremely strict as well making him totally unpredictable.

It was quite a shock for me after the subdued teacher I had in Japan whose every day training method would be exactly the same and in an almost meditative state. Here I never knew what to expect. It threw me off guard and I felt I couldn't focus on my actual skating. My jumps were a little steadier but my Canadian coach was clearly having his own skating career through me. He was finishing his career by coaching my skating and I started to have his nuances throughout my skating style. I am not sure if that was truly a positive thing or not, but again I was skating for others.

My new coach was an incredible artist filled with imagination and intelligence, extravagant in all areas of life such as food and clothing, and making the English language as eventful as can be. He was living a colorful and interesting life, a true artist dwelling on his paintings, but unfortunately he also dwelled on many other intense interests far from the skating world. It wouldn't have mattered if this hadn't affected me and, more importantly, my skating, but it did. I was clueless about what was going on since my mother always kept all problems other than what was happening on the ice to herself. I was getting annoyed, however, at the fact that we never knew if he was actually coming to the rink as we planned for him to teach me. Sometimes he would and sometimes he would not show up for days. I would just train by myself. It baffled us that a coach could be so irresponsible.

Injuries in my knees started creeping up because I was always over-training and my body was trying to grow at the same time. It would be painful to walk but I would force myself to skate. I was frequently at the physical therapy office to be packaged with ice, then heat, and back and forth. It was like going into a refrigerator and then a sauna! I felt like I was being electrocuted with all the instruments hooked up to me and constantly being prodded here and there.

The problems with my coach actually did relieve me a bit from my beatings though. My mother had so much to deal with that I was released from the harshness of my deep fear towards my mother for a little while, but not for long. We had no choice but to keep my new coach for a while longer since I was having an important competition coming up in September. There was no way of showing up at a competition without a coach. It would lead to more catastrophes.

The competition was in Austria and it would be the first competition of the season where judges sized you up. Especially the federation would be checking to see if you were in form. After leaving Japan I needed to prove that the move had turned out to be the right choice. We kept our problems to ourselves.

My mother and I were relieved to see my coach at the airport after fearing he would be on one of his travels again and not even appear. It was as if he was a magician appearing and disappearing whenever he liked and we were to play along with him. On arriving in Austria, my coach, as an artistic devil and angel mixed into one, rather than having us go right to the rink, took us to see the museums. Practicing and the competition seemed secondary to him while enjoying life coming first. Unfortunately my mother and I were so deep in skating drama that we didn't see the very valuable lesson presented to us here. It's only understandable that we were confused about this since we were in Austria for skating, not for museums but we did not see that life is more than that.

We did as my coach said, and in between every practice that we seemed to be late to every single time, we were at the museums. He lectured us about every painting and showed us every corner of Vienna that he knew in his majestic way as if he were a knight roaming the streets in the 17th century. He was in love with life and wanted us to enjoy life, too, but we were too scared of everything. We were frightened of not doing everything in military style as we had learned to do in Japan. That had been our life.

This freedom was so scary to us. It was unknown to us and we liked a strict diet of sorrow, work, sweat, and tears, and then maybe a dollop of happiness plopped on top that we would take off quickly so we would not feel guilty about our happiness. I actually skated quite well on the first day of competition, but totally fell apart on the next. The problem was that he had choreographed my long program in such a peculiar way as if I had the strength of superwoman, the power of fireworks, the speed of a gazelle, and the grace of a crane, all demonstrated by me in four minutes!

My program was like this: Perform all four spins, connective moves, spirals and steps in the first three minutes of the program, and then do eight jumps (triples and double axels) in the last minute. It was a wonderful and absurd idea with disastrous conclusions. At practice we had already tried to influence my coach to change the order of elements but there was no way of changing his painting he had created of me on the ice. How dare I change his work of art!

So you can only imagine the faces on the judges as they sat there mesmerized by my three minutes of really beautiful, graceful skating, and glorious spins to suddenly be awakened from their comatose state to find their beautiful butterfly turning into an elephant who fell eight times with every single jump. It was definitely fireworks on the ice I must say! We decided to have a dinner meeting that evening with my coach, my mother, my father (he had come to see me compete), the judges and members of the Swiss delegation, and me so that we could talk my program over together.

Judges told us and my coach how although they even had tears in their eyes as I skated because it was so beautifully done, it would be just impossible for me to do all those jumps at the end of the program when I was already so exhausted and dizzy from the spinning. They suggested to my coach that he change the order of elements in my program. My coach, as an artist in the extreme, could not digest these words of guidance in any way, shape, or form, and in his flamboyant style got up and without uttering a world, he left. We had no idea where he went.

The next morning we were supposed to fly to Zurich to see my sister and spend some time there before heading back to Toronto and we were worried he had just vanished. He was known to be very erratic and as far as we were concerned he might have even left the country already. We tried knocking on his hotel room door for hours, to no avail. We tried calling him in the room but received no answer. We even wrote little notes and put them under the door. They may have been read but we had no reply. My mother told me to write on them that I was sorry that I didn't skate well and couldn't make him proud of me and that I had ruined his painting. To this day I still have no idea where he was or what he was really upset about other than our wanting him to repaint his painting. I guess that was not to be told to an artist of such a stature.

Luckily he appeared the next morning at the airport, but he was frantic. He wanted to change his flight then and there to go immediately home to Toronto, claiming he was too upset to come with us to our home in Switzerland. He ran back and forth through the airport halls with his fur coat and lavish scarves moving in the wind he produced while racing past all the people. It was a sight to be seen, and although it was quite dramatic at the time I can't help laughing at it now. We were not going to pay for another ticket for him and to his great disappointment he had no choice but to come with us.

On boarding the plane my father offered my coach his first class seat back to Zurich. He arrogantly barked back that he could not be bribed and he sat in the back with a pout on his face. We were taking care of the coach once again instead of the coach taking care of me. He did not look or speak to my mother or me for the next couple of days.

On arrival in Zurich my coach said he would not stay with us at our home (I'm not sure where he was thinking of going to go but drama was definitely his middle name and he proudly lived up to it). However, my glamorous sister greeted us with a beautiful big bunch of flowers and the minute he saw her he quickly changed his mind and said, "Now I'll come to your house." In

Zurich he lavishly enjoyed the dinners at my parents' and our friends' houses and at beautiful restaurants, and he enjoyed my sister's company as well, but again not even once did he look or speak to me or my mother during the whole time.

On the morning of our flight back to Toronto my mother, wanting for me to be friendly, pushed me to play a game of chess with my coach at our home. I lost. I did not really care but he proudly held his head high. As the plane took off, my mother, wanting to gain my coach's forgiveness, presented him with a huge box of truffle chocolates from Switzerland. He gobbled the whole box at once as if he hadn't eaten for days! On the plane before we landed my coach wanted to play another game of chess with me, and this time, I won. He, for some reason unknown to me, suddenly started talking to me again. Now he respected me, since I won? It was a game for him but to me it was over. For me when someone toys with me, my skating, my intentions, or takes advantage of me, it's over fairly quickly. I forgive, but do not forget and really don't want that person in my life anymore. I knew inside I would not want to train with him anymore.

On our return to Toronto my training continued as my coach appeared at times and did not appear at other times, and I started feeling very uncomfortable with him on the ice. I didn't know how to have a discussion with my coach because I never had one before, so instead of talking I just wouldn't really do what he told me to do. One practice he sat me down on the bench and asked me if I wanted him to represent me at the next competition. It was a big Grand Prix event. For the first time in my life I had the courage to just bluntly say, "NO, I would not." He again, as he had at the airport, stormed off the ice with his fur coat swaying in the wind shouting all sorts of things that were quite incomprehensible. He threw his skates off in the lounge area, and then passed by my mother to scream at her that no one had ever spoken to him like I had in his whole life, and that he would be flying off to Mexico the next day. That was it. I was to never see him again. I think he longed for us to run after him, call him, and drop down on our knees to plead him to come back, but we did not. I could not trust him anymore but as time has passed we have become friends once more, and although he still blames my mother for not having pushed me to stay with him, he and I have wondrous and intriguing conversations over the phone. He has been a brilliant education for me.

A mere six months after we moved to Toronto my mother started searching for a new coach for me. The Swiss federation suggested a quite famous lady coach in San Francisco and we took a trip there for a few days to see if I liked it there. Of course this was the absolutely wrong thing to do. During a trial period of a few days the adrenaline is rushing through you and the new coach is on her or his best behavior since they want the business. So of course everything goes nicely and smoothly. It's a new environment, it is exciting, and it persuades you to think, "Yes, this is it. This is perfect."

Then, when you do move and he or she is sure you are staying and paying them well, the coach suddenly changes and the whole saga starts all over again. My mother now says she would never again do a national sport like skating outside of their country because you end up with no support, no one really caring, and pretty much struggling alone to make things happen. It has been said it takes a village to make a champion. I had only my mother with me and my father far, far away.

And so yet again, we had a home, a coach, one good friend, many new acquaintances from a new life in Canada that we had tried so hard to get used to, but found ourselves coming full circle to where we were only a mere six months ago in Japan. We were left with empty hands and once again with nothing left to grasp. When you refuse to see what is in front of you, refuse to understand what is causing the problem, and refuse to peel the onion layers so that your eyes can tear before you start cooking, you will only get the same results. Without changing yourself you will always end up at the same bus stop. But the fear of looking at the cause can be most terrifying of all. The day came, but only much later in my life, when the risk to remain in the bud was more painful than the risk it took to blossom. When death is by your side, that risk seems small compared to what you are faced with.

7

Misunderstood and Crushed to Pieces

(SAN FRANCISCO)

You can only give when your glass is full and no goal is worth the sacrifice of your most prized possession in life, which is your health.

Maybe I have led my parents on and caused my own pain and if that is solely what people think of my life and me, then I would never be able to forgive myself for it. People might never understand what I went through and my story is not to make them understand or force my ideals on them in any way. I mean for my story to help others going through similar experiences in order to let them step back to see more clearly what is happening in their own lives. Back then, I never claimed to understand anything and I still do not completely understand what happened. Maybe I was innocently leading my parents on by my own confusion about my aspirations and reactions to my circumstance, or maybe I was misunderstood or maybe we had been just unlucky.

While I was trying to be so good to others I might have done more damage to them than I comprehended. Skating (which had become my life-line) and I had a love-hate relationship. I did love skating but the fear of who I was and who I would become without my skating was much more potent than the fear of who I was and would become with my skating. I could not stop skating, no matter what. It was my oxygen and my food. It had become all of my identity and me. It seemed that to stop would be to suffer and to live in fear, but maybe if I had, I would have ultimately lived more in my own truth.

I think to feel misunderstood is one of the worst feelings someone can go through. If nothing is said of your turmoil, it scratches away at the surface of your soul and eats you alive, especially when you are misunderstood by your family, someone close to you, or a teacher to whom you so want to show how good you are. I feel my coaches have misunderstood me for most of my life on the ice. I truly laid out my heart, soul, and dreams in front of them very day and I prayed and hoped they would tread softly. It has been said that great people are often misunderstood. I never felt the need to have people understand me, think like me or see my vision the way I did since I realized it would be too arrogant of me to influence someone else. I had no right to do that.

I wasn't looking to be understood but I was looking to be heard and not to be condemned for my thoughts and feelings. But I knew even if I did speak, I would not be heard and I therefore remained silent. Silence is golden and can be the loudest scream I know of, and I only wanted to speak when I could improve the silence.

I owe everything I am and what I have achieved to my mother and father. In many ways they brought me up with delicate care and a love that cannot be surpassed. A whole book could be written just about how they were the best possible parents. They dropped their whole life, and their wishes and their dreams to fit mine. They followed me everywhere and gave me all they had. They sacrificed themselves and everything they believed in for me and ironically at the same time I was trying to sacrifice myself for them.

My mother does not like the word "sacrifice" because she says she did it because she loved me. Sacrifice to her has a negative connotation. But sacrifice can mean releasing something and my mother did release all else to free her hands so she was able to hold my strings. My mother and father never put themselves first nor did they ever second guess what they would have to do for my skating and me. They willingly threw themselves into the burning fire. I know that I will never be able to be thankful enough to my parents, although I have always tried my hardest to express this.

I have been fortunate in my life to have experienced increasingly diverse cultures with each coach that I have had. Each coach I had has given me a gift. My Japanese coach gave the gift of respect, focus, meditation and dedication. In Canada, I was given artistry, knowledge, and freedom. In San Francisco I learned to understand the human mind better, the need to assess a situation, and the priority of health. In China the lesson would be stillness, loving life, and myself and being a master of mind and spirit. In Switzerland I would find that it is still my true home to which I can return to any time, and in Russia I would receive passion, confidence, and the fight to win and, finally, in America I truly came to know freedom, freedom, freedom, and finding me.

To our disbelief we were inching our way back again closer to Asia by moving to San Francisco by the end of 1996. Once again a hotel would be our home for a long period and this time it was in Alameda, which was far enough from the unstable city of Oakland where the ice rink was. I had a full season ahead of me, including nationals and the world championships and all was going pretty smoothly.

My name was rising in the ranks and unquestionably in the media. I was getting standing ovations everywhere I went for my spinning abilities. The crowd loved me but the judges were harsher since skating was mainly judged on successful jumps that were still not my strongest point. Spinning was undoubtedly harder, and took more time and strength than jumps, yet spins were a side dish to the main meal. Skaters used the spins to rest. I used them to be the highlight.

I was training hard and since the team around me was new and I had consecutive competitions, I did not have the luxury of changing my technique to fit the new coach's way of jumping at that time. Yet this was the suicidal idea that would reveal itself it later. Everything was to remain pretty much the same until the season was over and when we could really work on making me stronger to work on new tricks. My new coach was accommodating about my training habits that came with the package and she taught me with care. She was proud to have me as her student and especially liked to accompany me to the many competitions in wonderful cities across the globe. It had been a while since she had been on the world stage and she felt comfortable being back. Meeting all her old friends suited her well. My mother and I slowly again moved into a new apartment. I was very much missing the quality of the Japanese lifestyle and missed the food, people, and all the childhood memories that were etched in the furniture I had grown up with. I missed my home and to me what were somehow still "my people."

As the World Figure Skating Championships in March of 1997 came to a close and my name was on the tip of the tongues of the people that mattered in the skating world, I was excited to return to California to start the summer training for the next 1997-1998 skating season. The next year would be the most important in my skating career and galvanizing because it would be the year of the 1998 Olympics. I was ready for hard work and great results.

To my dismay my skating training took an ugly turn. When the season ended my new coach had the opportunity to show her real self and she took over completely. The only way I can describe it was that she turned into a complete stranger and it felt like I had a new coach all over again and not one I would have wanted to move to San Francisco to train with. But as always, a teacher is to be followed and I continued to believe in her teaching. Believing is the almighty ritual of power and power was to be abused here. Her husband was a medical doctor and he magically seemed to have invited himself into the team to be my off-ice trainer. He claimed to have trained accomplished athletes and to have had his training method proven by doctors. He said he would work miracles and I would have to do as he said since I could not follow his wife on ice without following his lead off-ice. He said they came in hand in hand like apple pie and whipped cream and I would have to do as told.

So the training started. Looking back it was the most demonic schedule possible and I became a slave to my coach. I wanted to be perfect for them as I thought they knew what they were doing and that it would only help me. My mother and I were not accustomed to questioning the coach in any way. I wanted to skate and be the best so this is what I thought I had to do. Questioning was just not done in Japan, but only later on we did learn that in America questioning a coach or a teacher is allowed, and you do have the right to your own opinion! Having no knowledge of this we just plodded on as we followed their demands, not thinking twice about anything.

In Japan the coach is first on the priority list, then the parents, then the skater. In America it's the skater first, then the parents, then the coach. Wow, it would have been nice to grow up in the United States! We could have said NO, but we did not know that word.

The on-ice training and off-ice warm ups that I always did with jogs, ballet, Pilates, stretching, etc. stayed the same and amounted to about five hours a day, but what became so incredibly damaging was having the extra off-ice training. I was to do one hour of stationary bike every single day except Sunday along with a whole weight training regimen three times a week that when all completed would last about two and a half hours or more each time. The problem with the weight training was that I wasn't able to do the whole list in one day and then repeat it two more times a week along with all the other training I had to do off and on ice. I was way too exhausted and there really was not enough time in the day to do all of this. But since I have a personality that can never cheat or lie (truth is always written all over my face), I ended up having to do my weights every single day to be able to finish the complete regimen. I was in the gym for hours on end every day. I had a sheet of paper that I had to fill out and give to him to show him that I did it. I could not fill out an entry for the exercise if I hadn't done it.

There was another male skater who was on the same schedule and I didn't want him to do it when I did not, so I worked twice as hard. The problem was that I never saw him in the gym, yet his sheet seemed to be always all filled out and the off-ice doctor coach always praised him and I was not. I was puzzled but just thought I wasn't good enough, so I worked more.

A few years later he confessed to me that he never did that list of weights. He said he thought it was way too ridiculous and he wouldn't jeopardize himself. How foolish and naive I had been. I know now, that weight training is deadly for skating. It only makes the muscles heavy and slow. A little weight training is fine but exercising as I was doing it was like becoming a weight lifter. I was doing squats with incredibly heavy weights on the bar resting on my shoulders, as well as clean and jerks, and other extreme exercises. I mean the list was endless, and he would make me go up with the weight load every week. I was so proud of lifting so much. Little did I know how detrimental it was.

This weight training was exhausting. In the end I was doing about eight or nine hours a day of serious physical work. I was working out all day, but here is the thing, I also loved it. As hard as it was, it was also addictive and I loved working and working. I would feel incredibly guilty if I didn't do something. I was proud about going to the gym, and I felt my mother was proud, too, the more I worked out. I could focus with incredible intensity and nothing would distract me. Since I knew I was not ever allowed to gain weight, I thought all this time I spent exercising was also beneficial because if I ate something I could burn it off right away. Basically not having time to rest worked really well, or so I thought!

To add to all the pressure, the beatings and abuse continued and became much more severe. I was becoming very depressed, had constant high anxiety and was so exhausted. My body felt weak and I was feeling dizzy a lot of the time. A Swiss international skating judge had a house in Newport Beach, California and she invited my mother and me to come visit her for a few days of rest. Surprisingly my mother accepted the invitation. We went and the landscape was incredibly gorgeous. While my mother and she talked and enjoyed each other's company, I did not want to rest for fear that I would lose all my talents and all my strength in one day! No one ever said I was doing too much or held me back so I just continued. Since I would not skate for two whole days I went on long, long bike rides under the heat.

The last evening when we went out to eat I felt incredibly nauseous and hot. When I got up to find the ladies room, the next thing I knew I had fainted and was laying outside on the ground with pain on the back of my head where I hit it when I fell. When I got up and walked back into the restaurant I was oblivious to all around me, hearing nothing but my heart beating loudly and in rhythm to my footsteps and pounding head. I collapsed again into my mother's arms. The next thing I knew I was again on the ground in my mother's arms outside of the restaurant where I had first fainted. I heard my mother trying to wake me up and screaming and crying with tears.

Then I heard an ambulance arrive and I was quickly put on the stretcher. They could not find my blood pressure at first since it was so low. When they finally found it the high was only forty! At the hospital all I remember was feeling terrified and confused. With my mother and the Swiss judge by my side, they treated me for heat stroke, dehydration, and exhaustion, and after letting me sleep for a couple of hours they released me in the early hours of the morning. I felt extremely weak and disorientated but with my mother holding my hand we went back to the Swiss judge's home.

We were to go back to San Francisco that morning. This incident would have a domino effect and was the start of the collapse of many cards. The doctor told us I would need to rest for a few weeks and drink more water. Resting was out of the question so water was the only answer. I became obsessed with water and made sure I had a big bottle with me wherever I went. I would freak out if I did not. Flying back to San Francisco the body and cell memory of what happened was alive and I was frightened and scared that I could in any moment faint again. I was in terror over this for years to come.

For about two years after this incident I would not be able to enter a restaurant. I would have the biggest anxiety attacks. It is ironic how I recalled then that one time in school in Japan my classmates had a conversation about how they had fainted. I remember thinking to myself that I would like to experience that one day. They had made it sound so cool. Be careful what you wish for.

During the summer in San Francisco a Chinese coach came to train at the same rink as I with his two students. They all stayed in the same apartment complex as well. One student was high up in the ladies rankings and the other was a promising talent in the male category. He and I became very close friends. I took a huge liking to their coach and longed to be trained like he was training them, with such stillness and knowledge. He looked like a Chinese guru. He looked so wise, so kind, so understanding. He made me miss Asia even more and I longed to be taught by him. We had a beautiful connection as his eyes spoke volumes but we did not speak. The three of them spoke only Chinese with a few English words here and there.

Sometimes my mother drove them back to the apartment with us. The coach would often see me in the gym and had a huge questioning look on his face as he watched me. His look was full of puzzlement as to what in the world I was doing in there for so many hours. He looked more confused and sad for me than I was for myself. He would shake his head and continue on his way. I felt he disagreed with my training and I had a gut feeling he was right, but he was not my coach and I was to follow my teacher's orders. I felt at home around the Chinese coach and his students. I looked at how he trained them and I tried copying what they did. His training method seemed so beautifully created. He was truly a guru. Every word he spoke and every gesture he made was like a Chinese painting with no misplaced or rushed strokes, only those of brilliance leaving a beautiful painting. I was tearful when they left at the end of the summer.

In Japan I felt the training work had been tough but sophisticated and elegant, whereas here it was tough, rough, and bad. My skating did not improve much throughout the summer of 1997 in San Francisco, and actually I felt it just got worse. I was doing a lot of ballet training to add to everything else and I started having severe Achilles tendonitis. It mostly came from the weight training I was doing and the heavy load I carried and put on my shoulders and back as I worked my legs. To make matters worse, I did not have it on one foot but on both! They were so inflamed that the doctors were afraid they were both about to rip. I went through therapy, but it wasn't helping much because my team and I would not let me rest. Some days it was so severe I could not walk but I would try as much as I could to skate through the pain. When on the ice, I would manage somehow to put it in the back of my mind with all the rest of my issues, and only when the skates came off would the pain reality hit.

One day I got on the ice and started to warm up. I started with a single axel and to my astonishment I could not even pull in. I suddenly had excruciating pain that started in my back and went into my groin and then went all the way down my leg to my toes. I tried again and again, not accepting that I was in pain, but it got worse and was unbearable. It was the most pain I had ever had. I felt tears well up in my eyes. After all the things I had been through in this Olympic year, I did not want to now have to go through more injuries.

This was impossible, I thought. I stayed on the ice and tried to do other things, but to no avail. The pain was getting worse and worse. My whole leg was getting numb, plus my Achilles tendons started to flare up as well as I tried to avoid the back pain. I did not want to get off the ice and have to tell my mother what was happening. I knew she would be furious with me.

Ever since I started skating my mother always had the utmost rage when something was wrong with me, whether from some sickness or an injury. I would feel so guilty that I was sick. My mother would become so angry with me because she did not want me to be sick, and anger was her way of showing she was worried and felt so sorry for me. But by now my mother really frightened me, and I had so much fear about telling her because I did not want her upset. I only wanted to make her smile and laugh. That was my job. But I also knew she would be the only one to help me and she was the only one with my best interest so I had to confess. I apologized that I was in pain and cried.

We went to the doctor right away to take X-rays and the result was that I had pinched a nerve in my back and had sciatica. The pain was intense and I could barely walk because of my back. I couldn't cross my leg in front of the other when I was in so much pain. I was devastated. My whole leg was tingling and I couldn't bend backward or forward. The doctor suggested a lot of therapy and rest.

Now, for an Olympic training year rest was impossible. Would a back brace help? We then resorted to many therapies both traditional and alternative along with painkillers. My mother drove me constantly everywhere for this therapy and that therapy. I was amazed that she could drive on the huge freeways that we were not used to because in Japan everything was very narrow. The wide freeways with cars speeding by frightened my mother and I felt it, too. Sometimes we had to go into the emergency lane where my mother could stop the car. She would have heart palpitations and I would be scared for her life. She would be white and shake all over while taking a Valium to calm her nerves.

Unfortunately I couldn't help my mother with driving since I never had taken my driver's license test. We waited in the emergency lane as I tried to comfort her until my mother courageously continued on. A mother is the strongest person. A true mother like mine would do anything for her child.

To top it off, because of the weight training my right shoulder was bothering me a lot and I could barely lift my right arm. But with all the other serious injuries we were already consumed with I did not mention this one and just dealt with it somehow. As my injuries got worse my coach thought I was faking it, so she wouldn't give me any lessons. Her husband also refused to believe me and he did not even talk to me except to mention that I must continue to do my bike rides and weights. I was puzzled. I apologetically said that it would be impossible since it hurt both Achilles tendons, my back and groin, and the pain would go down my leg. He bluntly said that then I must do the bike lying down, basically putting the bike on the floor and riding upside down with my legs in the air. It was absurd to us but my mother and I tried and I was still in pain.

He suggested then that he would accept my being that lazy if I would swim every day. But swimming as well made my body hurt all over. Again, just to rest and let my body heal was not an option. We resorted to my wearing swim water training vest and running in the water for an hour a day. That hurt too, but oh well, I had to do something. I couldn't just do nothing and rest and rehabilitate. Rehabilitation was boring, an act of laziness and showed your weaknesses.

Because my injuries were so severe and debilitating we had no choice but to cancel all the competitions leading up to my Swiss Nationals. I would do as much as I could and take my time to rebuild so I could be ready for the Nationals and then the 1998 Olympics and the World's Championship. Having such great results on the world stage I had already given Switzerland a ladies spot for the Olympics and it was quite certain they would send me. I was now skating with a back brace and that seemed to help a little. Axel jumps hurt the most so I did not do many of them. I skated with pain all over my body but the Olympic dream was too huge to waste. I could skate in pain for that. It would be a good trade. I was broken in pieces but the Olympic dream would put me back together again.

I paced myself a little more and by the end of the year 1997 we headed to Switzerland for my Nationals. I wasn't a hundred percent in shape but ready enough to win and show them I was the lady for the Olympics. We had agreed that I would compete with the brace on under my costume because that was how I was training and I wasn't fully healed yet. So I am not sure what led my coach to do this, but on the day of the competition she told me I would have to remove the back brace. Well, that was not a bright idea. She probably did not want the judges to see my weakness. I did as told, but during my program I felt very weak without the brace and my back started to give way and I panicked. I was in first place after the short program, but the long program was the next day and I was in a lot of pain from the day before.

Again in practice I had the brace on and during competition I took it off. I actually skated pretty decently, but fell on just one jump when my back felt too weak and I felt no support without the brace. The other girl had done one more jump than I had but my spins and artistry were so much farther ahead than hers that we all thought it was a no-brainer.

To our huge shock the judges placed me second and the other girl won. Knowing the Swiss and what they had done to me over all these years, I knew then and there that this was their way of not sending me to the Olympics and I was devastated. My Olympic dream was crushed. I did not want to go on the podium. I wanted to disappear. The pain and sadness of this day will live in me forever. We would have understood what happened if the competition had been fairly judged, but no one understood what had happened except the girl who won and the demonic judges. They are truly devilish. It was a scam from the beginning. We even have a tape of this incident where we see two judges on the panel giving each other the thumbs up when they placed the other girl first. It was the tipping of the scale by these judges that caused me to be second.

I was crushed and so were my family and coach. The other girl was sent to the European competition, and the Swiss rule was that she would have to place in the top twelve to be sent to the Olympics. Not to my astonishment, she didn't even qualify in the top twenty-four. I mean what did they expect? She never had qualified so why would she this year? The whole thing was baffling. Actually, it was more disgusting. It was a game to the judges; it was personal and it had nothing to do with my skating. It crushed me to pieces in other ways than the injuries had. Now, nothing could put me back together again. However, no matter what I was going through in my life, I always did keep a little burning light of hope and trust in God in my soul and this is what would keep me going.

After all, my name is Lucinda, which means light, so I was destined to keep this in my heart. I was lucky I had that then. Otherwise I would have thrown my skates out the window. It was said that my American coach and the American federation and even the IOC called in to the Swiss federation to try to persuade them to send me to the Olympics. But they could not change the narrow-minded mentality of the Swiss federation delegates. They were stuck in the valley in between the mountains grazing on their luscious grass and nothing could be done. They couldn't see over the mountains. They wasted a spot. They just did not send any girl at all! It was absolutely ridiculous. There is no better word for it. They had ruined a girl's dream just like that, and then, they did not even give another girl a chance. In the end I would have felt better if they had sent the other girl. Or even the third-place girl or the last-place girl, but I felt like everyone was just begging them to send a female skater. For God's sake, it's the Olympics and you have a spot. Why not take it? Don't they have pride in their athletes? Apparently, not at all.

To add to my disgust, they did send their dance team and male skater who were all far less successful than me on the international stage, just because of their parents' and coaches' and judges' personal "behind the scenes" connections! It was despicable. I truly don't know how these people live with themselves and I truly don't know how I was able to face these people again. My parents confronted one of the delegates on a later date but he dismissed the fact coldly and my parents are not the type to fight for their rights or mine, and they backed down. In order for justice to be served maybe other skaters' parents, coaches, or agents might have set the record straight, but in my case nothing was done but having trust in life and God and that life would continue. My parents never wanted to succumb to what they thought were lesser actions and they'd rather walk away and walk the road of silence.

I did not watch anything of that 1998 Olympic Games. It was tearing me apart. For the first time I really let myself feel my sadness and I drowned in it. The Swiss again had somehow without an ounce of guilt asked me to go to the World Championships held right after the Olympic Games, and reluctantly I went. My coach wanted to go for herself not because of me. I wanted to stay home. I was training terribly and was just in too much pain emotionally and physically from my back. But like a good student I followed orders. I was embarrassed to skate at the world stage in the condition I was in and hurt that my coach would even push me to do it. To see all the Swiss federation again after they had been to the Olympics without me did not help the situation. Neither my heart nor my body was in it. Although not skating well, I competed and fought until the end and placed horribly. It felt embarrassing.

I had never in my life questioned myself about whether I wanted to stop skating until right after that World Championships. Even so, on returning to California I kept on going to the rink to train. You have to understand that skating and the ice rink was all I knew and it felt more like a home then where I slept. Without going there every day my sense of purpose in life was lost. All my injuries were still prominent and I was in knife-like pain throughout my body. I did not rest. I expressed all my anger and hurt on the ice. This period was very tough for me and I was very depressed. With the injuries, beatings, coach problems, and federation problems, I wanted not to quit, but to have everything stop around me. I was still too afraid to voice any of my feelings.

But my body wasn't afraid. It was speaking for me but that did not seem to catch any one's attention. Not even mine. All my senses had shut down. I felt like a lost cause. I would break down constantly and I was physically exhausted. I was so depressed that my mother wouldn't leave my side in fear that I would hurt myself even more and do something cowardly to myself. I could hardly get out of bed.

Instead of seriously contemplating whether I should continue to skate or take a break, the answer to what my cure should be was to get another coach. My worldwide reputation of success in spins held us back the most from my deciding to take a break. Because my unique spins were one-of-a-kind there was no way that I believed I should save my body and not spin. I must spin—more and better than anyone else for my whole life. My spins brought me so much joy, so how could I not spin! I longed to be back in Asia and maybe even with the Chinese coach that had come to our rink in San Francisco the year before, and had talked with us at the World Championships. We decided to try to contact him, and through one of his students, we were told that all was arranged with the Chinese federation as well. I would be able to train with the national team. The Chinese coach promised he could cure all my injuries and make me land all the jumps.

That conversation kept us alive and we felt we could do this one more time. For the sake of skating we could. We would pack and up, leave and go to China. Nothing would stop us from taking us away from the skating world. We must, must continue. Even if it were to be the far end of the world or on top of the tallest mountain we would be there. Nothing else mattered because skating would cure all. We thought if I could skate we would be all right. It was "we" who decided, "we" who skated. It was us in our own world for our own sake.

For what? I didn't know then. Now I know it was for the pursuit of our happiness. I was trying to make my mother happy and she was trying to make me happy. It might sound weird that this was what it was, but it was. But happiness starts within you and usually the only bird we cage is the most beautiful one.

8

Chinese Dumplings

(HARBIN, BEIJING)

A bad word whispered will echo a thousand miles.

There comes a time and place in your life when you don't know anymore whether to trust the people that you are surrounded with. My mother and I were at that stage in California and it was truly time to leave. I was broken into many pieces emotionally and physically. We felt the Chinese coach would be the one who could bring me back to health and to my potential. I don't know how my father agreed to everything my mother and I decided, but he gave us all the means and everything he could. I loved and missed him so much that I wanted to show my appreciation to him through my skating. He loved us so much by giving us all his trust. He knew how much I loved skating and anything would be possible for his little girl's dream.

But China? So far away? And not Beijing or Hong Kong or Shanghai, but all the way up north near the Russian border in Harbin! I mean it isn't just every day that you get to move to China. I was thrilled to go back to Asia and I felt in my bones that the coach would be able to teach me to perform miracles. Without the high hopes that I had for this Chinese coach I would probably have stopped skating. We thought that by our just taking off into oblivion we showed how focused we were on skating and, oh boy, were we focused. We saw one goal and one goal only and put all our eggs in one basket. That was for sure to bite us in the back.

A week before leaving for China in June of 1998, I was invited to do a prestigious farewell show of a famous pair-skater team and was delighted. They requested that I do a program with only spins. Tons of spins, one after another. I was happy. I loved to do that. I could have done only that for my whole skating career. I loved spinning forever, using the force around me to create all kinds of positions. I went to faraway places in my mind and became whatever I wanted—a bird, an animal, an emotion, a rainbow, even the mountains or an ocean. I used all my imagination to transform into all things and levitate in spirit and soul. I sometimes would literally leave my body and see myself spin. It was glorious. It was my trance, my meditation. I changed my spins all the time, never doing the same move twice. While doing a program I just did what I felt with the music. I immersed myself into the character and let my spirit guide me. I never knew what I would do next. I could never have skated with a partner, as I did not like skating to the rules. I skated freely. Spinning was my haven.

China, here we come. We boarded the flight and this time with no sadness. We were so glad to leave behind the torture we endured in San Francisco. The teachers there did not feel the need to apologize and rumor has it that for years to come following my departure they said incredibly nasty things about me, my mother, my training, and my personality to many skaters who followed their teachings. I cannot change other people and I feel sorry for them that they live in so much denial. I truly hope there are no other skaters who went through what I had to go through, but we understood what we had experienced, and not wanting to be immersed in that anymore, we not only sprinted out of there but flew half way across the world.

We flew to Beijing and on to Harbin. The Chinese skater who had arranged our arrival and stay with the national team had said that my new coach would come to pick us up, but having not spoken to the coach we were still unsure if everything would pan out. One thing my mother and I always did was walk the road less traveled, or furthermore one that had never been traveled at all, and we always had the courage to leap. My parents had taken risks since they were young and they were the first and only in many scary and unfortunate situations throughout their life and travels. We were the first and only foreigners at the ice rinks in Japan and now again we would be the first and only foreigners allowed into the training center in China.

We were never hesitant or scared of a new venture, a faraway land, or a foreign culture. We never feared anything. We just picked up and went to our new destination, trusting in the universe to give us all we needed. I think it is truly remarkable of us, if I may say so. I could also say it might sound totally crazy to others, but for us it was our life and felt completely normal. It was second nature to us and when you have such a purpose you will walk through fire to get to it. You do not see anything as an obstacle. I like to see the positive side of this personality trait and I think it makes us very strong individuals. We can adapt to any circumstance, any situation, and any surrounding quickly and we make our way in the world. It is however a very lonely road.

To our nice surprise, my new coach was there to greet us at the airport, and with our many suitcases in tow we were on our way to the winter athlete national training center in Harbin, China. My coach tried to explain to us in his very limited English that the campgrounds we were going to live and train in might not be what we were used to and it would a very simple life. As his words and teachings were as simple as the life he said we would lead, I can only describe my experiences there with simple words. It was truly barren and purely simple in the most profound ways. It was not colorful. We replied, "It doesn't matter since we were here for skating and not a party. We can live through anything." Little did we know what was to await us. The streets departing from the airport were dirty and uneven. There were livestock along the sides of the road with their herders and open fields for miles. This was most certainly rural China. It took about one hour to get to the camp.

As we neared the camp it was getting more city-like with rugged concrete buildings. The streets were bustling with as many cars as bicycles, people, and animals, pushed by everyone and everything. It was incredibly noisy and dirty with clouds of dust every way you looked. With cars and bicycles honking, animals barking, and people yelling, it was a disorganized jumbled mess, but it all seemed to work out in its own way and we safely made it to the campgrounds. We passed by track and field training grounds, basketball courts, and huge training buildings before we came to a halt. There was a big gate that opened to let us through as if it wanted to open the gates to happiness and paradise. But the reality was that it was inviting us into a government organized facility and it felt like we had entered a military camp. These two stark contrasting images were etched in my mind and it would feel like that all through my stay here.

As we passed through the gate we drove through a huge open space that was engulfed by five buildings. The one we drove up to in the middle, was where the athletes slept, the one on the right was where the coaches lived, the one on the far right was the off-ice training facilities, and the two on the left were the ice rinks. The bigger one was just an empty hall only used during the winter months when competitions were held there for figure skating, hockey, and speed skating.

As we were helped with our luggage, feeling like we had enough clothes for all the people at camp, many of the other athletes poked their heads out of their dorm windows and peered at us with big, round innocent eyes. Some were already outside waiting to see of what all the commotion was about. Who had arrived at their camp? Who was the new face? It looked to me like their expressions on their faces were of those who had never seen such a species as us! It was kind of intimidating since I felt like I was intruding in their space, and I was all too familiar with that feeling of always being the odd one out.

It was extremely hot as well and there was a heavy feeling to the air resembling a pressure cooker. The temperatures were to reach the low 100s in the summer but Harbin is known for its excruciatingly cold winters in the single digits. There did not seem to be any sign of air conditioning in the building as we entered. Luckily our days would be spent in a cold ice rink!

My coach, his son, his other male student who I had befriended in San Francisco, and his friends, all with their shirts off and yet still drenched in sweat, carried our luggage up a few flights of stairs, down a long barren corridor until we reached the last two doors far away from anyone's reach. He summoned my mother into one and me into the last room on that floor in the far end corner. He plopped my luggage down and said this was the best he could do and he had even managed to give us two rooms instead of one. Weren't we truly lucky! My room had one window, a meek metal frame bed with a very thin sheet covering a very thin mattress, and a metal rectangle shaped desk on the other side of the room. That was it.

My mother's room was the same except that in place of the table was just another bed and nothing else. They wanted to show us around the dorm, so we followed them. The floors of the hallway were filled with dirt, cigarette butts, and watermelon peels. The room opposite to mine was a communal area with a sink the length of the room and some broken mirrors on the wall.

Down the hall was a men's toilet, a ladies' toilet, and many consecutive other dorm rooms. We were on the second floor and the floors above us and beneath us had the same layout. The ground floor had communal shower rooms, one for the men and one for the ladies. We learned that there was only cold water throughout the building except for a specific time during the day that lasted for twenty minutes in order to shower with hot water for the athletes, delegates, and coaches. We would be naked with all ranks of the Chinese ladies affiliated with the teams. I was not so thrilled about this even though I had showered at

Japanese training camps before. However, there at least different ranks and ages were not be mixed with nakedness. Here in China, the young, old, athletes, coaches, judges, cooks, all had to shower together, as one. It would take some time to adjust to since I was shy, but it also gave a feeling of unity.

Also on the first floor was a little room where a tiny old Chinese woman sat like she had been there all her life. Wrinkled with wisdom she, not delicately at all, filled hot water kettles with boiling water that each athlete got once a day. No refills here! We could use this at our leisure for tea or whatever else we wanted it for. It would be placed in front of every dorm room door around 6:00 p.m. only once a day and only one kettle full.

Attached to the main dorm building was another little building and that was the cafeteria. The first floor was the kitchen and the second was where all the athletes received their food. I was however told that I would not be able to eat with the other athletes. I was to be an outcast, for whatever reason, if only because they were embarrassed that I plainly was not one of them. I was to eat on the kitchen level. It was a little and bare room with some rickety tables and chairs and that's where my mother and I would have to eat alone. It hurt very much since I had hoped to be part of them, but again I had to realize I never would be part of any nation. I had learned my poker face in Japan and was a master at it by now.

Everything worked very much like the training facility I had visited in 1988 in Moscow. It was government organized and regulated and all was free for the athletes. They did not have to worry about money at all. Athletes had lessons, received food and clothes, and great perks if they had international success. They were chosen from school when very young and put into the system. Most of the athletes, about two hundred of them that included all ice athletes, speed skaters, hockey players and figure skaters, were from Harbin, so their parents lived close by. Every so often since we lived near the Russian border some Russian hockey players would stay at the facility for a few days. But they looked more Chinese than Russian, leaving me again to being one of a kind.

If the Chinese athletes succeeded in their sport they would have to move to Beijing to the national training center that had better conditions. But the federation didn't move them there until an Olympic year because Harbin was the second biggest training Center in China and all the top athletes and coaches were there together already. Looking from the outside world many people might feel sorry for these athletes living in such conditions but being there myself I do not. In spite of living, training, and enduring the conditions there,

I would have liked to have had that support, a system that provided everything for me and where money was never an issue. In one way it is a very easy life. They don't have to worry about anything other than training hard and following a teacher's orders. It was a much better life than all the others living outside the gates of this compound. It felt like all the people who were not allowed within our gates longed to be one of us as they looked upon us with great awe and admiration. For the athletes in China no money was exchanged, but it had been arranged through my coach's prior famous skater that we would have to pay. And a hefty sum it was, considering the conditions. The sum had a reason behind it that we would not know until much later.

After the tour of the grounds my coach mentioned that for another two weeks there would be no ice. We would start with off-ice training slowly and I needed to recuperate from all my injuries first before I could train properly again. A secretary from Beijing from my father's company was to meet us that evening up at the camp, and stay for a few days to translate for us and get us acquainted with everyone and the customs and rules we would have to abide by.

She arrived shortly thereafter. She was to sleep in my mother's room with the two beds. My coach, his wife, his son, and some other coaches from the team invited us to a welcome dinner at a Chinese restaurant nearby. The courses came as they flowed out from the kitchen like there was no end and no tomorrow. The dinner was delicious even though we didn't know most of what we ate. We had been warned about the water there so I was a little hesitant since I did not want to get a stomach illness. The atmosphere was jolly and celebratory and drinks were on the house, bringing great humor from the coaches. Their cheeks turned red and all their troubles were drowned, making them look like little Buddhas wanting their tummies to be rubbed for good luck! Laughter passed around the table and it felt like good things were to come.

Since we were utterly exhausted mentally and physically, my coach took my mother, the secretary, and me back to our rooms to rest and settle in. Not more than five minutes after my mother and I sat on the beds, we broke down crying. The conditions were harsh. The rooms and the common areas were filthy. The food was different and interesting but I already missed the diet I had been on. The bed was so uncomfortable and hard. There was no television, no radio, and no privacy. We could not believe what we had gotten ourselves into. Again we were in a land far away with no familiar faces and we had to succumb to being total strangers. We felt like we were the only foreigners for miles and miles and we just cried. Even by the second night the secretary was crying for us. She asked us in bewilderment and confusion, "Why are you here?" For us it was just too drastic a change. Was skating worth it? Maybe it would build character? Maybe here we would learn the true necessities of life? Perhaps we would learn how little is needed to just live. Of course we stayed and we endured. I was a skater; I had to.

Just two months into our stay, my mother had to return to Alameda because our apartment lease was near its termination and it was time to clear things up. My poor mother was always cleaning up after me. She had had to do it all over the world for the family but usually with my father's company's help. Since we had left Japan she had been on her own cleaning up the mess her daughter had created in Toronto, then in Alameda and many more to come. I felt so guilty but my mother knew how important skating and training was to me and she never asked anything from me like that.

Not wanting to leave me all alone, my father came to replace my mother for a month or so. He enjoyed the hustle and bustle and he loved my new coach. I knew he loved him more than my mother did. They even went fishing together and had many evenings of enjoying beer and life stories together. My father did not speak Chinese and the coach spoke little English, but here language and culture did not matter and there were no boundaries. Two men of even more diverse backgrounds than could ever be described, bonded through life experiences. They saw something in each other that they found within themselves and my father trusted him immensely as a coach.

But even though my father had been in the military when younger he confessed he had never seen conditions like this. One time as my father and I were eating dinner in our dining area, a rat came over near our feet and just plopped down dead (hopefully from rat poison). The chef came to pick it up with his shovel and threw it out into the open space. That's all. No drama, no squeal, not even putting it in a trash can. And I have no idea for what other purpose he used that shovel and I don't want to know. But the others either did not see the dead rat in the middle of the campgrounds or it was just too common an incident to make a big deal out of it, but my father and I shuddered with disgust. We could not finish our meal.

There were cockroaches everywhere as well and they were humongous. The whole building was infested with them. They were behind all the mirrors in the common sink area. They were in our bedrooms. We used to skate late at night after the hockey players and sometimes came back to our rooms around 1:00 a.m. The minute I switched on the light in my room I would see hundreds of them scramble to the cracks at the edges of the room. It would sicken me but I had no choice but to go to my bed to get some sleep.

One night I decided that I would take the hot kettle of water that we got every day and pour it on them as I switched on the light. I followed through with my plan and tried with all my might to kill them, but to absolutely no avail. I don't think I managed to even debilitate one of them! But what I did manage to do was enrage my mother. She was furious because I had wasted the only precious water we had on cockroaches. We never knew if the next day would bring more hot water and I apologized for my stupidity.

There was much more this new life brought to me. First I had to get used to the smell of smoke everywhere I went. All the coaches smoked. They even smoked at the ice rink while teaching. Admittedly it did in fact give a relaxed atmosphere to the otherwise fear-ridden air looming above the skaters at the ice rink. Then my mother had to wash our clothes in the sink with a washing board as they did in the "olden" days. She bought some soap, washed and scrubbed the clothes, and hung them up in our bedrooms. I felt like I had gone back in time and did not know what year it was anymore! Most of the people would go into the shower with their underwear and bras on and take them off and wash them as they washed themselves. It was incredibly hard to get used to the new life we were in, but once again it was better than any history lesson or book could teach me about life.

During the heat of the summer that I was there, for a few days the city had suddenly no water whatsoever. The temperatures were very, very high and no water for the whole city, meant literally no water. No water for showers, for the toilets, for brushing our teeth (my mother and I actually brushed our teeth with bottled water in fear of water borne diseases) and for the Zamboni to clean the ice surface. So we trained on ice for almost a week with not one Zamboni run. But the skaters still did quads left and right. Because it was so scorching hot and all the toilets had not been splashed down for days, the biggest problem was that the air started to reek of urine and feces. I even tried holding everything in and refused to use the bathroom for the duration, but no such luck. Mother Nature is stronger and I found myself scouring the grounds for toilets not yet used!

My mother thought we would have to leave the city but we somehow endured it like everyone else and about a week later the water came back on. It was truly disgusting to all the five senses. But we survived. All in the name of ice skating.

The food was not to my liking and my mother searched outside of the gates of the compound for a Western supermarket to buy me some essentials. She found one and bought fruit and boxes of cereal and cartons of milk for me. She even bought a hot-pot that cooked with electricity and she made me soups and stews.

When survival becomes your main concern, bonds become tighter and my mother and I bonded together. My mother still lashed out at times and I was still frightened of her, but the fact that she had to look out first for my safety and health overrode all else. Also my coach was so incredibly supportive of me that some pressure was lifted from my mother. My coach was with me twenty-four hours a day. He made sure when I went to sleep, when I woke up, what I ate and when, and since he only had one other student besides me, he was our personal coach at our service. He did off-ice and on-ice training with us, and the whole time we were on the ice it was lesson time. It was wonderful and amazing. I felt looked after. I felt his method was not erratic but studied and mastered. It was being in presence of truly a guru in his own right. My care from my coach helped my mother, and my coach made sure my mother did not beat me as much anymore. His other male student and I bonded and we shared great experiences with each other. It was wonderful to train with him and laughter and smiles conquered the training sessions.

This coach was definitely different from any I had before. For the first time in my life I felt like my coach really cared for me. He was calm and that is what I needed. I did not need anyone pushing me. For the first time I felt my coach actually understood me. He saw right away that I always trained, worked, and tried way too hard. Where all my other coaches had always pushed me far beyond my limits, he actually saw that for me to do well he would have to hold me back and tell me repeatedly not to do so much.

He started off with healing my injuries. He had the acupuncturist and massage therapist from the team come to my room everyday to treat me. My coach made me herbal baths to soak my feet in and herbal medicine drinks that I had to swallow by holding my breath and my nose since the smell and taste was indescribably horrid. Somehow, like never before, it all worked wonders. My injuries truly subsided and I started to get my strength back.

However, during the time of less exercise I had gained a little more weight and it looked like puberty would soon start for me. It was the summer of 1998 and I was nineteen years old now. Although still flat-chested I was getting some curves. Again, my coach did not like this and maybe if we had spoken up about my never having had my period and that it was not healthy for me to lose weight, he would have understood and given me time. But we did not, and he wanted me to lose the little excess weight I had. My mother was actually furious at him for telling me to lose weight. She had suffered through my sister being anorexic and she could not handle it again. So to her dislike, I went on a strict and balanced but minimal diet. I chewed gum all day so that I would not eat and I lost the weight fairly quickly. I always did whatever someone told me to do since I would just do it without thinking it through. I lost the onset of puberty and my body went back to looking like a boy. Hormonally I was not balanced and I was to suffer the consequences of this later on.

Since Harbin was the home to all the athletes at the training center, their parents visited often and brought food for their children and kindly brought us some as well. I was speaking pretty well in Chinese by then and had fun conversations with my teammates. The Chinese invited us much more into their culture than the Japanese had done. On the weekends after the morning practice on Saturday the athletes went back to their parents' home and returned to camp on Monday mornings. Since my mother and I had no other home but the campgrounds, in the beginning we just stayed there on the weekends too. It was desolate, lonely, intolerably quiet, and you would hear the uninvited cockroaches scurrying! The kitchen would of course be closed as well.

During the week, when I rested in between practices, my mother ventured off to explore the city. She found a beautiful hotel, the best in Harbin, and some days we would go and have a proper (for us) dinner, and it just was so amazing. To eat with a knife and fork and have a piece of steak melt in your mouth was just heaven. It felt like a dinner fit for a queen after eating at the cafeteria. I wouldn't want to leave the comfort of the hotel. To come from nothing and then have a dinner on a nice plate in a clean dining room felt incredibly indulgent. The contrast could be felt in every vein in the body. Even the sight of a few foreigners here and there and to hear some English being spoken brought us some sort of familiarity.

My mother had a marvelous idea! She decided she would treat herself and me to weekends at the hotel! So every Saturday afternoon we packed an overnight bag and went to the hotel. Ah, you don't know how good the clean sheets and the big bed with the bouncy mattress felt, and oh, the bathroom was just marvelous. I never appreciated all these daily things as much as at those times. I would soak in the bathtub for hours scrubbing off all the dirt from camp. I would lie in bed cuddled in the clean white sheets all afternoon watching television, and we would just order room service. This was the life! It wasn't glamorous at all but after camp, oh my goodness, it felt glamorous! We felt like queens.

On Sundays we had a big brunch and would stack away a few breads in our pockets for the next week. Sunday afternoon, like good soldiers, we would be back on the campgrounds and back to Chinese reality. At least now the weekends were something to look forward to and made the week more bearable. It was like a special treat!

The city outside the grounds was stimulating to say the least, in many different ways. Huge trash bins circled the gates and the trash was overflowing and had a horrendous stench to it. There was a huge market with a tent above it that sold everything you can imagine for very little. My parents and I would explore it often and have a blast. We used to buy tons of these colorful hackisacks that had a metal base and feathered heads. My teammates and I would play with them for hours. One time the sellers even wanted to buy my father's pants off of him! There were bicycles and people everywhere. I have never seen that many people, not even in Tokyo. Or maybe I have, but in Tokyo everyone walks, and goes in the same direction in his or her own little bubble. It seems cold and distant, everyone camouflaged as if they all look the same. In China everyone was going everywhere in no order or manner, everyone pushing each other out of their way. There were barbers lined up on the street giving haircuts. It was alive and there was a sense of urgency in the air that all must keep on moving. Nothing must ever come to a halt. It was bustling with excitement.

My coach had seen me compete and train before, so he knew what I was all about. The first few days I was getting back on the ice were terrible. I was still healing from my injuries and I wasn't landing any of my triples, but I was doing them over and over again. After studying me for a few days he came to a conclusion. It was July by now and he told my mother and me that he would allow me to do only doubles for three months! Not one triple. He said my timing, rhythm, and coordination were completely off, and my falling repeatedly and landing one out of ten jumps was not going to do me any good. He said that we would see that after three months, when my doubles were performed to perfection, I would land all the five triples in just one day. My mother and I were dumbfounded. We couldn't fathom not working like a donkey, even if that meant falling over and over again. But I trusted this coach more than I ever had, and to finally have a coach that understood, and for someone to finally step up to my defense and not push me, was such a God-given gift that I knew I needed to follow his teachings. It was pleasing to me that he calmed down my mother; it wasn't my job anymore. He took care of everything. Everyone was living so close together that it was impossible for my mother to lash out. Since she and I were tightly watched, she no longer had the freedom she had previously. It was so good for both of us. My father having so much trust in this coach also helped my mother to relax. It started to feel like my skating life might finally come together in peace at last.

My coach believed in me. I felt it and he knew that I had to be excited again about skating and that falling time and again would only put me more in despair. He later told me that all the other coaches had told him that I would never ever be able to land my triples. That is how much negativity goes on in an ice rink. No one except your mother or father (whoever is there), and your coach (and sometimes not even your coach), believes in you. The rest are all against you. Lo and behold, the other coaches would be wrong.

For three months I was only allowed to do doubles and that also allowed time for my injuries to be healed. But I needed to do the doubles with such care that each and every one of them could have been a triple if I had pulled in. He made sure I felt no pressure and that skating was fun again. He made sure and worked with me tirelessly until the timing was just perfect ten out of ten times. I did program run-throughs with doubles. When I started to enjoy skating again I was getting back to my center in life, too. I skated with all the top Chinese pairs-skaters and single skaters and it was a joy. We were not really friends but were training companions, and because there were no other good single-lady skaters, they saw me not as a threat, but as a treat. I could live with the bare living conditions while the skating was going so wonderfully. I loved it.

One day in September of 1998, after the three months were up, my coach felt in his bones that I was ready, and he told me on that day, that we would do triples. He gave me permission to fall and make mistakes and not to worry at all about the outcome. To all our amazement I went on the ice and after a few doubles I landed every single triple in the book! All five triples and just like that. Not one fall or mistake. They were so easy! I felt like I wasn't even trying. It just happened.

For the first time in my skating life I loved to jump. I was landing each and every one and was even going for triple–triple combinations! It was wonderful, exciting, and freeing. It was purely a slice of heaven. My coach was not surprised since he had felt I was ready, but he was so proud of me! He never ceased to be my guru. Whatever he did he was never in a rush. He was as if in slow motion soaking up every second within every second. He was always living in the moment and like a true teacher he had formed a champion. I felt like one for the very first time in my life, exceeding any happiness I had felt earning a gold medal. I was happier than ever. I could have stopped skating then and there and know I had accomplished it all. My mother and father were elated. My triples would stay with me, but unfortunately only as long as I was under his watchful eye.

Skating would be bountiful for me for some time but the living conditions would catch up to me physically. Either because I lost a lot of weight or my immune system had never been exposed to what I was eating and drinking, I became incredibly sick. It felt like whenever one part of my life was getting better everything else would collapse into heaps in front of me. I truly did not know what God was trying to tell me. All I knew was I had to fight on. I would start feeling nauseous, losing my appetite, and dizzy with a headache. Then my stomach would inflate until it looked like I was nine months pregnant. I could not see my toes. I would not be able to eat for a few days and just lie in bed, not able to train. Then on about the third day I would explode in both directions with extreme diarrhea and vomiting. This would continue for a few days and then a few more days of feeling better and then back to training. The whole cycle took a little more than a week.

When it first happened during the summer, we went straight to the hospital. Unfortunately the hospital was not a hospital with Western standards. There were people lying all over the floor, in the hallways, and in every room all huddled together. The doctors had more holes in their white gowns and more missing teeth and hair than their patients. It reeked and was filthy. The doctor wanted to inject me with something and I firmly declined, not knowing what they were going to inject me with and not sure if all their needles and equipment was even clean. Having received no treatment we went back to the camp. The secretary who had come up to help us in the beginning called a few places and found a good doctor nearby who spoke a few words of English. We paid a visit and all I received was a dose of antibiotics and those cute pink tablets that you can suck for stomach discomfort. Now, compared to how I was feeling this treatment seemed more suitable for a little stomach ache than what I was going through, but we had no other option at that time. My Chinese coach had never experienced this before so he did not know what to do either.

To my dismay this cycle started happening once every single month! Instead of the monthly women's cycle I experienced this kind of monthly cycle. I can tell you I would have rather have had the other one! Luckily my training and its method was going so well that it did not really disturb my skating, but I was getting weaker from it. Feeling this unwell and not knowing why, was exceedingly scary. My mother was fine. Always was. Lucky her. God had sent her to me because he knew she would take care of me best. I was thankful. I do not know what I would have done without her.

As the winter approached it was quite freezing and people were dressed like Eskimos to keep the warmth in their body. The grounds were frozen over and at least I was happy that the insects and rats might have been frozen too! My stomach sickness was continuing every month and to top it off I got a terrible flu. I had an extremely high fever, over one hundred and five degrees for two days. I did not feel anything, actually. I was feeling completely fine. That's when you know it's dangerous. I just remember going in and out of consciousness and seeing many people huddled over my bed trying to give me all sorts of medicine. My coach's wife came with bowlfuls off watermelon (I do not know where she found it in the middle of winter) to lower my fever. My coach poured gallons of vinegar on the floor of my room and wrapped my feet in towels soaked in vinegar as well. They were all trying to get my fever down. They really thought I wasn't going to make it, but my mother's prayers were answered, and after a few worrisome days my fever settled down. I stayed confined in bed for another week before I could start skating again.

There was another incredibly important situation going on at the same time. The main national training center was in Beijing, but since the Olympics were over, my coach did not think that the federation would call the skaters to live, skate, and train there to prepare themselves for the season. I, of course, wanted to go there because I wanted to experience Beijing as well, but for some reason whenever I brought it up, my coach dismissed the conversation and said he did not want to go to Beijing. My mother and I had no understanding of why, and of course we thought if there was something he was hiding he would most likely not admit to it anyway.

Unfortunately for him the athletes were called in, and we were told we all had to go to Beijing to train for a while. There was a change in my coach's demeanor and he became uncannily tense. We were to all go by train to Beijing on an overnight trip. It was thrilling when my mother and I and all the other top skaters and their coaches were together on the train. The other skaters and I played cards and finally fell asleep in the bunk beds all lined up, one after another. My mother and I had contemplated flying to Beijing but we thought the experience of the team and the train was more valuable than the luxury of flying. It was fun, Chinese style! Oblivious to it all I was thrilled to be going to train in Beijing!

The training grounds there were similar to Harbin but a little more upper class in terms of conditions and much cleaner. At least, inside the buildings it was cleaner. Outside the people still spat and threw things everywhere. There was to be an international junior competition held in Beijing at the facility. I remember for that one week when all the international skaters were there, not one Chinese spat on the ground. It was a rule for that one week. The second they were gone it started all over again! It was remarkable to observe. You can change a man but never the culture within him!

I had some competitions I would have to attend in Europe. The Chinese skater who had organized our training stay had promised my coach would be able to travel with me to them, but as life would have it he was not able to leave. The Chinese government and federation had him on a tight leash and muzzle. So I went to the competitions alone, phoning in every day to my coach to ask how I should train that day and calling him with results right after I got off the ice. He coached me on the phone.

Even with no coach physically there, I never was more confident. I had to do a qualifying competition for Swiss Nationals in December of 1998 and I was excited to show my new jumps and amazing skating to the judges. The competition was in an ice rink as cold as Harbin had been! It was so freezing that I would have loved to compete with a ski suit on. It was in the Swiss Alps and in an open ice rink! For the six minutes warm up, I did just doubles. I felt the whispers of people talking to each other remarking coyly that "now Lucinda could not even master one triple!"

As my turn came I completed every single triple in the program, even with numb toes and fingers and cold air steaming out of my mouth! I was a huge success and judges came up to me afterward, saying they were puzzled as to why I only did doubles in the warm up and they wanted to know why. I felt I did not owe anything to them and pretended not to understand their question and walked away. These were the same people who denied me my Olympic spot. I did not feel I needed to explain anything to them nor did I wish to speak to them. Whatever the result, I just wanted the skating to speak for itself.

After this competition on our return to China there was more drama than I could have expected. I was still getting very sick every month and it got so bad sometimes that my mother and I honestly thought I was going to die. Really die. My mother was very scared and so was I. I was that sick and felt that horrible, and no one could help me. On the other hand, my coach had the other male skater and he was extraordinarily talented, doing quads left and right. He was the first skater ever to land two quads in one program. He was so talented and he was also so lazy. Whereas I was a workaholic, he never wanted to work. He was a very good kid, funny, and so kind hearted. He liked me more than a friend and we had a great relationship. He would sneak out of the campgrounds in the middle of the night and not return until sunrise. He would go to the game centers and play arcades all night long, have a couple of smokes, and maybe some alcohol. Nothing really bad. He just wanted to play all day.

We all longed to have his talent, but sometimes your greatest strength becomes your greatest weakness. My coach had hoped that my being there would motivate him and make him work, but my dedication did not influence him and his bad results at competitions were an indication of lack of practice. He was even starting to lose to his Chinese teammates. My mother and I knew if he did not skate well the federation would blame my presence for hindering him and taking time away from his coach. It would be my fault, so we always tried to help and support and push him to skate and train but he just wouldn't. He was so happy with his life and himself that he did not see the need to push himself. We were two opposite people and I think in the long run he taught me more valuable lessons than I could have ever taught him. He put life and enjoyment first and unfortunately it was at my expense.

There was another unavoidable problem. Money. My coach was the team leader in Harbin so he was in charge and could pay off the other team delegates to keep quiet, but in Beijing he would have to report to others. Now it was making sense to us why he hadn't wanted to go to Beijing. Since there had been no choice but to go to Beijing on their orders, word got around and everything fell apart. The federation and government were furious at my coach. It turned out he had taken American dollars and he been training me without telling them first. My parents thought everything had been properly arranged and when they found out, they were fuming at my coach as well. My mother and I were told that I would have to leave and he would not be allowed to teach me anymore.

My mother after practice one day went up to my coach and put both of her hands on him and just shook him before she collapsed into tears. She screamed at him, asking him how he dared to do this to such a young girl. How dare he ruin a dream and a life? It was the first time in a very long time I saw my mother so livid at someone else. I remember when I was a child in kindergarten, some mothers had gone behind my mother's and my back to do some awful things, and I saw my mom shake them too. But this was the first time I saw her fight for me over skating. I felt so loved and cared for. At that time I did not really understand everything. As I have said time and time again my parents were great about keeping all the surrounding organizations away from me. All I knew was that my favorite skating coach would be taken from me and not be able to teach me anymore. We had to leave.

Leave. That seemed a good idea. Leaving, I did that a lot. But it had always been my choice to leave, usually because I was in a terrible situation. No one had ever made me leave. I was told to go home and leave the country many times in Japan, but they were just threats. This was real. We had to leave since we knew the Chinese federation really wanted us to leave. They knew I would not take another coach and I am sure they would not have let any other coach train me anyway. It was their way of saying, "Please go. You do not belong here and you have caused enough damage."

Having no choice, my mother and I solemnly packed our bags to go back home to Switzerland. We had no other place to go. This was all so sudden. Yes, Switzerland was still our home no matter how little we had lived there. No matter how much we denied it, it still was our only real home and in despair our only place to return to. My father was still there and we would reunite with him.

I could not believe that just when I had found the coach I wanted and liked so much, and just when my skating had become the best it had ever been, the carpet was ripped from beneath me. Why was this so hard? Was I making it so hard? Was I the culprit of it all? What was God trying to tell me? I was utterly speechless and disappointed beyond belief. I was even more devastated than when I was denied the Olympic spot. China had more impact on me in six months than Japan had on me in thirteen years. It had been an enrichment of a masterful six months. I believe there is a reason for everything and God must have known that six months was enough for me. China was not to be experienced longer and there was nothing I could do about it. Its run was over and now I would go on with my life to new experiences. I always believed in letting go of everything and every moment. When the time has passed it has passed.

In one way that is why I do not like pictures. I don't feel memories should be kept on material. They shouldn't be documented. They are to be experienced then and remembered only to help others in the world but not to be hoarded as a be-all and end-all. Living in the moment is what I learned from my coach in China. Around the world we had flown and it was time to now go home. Yes, to a home I did not know, but home it would be.

9

Unknown to Known

(ZURICH)

A short day of sorrow lasts longer than a long month of happiness.

With sadness tucked away firmly in our hearts, by the end of December of 1998 we said our goodbyes to our Chinese life. We felt like gypsies, nomads roaming from one place to the next. Goodbyes are not easy and we weren't getting any better at them. Hiding our emotions we thanked everyone and were on our way to the airport. Since we could not take all our belongings back with us at once, we decided to leave some suitcases with my Chinese coach to retrieve at a later date. We thought maybe my mother would go back and once more clear up the mess I left, or maybe it was more of a sentimental feeling that we wanted to believe we would be coming back and wished to leave a part of us there. To this day we have not retrieved our belongings. I actually have no idea where they went! That is the beauty of it though. Maybe some Chinese people are relishing the clothes we left behind. Maybe some part of my mother and me is still looming somewhere over China. Our spirits live on.

I like to believe that I have left a little part of me everywhere I have been. It had not been taken from me nor had it emptied me out, but rather I willingly gave a part of me. It made me even more whole since at the same time I received so much from everywhere I had been, and everyone I had met. I want to be remembered and to leave my footprint. To me it is all an enrichment of life and an education of the spirit.

Surprisingly I somehow felt relieved and relaxed as soon as we touched down in Switzerland. It felt like this was my home after all. Please be aware here I am not talking about the Swiss skating world. Usually when I went to Switzerland I despised it since I was always there for only a few days for a competition and that was it. Here I am referring to the country itself away from skating. I had never experienced it before. Maybe, too, it was different this time because my father was living here. I felt I had my family again. It was after all my birthplace. It was more a feeling of a force beyond the earth's realm and more spiritual and unconscious than something I saw. I was relieved to be home with my father again and to sleep again within my own furniture and memories that I had grown up with. It was magnificent.

It felt like I had come full circle and God had been waiting for me to come there. As all of this was giving me back my soul I also was utterly mentally and physically exhausted from life's experiences so far. My mind and heart and soul were feeling like they were all going to explode. I had been around the world, moving, packing, unpacking, and living out of suitcases with illnesses and injuries. I just did not know if I could handle anything more. It had been a whirlwind tour and I had come back to the starting point. Once again, I was empty-handed with no coach.

My illness that I had conceived in China unfortunately came with me. Instead of having once a month bouts of the illness, I started feeling sick to my stomach every single day. My diet became so limited as to what I could and could not eat since everything made me feel sick, causing me to become very skinny. I was constantly feeling gastrointestinal discomfort as well as, feeling weak, tired, and experiencing pain throughout my body. At least my injuries had all healed! One step forward two steps back. I was not getting anywhere!

My mother and father started pursuing different ice rink and coaching possibilities. One seemed very promising in the French part of Switzerland in Geneva. My mother and I decided to take a train ride there for a day or two to try it out to see how I liked it. I missed my Chinese coach, his care and masterful teachings incredibly, and every day I was on the ice I cried because he wasn't with me. I was also traumatized from everything I had been through and was still going through. I was not in a good place. I knew that his teachings and guiding me only on the phone was great but I needed a coach by my side to give me the support and attention any athlete would need at the world skating level.

We stayed a day in Geneva and I disliked it to the utmost degree. I didn't like the coach. I didn't mind where the rink was or how the rink looked. Only the coach mattered to me. I had been so spoiled by the knowledge of my guru in China that no coach would be able to surpass that. It could have been my stubbornness that I just could not accept anyone else of a lesser caliber. Well why would I though? Why would I go backwards when I could have the guru teachings on the phone? I did not want my parents to waste their money on someone I felt was neither worthy to teach me nor worthy of my skating.

I must admit though, that they were incredibly kind there and only wanted the best for me in terms of accommodation. I would have been able to skate for free, live for free at a prestigious family home, and everything would have been taken care of. I was a celebrity in the skating world and they would have waited on me hand and foot. But that never ever pleased me; nor was I fond of that or intrigued by that. I wanted a good coach who knew how to teach me, understood my body, and after all I had been through, I knew the coach there had no clue. I could feel it. Maybe this is my dangerous trait, but I always go by how I internally feel and the intuition I get, and I make my conclusions according to my feeling about a situation. It may drive people up the wall, as it may not seem rational but I'd rather do what I feel than what the outside world sees as perfect. How do they know what they are looking at and judging, anyway? I never judged a person or a situation. I always accepted it for what it was, but that did not mean that I did not live through and feel the pain of the emotional trauma it produced on me.

My mother, on the other hand, did not see the situation like I did. She was so happy that they would take care of me, and for once I would have privileges that I deserved after representing Switzerland so well abroad. After all the experiences and turmoil we had gone through, this reception was heaven for her. Being exhausted from everything, she deserved a break. She advised me to take the chance. My parents had been my only sponsors. To have the whole rink and their people stand up for us and want to help me made my mother elated. And she was absolutely right. It was wonderful to have a village behind me. So for me to tell her that I in no way would accept this coach, and there was no other coach good enough in Geneva, filled my mother with rage. So much rage that it turned her into a mad woman.

The whole train ride back home that lasted about two-and-a-half hours was outright torture. She took me into the area where the two train carriages meet and beat me hard for the longest time. I cried quietly since I did not want anyone to see, and I knew my mother did not want that either. The thought went through my head that my mother was going to kill me. Really kill me. I was so frightened and hit so much that I felt like I was going to die. I was defeated and crushed when we reached Zurich and my father met us at the station to bring us home. My sister had come to visit us from England where she was working at that time. I did not speak. I was hurt like never before. I could not look into my mother's eyes and I could not muster a word.

My father, sensing something was wrong asked what had happened and I told him, but he just kind of dismissed the fact, not taking it too seriously, and even my mother was surprisingly able to put on a happy face. I did not. For about two days I could not voice a word. I was frozen in time and in emotion. I could not believe what just happened. I wanted not to speak for longer but I always managed to feel sorry for my mother and couldn't forgive her quickly enough. I did want everything to stop. I wanted time to stand still. I wanted not to be alive in this way. I knew it was never my parents' fault. I never blamed anyone but myself. But at that time to feel like you were going to be hurt by someone you loved so much was unbearable. Maybe parts of me did die. I don't write these words freely either. I write them with care and precision expressing only what I truly felt and what was going on at that time. I do not intend to hurt more when it is time for joy, but the truth must be written in hopes of healing others now.

I had to compete at my national championships and since I could not change my surroundings, I changed my hair color. I went from blond to fiery red. I often would just dive into things without any fear. So my hair was red, red. It looked gorgeous and many said I looked like a model or a sophisticated actress but the national Swiss Figure Skating Championships was a disaster.

It was the first time in my life I did not want to get on the ice to compete. It's not that I did not want to, but I could not. I could not force myself to get on that ice. I knew I would eventually have to when I had no choice, but I was so tired and sick at the same time. I was crying most of the day and even told my mother, "I just can't anymore, I just can't." No other words could express what my body was telling me. I had turned into a little kid who just looked up to my mother with tearful eyes wanting guidance and I was crying with exhaustion. I looked very pale but I knew I would have to skate. And I did. I went on that ice, with a big smile on my face and did my programs with no coach by my side.

My mother actually stood there for me. She in the end was the only one who had gone through everything with me so who would be better than her? I went through the motions emotionless like a puppet with someone pulling my strings. I felt nothing. I was dead inside. No one outside of my family knew what had happened. We did not explain and how could anyone understand what I had gone through the last ten years? Some things are better left unsaid. I placed fourth. I was still the best skater in Switzerland if I could have done what I knew, but I did not land one jump. I wasn't disappointed, sad, or angry at all. I was frozen. I was thrilled to not even be on the podium so I wouldn't have to go out there again. I was thrilled to get out of my costume and out of the rink and go home. I was thrilled it was over. I was thrilled I did not have to fake my smile.

True exhaustion is detrimental. When you start not feeling anything anymore you know you have hit rock bottom. I did not care anymore. We arrived back home and unpacked. I decided this was it. I would stop skating. It was not worth it anymore. Not worth the pain, the illness, the hurt it was not only causing me, but my whole family. It was not worth the work, sweat and tears just to be judged by nine people giving you numbers that would be erased from the face of the earth with tears of sadness. No, it was not worth it anymore. But somehow it was all I knew and if I did stop what would I do? I did not know myself without skating. Who was I?

So oddly enough, or actually not odd at all, I kept on letting myself be driven to the ice rink near our home. I would lace up my skates, left foot then right foot, and like a good soldier go on the ice and train. I had no more purpose to live, no more goals, no more dreams, yet I plodded on. I continued like a man at war who has lost all he has, but just keeps on going with the beliefs he first had, when he joined the military. The reason I first skated was tucked away in my heart. Maybe for that reason I skated on. My heart and brain wanted to stop but my body just continued. It had been doing skating routines for fifteen years; it could not just stop at once. If it is stopped cold turkey it could be even more detrimental than to continue with the addiction. So there it was. It seemed I wasn't going to rehab yet, because I didn't realize my addiction at that time. I was just going through the motions as I always had done. It was more comfortable to stay in the pain I knew then break from it into unknown territory.

At the Swiss national competition many coaches had come up to my mother offering their teachings to us. One Swiss coach that stood out for her was a coach at an ice rink near our home. We decided to go pay him a visit. Being totally out of it at that time I don't remember much of what was said. But what I did hear and remember was that if I wanted, he could make it possible for the federation to give me another chance to be the one chosen to go to the world championships to be held in about two months time. I felt lightness in my heart.

The 1999 World Figure Skating Championships were around the corner and I still wanted to compete in them. I decided to give the coach a try. I did tell him one thing though: that I would be in contact with my Chinese coach every day and I would train on and off ice exactly as my guru said. I would not follow his training regimen. He agreed and we started to work together.

I really have to give him credit for accepting my proposal and for instilling in me hope and enthusiasm again for the sport. He gave me confidence and joy again. He did not pressure me into doing anything I did not want to do and let me do exactly as the Chinese coach instructed me. He gave me weekly plans for my training regimen and off-ice I would do on my own. My new coach had patience and things were looking up. The feeling of working hard on the ice was always an upper and when you do it full force it masks a lot of sorrow and pain. The more you do it the more you start feeling good again, at least when on the ice. I also knew that he was more of a manager and agent to skaters than a typical egotistical skating coach. He was always on the phone while coaching. It took the pressure off of me. He had shows he was producing and they were his first love. It felt like we were a good team. Our relationship on the ice worked well.

Badminton was one of the off-ice exercises I had done in China and my new coach willingly played with me even on the weekends, not to the liking of his wife. He really cared for me and he arranged makeup lessons for me so I would know how to do it at the competitions. He even had me going to tanning sessions to look healthier and have a glow. He went with me to a famous Swiss fashion designer to have new costumes made. He made me feel like Cinderella. He was producing me into a whole package ad I appreciated it very much. I liked that he let me do my own thing but supported me fully throughout it all.

I did not, however, ever listen to his technique suggestions while on the ice. His mouth would move but I heard no sound. The only coach that could make me land all my triples was my Chinese coach and I was not to have any disturbance with that technique that had worked wonders for me. Unfortunately due to not having my guru physically with me and having gone through so much turmoil, I was back to doing three triples out of the five but for me it was good enough at that time. I just wanted to be happy on the ice and do what I really loved to do. I was injury free, although my stomach illness still presented itself and hindered me in many ways.

Life off-ice was great. I was so happy to be with my mother and father and to sleep in my own sheets, eat food that I liked, and look at for hours and hours the albums upon albums of old memories printed on pictures of lands of my past, as I relived the good times. The peacefulness of Zurich and its beauty instilled a calm in me and I felt comfortable and confident. At last I felt at home and I felt Switzerland was supportive of me. My parents had their many old friends there and they all wished me so much luck while truly wishing the best for me. I felt loved.

As the 1999 World Championships were approaching and Europeans had ended with bad results from the Swiss ladies skaters, a judging critique session was set up so they could come to see me at practice to decide whether or not to send me to the World's competition. Now, I am never very good under pressure. I do not like any pressure at all and, oddly enough, I do not like people looking at me. I don't mind if I am under the spotlight when it's dark and I can't see any faces, or they are so far away that I don't know who is in the audience. But the minute someone comes up to look at me, or even just to have a social conversation with me, I am incredibly uncomfortable. Still to this day I am not good in intimate settings, but am great with big audiences.

The judges finally came around seven in the morning and the pressure was on for me to perform my best. I like to perform when I feel like performing. When I feel my spirit and soul is ready to move I am able to do it. I can't switch it off and on like that. I never could and never will. I do not feel that doing this is art, and for me skating is an art, not a sport. I never wanted to be an athlete, just an artist. So the constant fight continued between what was within me and what was needed of me in this sport. However, this was my only chance to prove to them that I was good enough to be sent to the world championships.

In the beginning of the practice I was skating not too badly, but my coach was furious with me because I had not listened to him about something he said. I probably did not hear him and he had been fine all along with my not listening to him, so I was puzzled because I didn't know why he wasn't all right with it that morning. Suddenly he became enraged and left the ice rink. He was under pressure too and he had cracked. A coach is not supposed to leave a student behind but I continued skating and actually felt better and less pressured without him and skated wonderfully. The judges loved what they saw and it was decided I was to be sent to the World's competition. I was excited and so was my coach after he apologized to me.

For me, landing a triple or not was honestly insignificant to me. I don't think I really cared, thinking it didn't matter in the big schemes of things if I succeeded at it or not. Perhaps only fear made me land it more than anything else because I knew it mattered so much to my mother. But truly for me it was always more how you landed a triple, not whether you did or didn't at a particular time, so maybe I was never a true athlete, just an artist that happened to be a skater.

The World Figure Skating Championships in 1999 would be a display of the best skating and spins I have ever done during a competition. I felt amazing, confident, and ready to show the world my art. My Chinese guru was there as well with his student. Although I asked my new Swiss coach if my Chinese coach could sit with him at the boards my new coach refused. He wanted to be the only one there. I respected his decision but I compromised by having my Chinese coach sit with my mother at every practice and from afar he would give me signals as to what I was doing wrong or right. He set up for me what I was to do in each practice, did off-ice with me, gave me mini massages and I heard only his voice in my head. I must say a thank-you though to both of my coaches I had then, since without them I would not have succeeded.

I skated wonderfully and Dick Button coined his famous quote "Good for you, Lucinda Ruh." I got standing ovations at every practice and even more for my short and long programs at the competition. I received many gifts but a stuffed lion animal for some fateful reason would be the one to land on my lap and in my arms at the "kiss and cry" bench. My mother is the sign of a Leo and so is the man that I would marry much later in my life who remembered seeing me with that lion on TV. Leo, a presence I was always to be reminded of.

Once again, to all of our dismay, it was a disappointment when I placed thirteenth. It was said then, and is still said among those in the skating community that I should have been placed on the podium. But to me it did not matter. The judges did not like that I was so good at something they did not know how to give marks for. So they kept me in the middle where they thought I wouldn't be noticed. But instead, the opposite effect happened. My results sparked conversation and were questioned and written about all over the world. Soon after this event, my name was in all the International Skating Union books and spin rules changed because of my spinning. All my creations became a necessity for high level points at competitions.

I was even asked to do my spins at the finale exhibition where only the top three in each discipline were invited to perform. I was placed in the middle of the ice, doing my spins with all the medalists around me. I was the star. I felt like a champion inside and out and it had nothing to do with medals or placements. The fact that I had overcome such adversity and that my spins were so appreciated brought happy tears to my eyes. I am not proud or arrogant about it or myself in any way. Please do not misunderstand me. I was just truly happy that God's gift to me had finally been appreciated even a little. Looking back at my life, I think I should have been more proud of myself. Maybe then I would have had better results, but because an artist's insecurity often produces more art I did not want or feel the need to change myself for something I did not believe in, a medal.

The producer of the famous German skating tour at that time was enticed by my performances and invited me to skate in their shows that would begin right after the championships ended. I remember being so excited to receive the invitation. I had the chance to do what I loved most, which was to spin, and this time with no judges to judge me. My Swiss coach and I accepted gladly and I was to leave to Germany right away for rehearsals. I went alone without my mother and it made me feel independent. I was in a good space. The tour lasted for almost three weeks all across Germany. In the beginning of the tour I was a little nervous, since I had no experience whatsoever of performing under spotlights. The producer at first had me skate twice, always near the beginning of the first and second halves of the show. I fell the first few times but after that became incredibly comfortable. I would be one of the only ones to receive standing ovations for my performances, which resulted in the audiences wanting many encores from me.

Since the show could not have encores in the middle of the show, the producer had to switch the skating order so that I was the last female single skater to skate in both the first and second halves of the show. That was a huge compliment and I basked in the spotlight, not for the fame but just because I could spin and spin. With the spotlight on me while I spun I felt even more in heaven as the bright light surrounded me. Many famous skaters were on the tour and it was exciting to be in their presence. I was nineteen years old and for the first time was on my own skating. I was growing a little part of my wings. It was so interesting for me to understand my habits and decide for myself my training schedule. I felt in control at last.

My mother and father visited me often on the tour and they loved that I was so happy and was skating so well. Even my sister and her boyfriend at that time (now her husband) came to enjoy the show, and that was a surprise since my sister rarely came to see me skate. She had her pain of not succeeding in a sport that she loved even more than me, her little sister. It was too painful for her to watch. I was thankful she came, as I knew how hard it was for her. For me it was a fascinating time. To add to the dessert, there was a very enchanting man on the tour, a famous Olympic champion, and we started to flirt a little with each other. He was much older than I was and for me it was all new, pure, and sensitive. News of our young relationship spread quickly though out the skating world. The relationship was truly charming. I did not want the tour to end but reality always hits and it was time to go back to Switzerland.

My celebrity status had grown enormously in the skating world and I was in almost every newspaper. Interviews of my performances and me were constantly on the television around Europe. I was dubbed the Queen of Spin and recognized as the fastest spinner in the world. I wish I had named all my creations at that point because now they are referred to as the "pancake spin" and many other names instead of the "Ruh spin" or the "Lucinda Spin." I do hope that the skating world can now name my creations after me so the legacy continues. At a young age journalists and television commentators around the world had called me the "ballerina on ice" and now, "the queen of spin."

Interestingly enough, "spinner" in German means the crazy one! Maybe my spins would be more than just spins in my life. They would be a metaphor for what I am and would become. We truly are what we do. It had been such a sudden change from such sadness, desperation, and depression to elation and fame that it was unbelievable. I was on a roller coaster and what goes up must come down. After all the pain and terrible experiences I had gone through I thought I was no longer on the bottom emotionally, and I prayed that my fame, good luck, and good fortune would stay with me, not forever since I did not expect that much, but at least for a little while.

But as my luck would have it, it would not, and I was to even experience more despair and tragedy for years to come. Why was I so unlucky? Was I making my own misfortune? Or was this all happening for a reason? Was it happening in order for me to understand more about life and myself in order to be able to find my destiny? I thought that by giving so much joy and happiness to the world with my spins maybe there was none left for me to soak in. I believed and still do that the more you give, the more you receive, but I have learned through the years that it only happens when you have a lot of what you are giving. I was giving all I had and was emptying my tank like there was no bottom and no tomorrow. Without the replenishing refills, I had nothing left to give myself. And soon I had pretty much nothing left to give to others.

10

Pains of Error at the Expense of the Innocent

(ZURICH, SIMSBURY, ZURICH)

A gallon of tears

When someone can make you laugh and cry at the same time you have found the one who truly loves you. My parents were always able to do this for me, in times of despair and utter devastation or in times of glee and exhilaration. My parents lived through so much with me and it was never the words we said that mattered most but rather the feelings we were able to give to each other. We were never a family of much talk but we always were a family of much depth in feelings and philosophy. In my family everything always had a meaning to it. For every action and reaction we had, there was a deeper reason behind it all. I feel this is how I skated as well. With a deep understanding about life and our journey I lived through my life experiences on the ice. The ice was my blank canvas that I would feverishly paint my emotions on.

Every day I painted a new picture and in a new way. I wish it could have been documented like a painting that you could look at forever, but maybe those emotions were to be let out and forgotten and to be imprinted only in the eyes and in the hearts of those who saw the painting enacted at that time and place. It was always raw emotion for me, and even if people did not understand my story it touched them and made them see something in themselves that I had awakened. This is what I had always hoped to do on the ice. If I could bring my audience to tears or to jubilant joy or for them to shed that perfect tear, I had done my service and healed myself in the process. Without the ice, I would die.

I was back in Zurich. The skating season was over and conquered. Flowers and trees replaced the snow as summer arrived. I feel summers are tough in a way for skaters because all the adrenaline from the season has worn you down, yet all the events were so exciting you did not want it to stop. Then you have to unwind and start up again to prepare for the upcoming season and wait and wait for the right time to pounce. It was a strategic game and I did not like those games. It was, however, always a magical time, too, as you created new costumes and new programs for the following year. You were creating a new character on ice. This summer would be quite a new experience for me and tragically not at all in the good sense.

In Switzerland during the hot summers a lot of ice rinks close down. As a result, many skaters go abroad during this time and we found ourselves driving every day to far away ice rinks to try to get my practice in. It was not convenient. I was also getting very impatient with my Swiss coach. His wife had come in between us a little and he now seemed cautious and restricted about how much attention he could give me. I also felt the void of not training with my Chinese coach and missed him more than ever. I felt I needed him to help me again with my skating. I was skating on my own and I was trying to teach myself with my Chinese coach's words in my head, but since I did not have him there to point out my mistakes, I ended up fixing the wrong problems and this resulted in uprooting other problems. I wanted him to teach me again.

Skating is a repetitive sport and skaters need constant reminding of what they are doing wrong every single day or they can lose their edge. Skating is very delicate. At least it was for me. Not liking the exercise of being repetitive was my shortcoming. I despised it but knew I needed to repeat things exactly the same way over and over again to get consistent. I never wanted to repeat it the same way. I thought that was a waste of time because in my mind it was not creative in any sense. My coach in Japan used to tell me he would like to just play a tape over and over again to repeat his teachings instead of having to stand there and voice it! He used to complain he was so tired of repeating himself. But that is the sport and without the repetition there is no consistency.

We found out that my Chinese coach along with some other Chinese team members, (coaches and skaters) would be in the United States in Connecticut that summer for about two months of training. We asked the Chinese federation if he could also teach me if I also went there. They said he would be allowed to since it was not on Chinese soil. My Swiss coach with no hesitation agreed as well because he wanted me to be the best I could be and he

PAINS OF ERROR AT THE EXPENSE OF THE INNOCENT 139

knew I missed my Chinese guru. Our plan was to just stay for the two months and then return before the new season started. I wanted to stay in Switzerland during the competition season. I never had felt more support from my country than I did when finally living there and it felt good.

When we arrived in Connecticut, I was absolutely revved up and ready for great summer training. I was excited to be soon again landing all my triples and getting my confidence back. We arrived around noon at the skating camp accommodation. The whole Chinese team was supposed to arrive that same evening but due to some delays they arrived in the wee hours of the morning. I rested, settled in, and fell asleep for the night. I couldn't wait to see my coach in the morning. I went to see him as soon as I woke up and he was oddly in a suit and tie, not his usual attire. Something was up. My mother and I felt it.

My Chinese coach took us aside. He told us firmly but with a tear in his eye that the Chinese team and federation delegate that was traveling with them had told him in the plane on the way over there that he would not be allowed to coach me, whatsoever! He would not even be allowed to speak to me. We were shocked, dumfounded, and speechless. We had travelled all this way just for him and once again been cheated and taken advantage of. I would, as always, it seemed, be training by myself. After all these incidents was God trying to tell me to stop skating? If so, then why did he give me the gift of spins? I could not comprehend this.

The delegate had apparently told him of their decision on the plane in fear that if they had told him earlier he would not have come at all. He had only one other student, the same one he had when I was in China, and he could have easily stayed in Harbin and trained him there. So this is how they tricked him into coming to the States and how they had tricked us along the way. We were hurt and I was just incredibly devastated.

But as we had always done and always continued to do, we rose up to the challenge God presented us. We were like those dolls in Japan, that no matter how much you push them over to one side they just spring right back up. We were like the indestructible daruma doll or the one drop of dew on a thin blade of grass. We saw every situation as an opportunity to rise above and be the bigger person. I cried and cried. Life seemed to be a whole lot of crying lately. A gallon of tears it soon would be.

After the initial shock, my mother, the Chinese coach, and I decided to make a plan. We would not back down and just retreat into our shell. We would take matters in our own hands. He would not and could not teach me out in the open but he promised me this: On the ice he would make his hand signals to me after my jumps when I looked at him from the corner of my eyes. If I skated past him he would whisper some corrections to me. We both would make sure no one would notice. I made sure I always skated by him and he made sure he stood in a convenient spot with his back to the delegate members where it wasn't too obvious that he was giving me corrections.

Then off-ice, we also had a plan. He and I would meet in a specific spot in the woods that surrounded the ice rink and campgrounds at a specific time each day. He went a different way from us to the spot and we left the campgrounds at different times so no one would be suspicious. After the training he went back first and we would run some errands before returning to the camp. It felt like we were in espionage and this was a secret mission. It seemed crazy but also added to the intensity and the excitement of the training, and it worked wonders. I felt special and taken care of and the thrill of making sure no one noticed was fun in a way. It was crazy but worth it.

It was truly sad that this is what our relationship had become but I was improving so quickly on the ice that I was elated. In just those two months I was back to landing all the triples and triple-triple combinations. I loved training again with the Chinese team members and my mother even taught my coach's other Chinese male student how to drive. It was fun and the experiences were raw and human. Memories of our time in China were awakened once more. To my dislike, so did my stomach illness I suffered from when in China, and it still caused many problems. My diet was so limited from my problems with digesting food and so lacking in vitamins and nutrients that it caused my bones to be more brittle and prone to injuries.

Meanwhile, there was a Russian coach at the ice rink who took a big liking to me. She thought that I did not have a coach and wasn't getting any lessons so she took my mother and me aside and said she would like to coach me as long as I was there. We innocently thought: why not try her, try a new experience and see what I could learn from her as long as we were already there? We always had a hard time saying "no." We were ultimately "yes" people trying to please everyone and always wanting to be better and better. We were never satisfied with what we had or how I was doing. Now looking back, I think we should have just stuck with my Chinese coach, but greed is a dangerous trait and wanting more and more and wanting to be better and better always dominates and clouds judgment, so we decided we would try her. We thought there would be no harm in this. Later we thought about how wrong we had been.

Nothing changed with the Chinese coach but I now had extra lessons with her every day. I did not listen to her jumping technique but soaked in the artistry and passion she had while coaching. Her daughter helped me with the choreography and I had a lot of support. They were Russian and their strong dominance did not quite suit my personality. I felt they talked too much and their energy was just over the top for me. However, they were incredibly accommodating and she even invited my mother and me to live in her house. So instead of staying at the campgrounds my mother and I took the opportunity to stay with her. It was wrong and overbearing, and in consequence made me feel suffocated, but at that time we took what we could get when we were feeling so lost. The Russian coach was lonely as well. I had given her a reason to teach again and I knew it. I wanted to please her and bring her happiness.

The summer was ending and there were just a few more days left of the Chinese team's presence before it would be time for us to return to Switzerland too. My Swiss coach had been calling in often to check on how I was doing. I started to feel exhausted again since the Russian coach was pushing me too much. I should have just kept the Chinese way that I knew worked for me but my coach let her ego get in the way, and was being greedy about wanting more and more from me. With all good intentions since she loved my skating and thought I would be her next Olympic Champion, she pounced heavily on her prey. There was a price for this that again I would have to pay. My downfall was that I would fall very quickly into over-working mode. I would push myself until I fell off the cliff. I never did anything in moderation.

On the last evening before my Chinese coach went back to China, he and I talked. I was sad that I would not be able to go with him and I cried. I was also very tired. My Russian coach wanted me to skate the next morning because her son-in-law was back from his tour as a professional skater and she wanted me to be present so she could show off her new pupil. She said he would be instructing the class mostly about stroking and footwork. She said it would be fun and she wanted me there, ultimately but unspoken, for her. I hesitantly asked my coach his opinion about whether I should rest the next morning or skate. My Chinese coach was firm with me, saying he thought I needed to rest, sleep-in the next morning, and maybe even take a few days off. Otherwise I might get injured again. I said my good-byes and felt I would not see him for a very long time.

Unintelligently, I did not listen to him. I had always done what he told me. Why not this time? It is nobody's fault but mine. But at this time he was not my coach. She was, and the present coach was the one I followed. There was only one captain of the ship and I listened to that captain only. He was gone but she would remain. I see now that I needed to understand that I was the captain of my own ship. Listening to myself would have been a good idea but I was used to following other people's orders. I needed to be stronger in life, take responsibility for my own body, and stand up for it. But I had never been taught that so why would I do that now? I was truly ignorant that day and it would be hard to forgive myself for it.

The next morning, half awake, I dragged myself with my mother to the ice rink. My legs were feeling weak and wobbly. I laced up my skates and on the ice were the Russian coach, and her daughter and son-in-law who seemed like a pack of wolves waiting for me to arrive. I greeted them all and smiled meekly. I knew she wanted to show me off so the pressure was on and this skate would be for her. Everything was going fine and her son-in-law liked me. About a half hour into the session my legs started shaking. I was a little dizzy. We were doing some footwork and suddenly I fell to the ice and was frozen in pain. My knee was burning up. I had been doing a step and since I was so tired my body wasn't as quick as my mind that morning. I wanted to turn but my blade got stuck in the ice. My upper body motion did follow through, but my legs had stayed still, and so my knee was totally twisted.

I thought I had broken my leg. It was that painful. I am not one to complain or fake an injury. But this was a pain I never felt before. Her son-in-law carried me off the ice and with tears rolling down my cheeks we were off to the hospital. Not again, I thought! Always the hospital, always injured Lucinda. I feared that my skating career was over.

My knee, after many tests and X-rays and MRIs, was diagnosed as having a big ligament tear and rip. My knee was so inflamed that it looked like a big hill on my leg. This diagnosis may not have sounded so bad but the pain was excruciating. The doctors told me I would need at least a month of staying completely off my leg. As a skater, resting and following those kinds of doctor's orders never made sense. I would stay off the ice for the bare minimum time necessary to heal and rush back onto the ice as soon as I could walk a little. So a month was a month for the doctors but about a week for me even though I was on crutches.

My mother and I stayed at the Russian lady's house. The summer was over and we should have been headed back to Switzerland but something held us back in the States. We used the knee and the doctors here as an excuse. We also let the coach make the decisions since we thought coaches should instruct their pupils and she wanted me desperately to stay. At that time I also was no longer looking forward to returning to Switzerland. I had gotten a taste of the American life and liked it. We had to call the Swiss coach to tell him I had now an injury and we were staying over here for doctors' care. My mother was scared to make the phone call and was not looking forward to that conversation to relay the bad news to him. But it had to be done and thank goodness my mother had to do it and not me. Maybe unconsciously we felt guilty and thought that we were doing something wrong and we felt we really should just stick to our word and head back, but nonetheless we succumbed to the situation and stayed in the states. My Swiss coach was devastated.

A week off the ice became a month like the doctors advised. We stayed at my coach's house and I went to doctors and rehabilitation for my knee every day. I slowly returned to the ice. My Swiss coach was furious we were not returning but I wanted to stay in America. To me it wasn't even about the coach. Neither coach was my favorite, nor did I trust the techniques of either one. But I liked the American lifestyle better and I was too tired to go back. I was exhausted mentally and physically. The going back and forth was too much for me. I just wanted to stay where I was, wherever that was, and did not want to move. This feeling got worse in years to come, as I never recovered from my exhaustion.

I was twenty years old and still had not gone through puberty and friends were not really a part of my life. Where we were in Connecticut was a lonesome city with nothing but the woods, the ice rink, and a supermarket. It was great for training since there was not one distraction other than squirrels and wild life roaming about. The woods were eerie and although in a way I loved them, there was something about them that just seemed to expel ghosts and evilness. Even the ice rink smelled of fear and disaster to me. Ever since the first day there I was scared of the whole area. Something seemed not right and it felt haunted.

At this ice rink there was also a memorial for my all-time favorite team-pairs who I had wanted to visit in Moscow when I was nine years old. Their training home was in Connecticut but her partner had horrifically and unexpectedly passed away on the rink in Lake Placid, shocking the whole skating world. To be within its lingering memories made me feel very uncomfortable and I was spooked by the whole situation. My fifth sense was in overdrive here.

As my knee healed, but would never again not be painful, I was getting ready for my next skating competition, a grand prix assignment in Russia arranged by my federation. It was the last skating practice in Connecticut and my last evening in Connecticut before flying off to Russia. I was excited and looked forward to continuing the success I had at the end of the last season and at the world championships a few months back. Why do things frequently happen on last evenings? Maybe it's our desperation to fit everything in and fix everything in the last minute, or to give it our all one last time before a big event? It is greed again, I think—it is the greed for success, greed for wanting to leave the ice with a perfect practice before heading off to a competition. Greed for wanting good luck. It is never a good thing.

That last evening I fell one time, very heavily right on my coccyx on a triple lutz. I felt a jolt all the way up through my spine and neck and up to my head. I got up and continued to skate, not thinking much of it. I have fallen so many times, so what was one more? I had banged my head on the ice so frequently and had heard my head crack many times before, so what was one more time?

Perhaps I was clumsier than other skaters. I was also taller than most and had long legs. The higher your center of gravity, the harder it is to skate, let alone jump. Even when I did my spinning, I sometimes fainted right out of it when there was no oxygen reaching my brain. I used to hear my neck and my head crack all the time while in spins. I would get blood clots in and around my eyes, face, and all the way up and down both arms. I would look like I had chicken pox. So I was used to falling, and being banged up, and bruised and polka-dotted. As long as I was still alive I could skate through it.

The next morning I boarded my flight to Moscow with just my coach. My mother went on a different route because she had to go back to Switzerland first and would then fly to Moscow. After takeoff I needed to go to the bathroom and stood up from my seat. But I could not move. My legs froze. I felt dizzy and both of my legs felt numb. I had no pain other than a knife life sharp pain in one specific spot in my spine. I could not move my neck or back. I sat back down. Usually when I had back pain, which I normally had every day, the pain radiated throughout my back around the area from the one spot it stemmed from. But this was different. The pain just dug into me from only one small spot in my spine. Then the rest of my body was numb.

I panicked, as I thought, *oh, dear God, no. Please no.* I did not say anything to my coach. I was in fear the whole way there and the nine hours it actually took felt like forever. I slowly slid back down in my seat and thought I would try again in a few minutes to get up. I ended up trying many times but with no success. Luckily, I eventually made it to the bathroom without bending my body in any direction. I just moved in very slow motion. Finally the plane touched down and competition mode would need to set in. I was terrified I had broken my spine. I would have to work through it, I thought. I could not look weak now. I would have to compete. Then we could figure out what happened. I could not look foolish and say I was injured again. This could not be done. It would be a disgrace for me.

My mother arrived at the hotel and I was so thrilled to have her by my side. I told my mother I was in pain but did not say more. I had my first practice and I was extremely cautious. Usually I just skated through the pain and ignored it, but this felt different and my gut feeling and intuition were telling me to be very careful. My coach noticed I was not doing much since I could barely move my legs, and she called me over. She asked what was wrong and if my knee was bothering me again. I said that it wasn't and told her now my back was hurting. I felt so bad but I had to tell her. She got angry and said I better just deal with it and push through. It was a competition and this was not a time to feel sorry for myself and have excuses. She was in her home country and I was to make her proud. I was her prized animal on show.

But I really could not move. I tried some jumps and just could not even pull in. I was too scared to fall again on my back. Something was really telling me this was a serious injury as I felt paralyzed from my back down and I was trembling inside. The practice ended and my coach was furious with me. She ordered the chiropractor to help me. That was the wrong thing to do but we tried it all. I got pills and cortisone injections to numb the pain. I wanted to pull out of the competition but the Swiss told us that if I did not compete here they would not send me to my next grand prix in Japan. How foolish of them.

But orders were orders. I had already missed the Olympics in Japan and did not want to once again not be present for this one in my so called-home, so I forced myself to compete. I did nothing at the practices, absolutely nothing, except skating around a bit. The pills and injections were not helping. They were actually making it worse because now I could feel even less of my body. Almost everywhere was numb and I was scared not to feel the movements of my body and injure myself even worse. To counteract what I felt I was given more pills and more cortisone injections. Somehow I competed. I just went into the zone and did what needed to be done at my own expense.

We were told much later that my spinal injury was so serious that I could have cracked and crushed my entire spine and been completely paralyzed, but at that time competing in Japan was too important for me. Luckily I did have angels looking after me. I was so in my skating bubble that I would literally have even died for it. Kill myself for it. Nothing seemed more worthy than getting on the ice to skate. After my short program, more injections were administered and after my long program I could barely sit at the "kiss and cry" bench. The competition was over and of course the Grand Prix competition in Japan was now out of the question because of the intense pain that I was in. So either way I would not have been able to go to Japan, but this way I was injured for life and the other way my career might have continued. The Swiss team did not seem to be of good guidance to their athletes. More tears were to be shed. Maybe it would become two gallons of tears by the end of the year.

My Russian coach wanted us to return to the States and be treated by doctors there, but my mother was completely stubborn. She decided that the smart thing to do would be to return to Switzerland. She thought there I would have the support of the Swiss team doctors who would be able to help me the most and hopefully diagnose me properly.

When we arrived in Switzerland we went straight to the doctors. Hospitals and doctors' offices were becoming my second home and undergoing tests were routine for me. It is truly depressing going from one test to another but humor is needed. My mother went through everything with me, bless her soul, and we put brave smiles on our faces and did what was needed to do.

After about a week waiting for the results we were called into the doctor's office. By now my legs, toes, arms and some fingers were still numb and I could not bend backward, forward, or sideways at all. I was just in my bed at home lying down and not moving. My whole back from my coccyx to the start of my head was now as hard as a rock. No one could touch me because I would yelp in pain. You could also feel a bone protruding in the middle part of my spine and I quivered every time my fingers would feel it. My mother and I entered the office and sat down. We had not uttered a word the whole journey there. We could not think of anything to say. We were scared. The doctor looked filthy and disorganized. Papers and x-rays were everywhere, making his office look as if someone had raided the place. Everything was turned upside down and he himself looked like he hadn't showered in a week! The hospital on the other hand was gorgeous, impeccable. Walls smelled like they had been freshly painted just that morning! It looked a five-star resort.

The doctor sat down and from beneath the rubble he somehow pulled my file out. He put all my x-rays and MRIs on the board with the bright light shining behind them as if either grabbing our attention in a good way or with the light of death. I swallowed hard, not wanting to hear what was wrong. The doctor seemed strangely calm and had a "je ne sais quoi" expression on his face. It looked like he was amused at something. The words came out of his mouth: "It's nothing," he said. "Nothing is wrong, just a torn muscle. It's in your head. All in your head, Lucinda." He said it in such a condescending way and with such a nasty chuckle that I could have thrown his computer right in his face. How dare he belittle not only me, but my mother as well, and the whole situation. This was not a game. This was real, a skater's life.

The rest I did not hear. "All in your head, Lucinda" is all I heard repeatedly over and over again. This doctor was supposed to be knowledgeable and intelligent and he was the Swiss team Olympic-appointed doctor. And he said that all the pain, the bone protruding, etc., was all in my head?? Now, I have a great imagination but this was too much. Was I utterly and truly that delusional? Then he said something to the effect that I needed to exercise! Exercise? I couldn't move. He said I needed to swim and have massages every day. Massage? No one could even touch me a little. Why in the world would I have someone massage me? I was outraged and confused and what the doctor said made absolutely no sense to me. My mother and I walked out of there with all the X-rays in tow. I never wanted to see him again. My gut intuition knew he was wrong and my good-girl nature of following people's orders would not work here. My mother on the other hand seemed to want to persuade me to follow his treatment. I truly thought my mother was out of her mind!

Once again it was "should have." But it's so true. I should have gone to numerous doctors for second opinions. My Russian coach and her son-in-law repeatedly called us, wanting us to come back to them to go to Boston where they knew of wonderful doctors that could help me and figure out what was wrong. But my mother and father believed in the Swiss doctor and they did not see enough reason to go there. It was my mistake too that I expected them to know what I was feeling and I did not push.

Now we all see that there was way more than enough reason but at that time we did not see. I wanted them so much to believe me, their daughter, not some stranger or some doctor. I wanted my mother to see that I was in serious pain and I wanted her to take me to other doctors to see what was wrong with my spine. But nothing was done. They had accepted the diagnosis and once my parents agree on something they can't be swayed and I believed them above anyone, even above myself. I was misunderstood once more and I did not know what more to do to get my message across. Die? Be permanently paralyzed? I was truly foolish for not speaking up. I was not used to voicing my opinion on a situation when everything always was decided for me. I thought it was enough to just show that I was injured. The rest of the things in my life I was accustomed to my mother handling. If she did not take me to another doctor, it meant no other doctor needed to be seen.

But maybe these were just excuses. Maybe deep inside I also did not know what I would do without my life on the ice, and wanted to keep it going as well. I had no voice of my own. I was confused. We all were. My mother and I were one person. She was the puppeteer and I was the puppet. We were a great team with great consequences. How did we know that this doctor had not been prompted as to what to tell us by the Swiss skating federation? Or was this doctor naive and was this a misdiagnosis? To my expense we would not find out until many years later when the pain and destruction from this injury was so intense and severe that I could barely walk once again. It would ultimately end my career and in many ways my life the way I knew it. But it would be a blessing in disguise. A beautiful blessing in a horrendous disguise. Little do we know why things happen to us. Little do we realize what goes on around us let alone within us. Just how awake are we really in this world? What does it take to wake us up? We close our eyes, our ears, and our mouths, close tightly our hands and make them into fists and fight. Fight for what? For whom? To prove a point or to save our own ego or maybe to save others. I would later learn, however, that to fight for what you believe in is truly empowering and I had never had the chance to do it. We become senseless in more ways than one.

I was confined to my bed once more and not able to move. I stared at the ceiling praying for guidance. I had no other help than my mother's and father's support that "all will end well." They saw me go deep into a world of tears. I was in desperation. I longed for help, for guidance, for someone to pull me back up. I see now that most of all I was longing for my mother or father to lift off all the pressure and let me stop skating and everything that came with it. I wanted them to say it, so that I would not be blamed for anything. I know it was cowardly of me, yet when you believe in someone else other than yourself, you can also start to not believe in yourself at all. And this happened to me. I cried myself to sleep every night.

This was the end, I thought. Everything would have to stop. There was no way in the world this could go on. I was now critically injured. I could not go on and I was sure my parents would never let me go on. This was rock bottom, I thought. I had reached it. All these were merely thoughts and thoughts, nothing much more than energy flowing through. The whole world, it seemed, was determined for whatever reason to prove my thoughts and me wrong. I would have to figure out why by myself when I was truly ready. God saw I was neither ready nor ripe. I was still a child in body and soul, trying to be an adult. I was not to be freed from my misery yet.

I am featured in a Ripley's "Believe It or NOT!" comic strip on 4/27/03.
(Copyright 2003 Ripley Entertainment)

Photo shoot on the famous Dolder Rink in Zurich, Switzerland, 2005
(Photo by Christian Lanz)

The speed of my Biellmann spin created a blurred image during the Art on Ice show in 2003. *(Photo by Erwin Zueger)*

My famous self-created "Lucinda Spin" at the Ice Theatre NY show (www.icetheatreny.org)
(Photo by Diane Bidermann. © Ice Theatre of New York and Diane Bidermann)

Skating on tour with one of my favorite dresses
(Photo by Gerard Vandystadt)

My famous layback spin photographed from above shows a wonderfully interesting angle.
(Photo by Gerard Vandystadt)

A striking ending pose in my famous, statuesque Gold Oscar costume
(Photo by Gerard Vandystadt)

Another one of my spin creations performed on tour around the world
(Photo by Gerard Vandystadt)

Here I am performing a Biellmann spin at my first and favorite professional competition, the 2000 World Professional Figure Skating Championships in Washington D.C. I received several perfect scores of 10.0 and was the Hallmark moment of the day. Soon after this success I received an invitation to be a guest at the White House.
(Photo courtesy of IMG)

Photoshoot 2003 *(Photo courtesy of Lucinda Ruh)*

Photoshoot, Los Angeles, CA, 2003
(Photo courtesy of Lucinda Ruh)

Doug Aitken photographed my spinning for his "Sleepwalkers" exhibition at MOMA.
(Doug Aitken, Sleepwalkers, 2007, courtesy of Museum of Modern Art, 303 Gallery Eva Presenhuber, Regen Projects, Victoria Miro Gallery)

Antonio and I walk across Fifth Avenue on our wedding day after the ceremony held at St. Patrick's Cathedral in New York City, October 16, 2010.
(Photo by Michael Vernadsky, courtesy of Lucinda Ruh)

11

Beginning of an End

(ZURICH, TOKYO, HACKENSACK, SUN VALLEY)

The blind were leading the blind.

I must admit looking back that I think I was completely, truly, and utterly insane in many unclassified ways. No question about it. I did the same thing over and over and over again and I expected different results each time. It was not just me; it was all those around me who orchestrated and conducted my life. We continued in our ways, yet we were always hoping for a completely opposite outcome. You just try even harder than before, while never getting what you hope for, and all you do is ask "Why when working so hard, is so little achieved?" We never think to re-evaluate "how" we are doing it.

There could be many various reasons for the mistakes of a failed execution, but if no one is able to pinpoint the core reason of why it failed, you will never ever be able to fully correct it and succeed. If we can't see for ourselves the reason for our mistakes we need others to discover it for us. Yet when the others around you are living in your bubble as well, it also becomes impossible for them to see it. Sometimes in life stepping back is much more important than trying to move forward. This is when you learn the most about yourself. I was trying so hard with all my might to move forward yet just like I did with my famous spins, all I was doing was spinning in one place. I would never move from one place where I was digging a hole in the ice.

That is what my life had become. I was drilling my own hole deeper and deeper into the earth, deeper into despair as I spun around and around, always returning to where I started. How ironic that my strongest trait on ice would be the way I live my life unconsciously off the ice as well. It was a mirror image not to vanish until I fell so hard right through the glass and shattered it to pieces.

I longed for happier times. I wanted so much to go back to the time when I was little and engulfed in the fairy-tale life my mother and father had created for me. They were and are perfect parents in an imperfect world. The life they gave me had been so beautiful, so magical, so like a fantasy, and so angelic. Their hearts and souls are made of gold and they had been forced into a world built on mistrust, wrong judgment, and petty criticism. It was not my parents' choice, yet skating had warped them into people they were not, and forced them to make decisions that no parent should have to make.

I understand the famous singer's wish to be like Peter Pan and never grow up. Long before this, I had thought that, too. I wanted never to grow up. My life as a kid was so glorious, so enchanting. It was what I, and children around the world, envision life to be and it wasn't growing up that changed it, it wasn't even skating. It was everything that surrounded skating in our world. Movement on the ice is pure. The frozen water that the clean sharp blade paints on is pure. The intention is pure. The face is pure. Yet every single thing that surrounds the outside of the circumference of the ice is not. Our bodies are made mostly of water and water holds every emotion within its structure. I wonder what kind of emotion each patch of ice held packed so tightly?

It was just the start of the skating season yet my competition season was over. The injury that was so serious from pain and debilitation, yet had no diagnosis, would hamper me for a long time. I wasn't talking much at all, not knowing what to say, and I started questioning my life. What was I to do if I could never skate again? My sadness and frustration was plainly visible and my parents thought that sending me to Tokyo for ten days would cheer me up. They knew I really missed my life there and they wanted me to just have some playtime. In Switzerland the physical therapists were not doing any good since their orders were to heal a torn muscle. They could not even really touch me when I was in so much pain, so they and we were at a loss.

The last few years I lived in Tokyo I was treated by a famous Japanese doctor who worked with the best baseball and track and field teams as well as other athletes in Japan. I remember his office well. He was a very prestigious doctor with about twenty employees following his orders. He did massage, acupuncture, and all sorts of therapies. He had about five people on beds on which he would work at the same time, going from one to another all day long. He was a tiny guy with the most energy I have ever seen. He worked for about two hours on each patient. The minute your therapy was done another patient was waiting in the wings to take your place. You would think his office would be a palace but it was in the busiest part of Tokyo in the Shibuya area and crammed in between two high-rise buildings. It was a shack three stories high that looked like it could fall any minute. I remember vividly that whenever a big truck passed by the whole building and the beds would shake feverishly. Every single time before I entered the building I said a prayer and made the sign of the cross praying that there would be no earthquake while I was in there.

I was in constant pain and could not truly bend in any direction or do any sort of exercise, but I could walk and I was excited to go back to my home. I was excited also to travel for once in my life without my skates. It felt awkward to not pack them but was secretly a little freeing as well. I needed a much-deserved break. Tokyo was wonderful, rekindling memories. Eating the food I had grown up with and revisiting my old school and teachers there was fantastic.

Right away I took time to go to the Japanese doctor. He was thrilled to see me and mentioned how much I had grown. I had left Tokyo very tiny and I kept on growing since I left. I was twenty years old by now and my growth plates in my spine had still not closed. There were many reasons I always got injured so quickly: my height, my restricted diet, my imbalanced hormones, my not allowing my body to rest or heal, and my following bad coaching techniques. My restricted diet made my bones more brittle and did not let my body go through puberty, causing a domino effect in other areas of my body. Not resting and not allowing myself to heal and grow also stopped a lot of processes a woman needs to go through, and so my body was frozen in time. I suspect all this caused a lot of my problems that later escalated and caused major havoc in my life.

I explained to the doctor what had happened with my back. I told him how much pain I was in and that the diagnosis did not seem to fit what I was feeling. He told me to lie down on the bed. He took one look at my back and stepped back. I knew he had seen everything, and in a land where no injury is really serious enough to stop you from training, I did not expect him to think much of my spine.

He asked me if I knew that there was a huge bone protruding from my spine, and I told him I knew this. He looked completely stunned. He told me he couldn't understand how I could even walk. He said I needed to get more X-rays, a second opinion right away about the nature of my injury He said he would not be able to do anything for me since he did not want to touch or treat someone with something like that. He said my whole back from the coccyx to the neck was now so tight and so cramped he would not be able to touch me. I left there feeling at least that someone saw something that matched what I was feeling and it confirmed that I was not crazy and delusional.

I relayed the news to my parents and you could tell they were covering up their emotions as they told me, not to worry, just to have fun in Tokyo and that they would take care of it when I got back. I enjoyed the rest of the trip but I had this intense fear within me that if I moved the wrong way, in any minute I could become paralyzed. I did not want to voice this because I would sound like I was complaining, and since the medical doctor in Switzerland had said nothing was wrong, people would think I was talking nonsense. I kept the fear to myself but it was stronger than ever. I usually just dismissed an injury but this one struck a chord in many ways.

Once back home in Zurich, I knew it was time to discuss what our next step would be. A second doctor's opinion never came up again. My parents were adamant that the injury was nothing serious and in a short while I would be fine again, and up and running, or more like up and skating, in no time. We always thought injuries would just heal on their own, as long as we did not think about them, touch them, or even mention them. My parents did not seem worried at all but maybe they were very good at hiding it. I hid it well too. They thought the less they talked about it the more I would forget about it, and the more quickly the injury would go away.

My mother and father share the philosophy that a lot is produced in the mind and if the mind doesn't accept the injury then there is none. Voilà! Just like that they desperately wanted the injury to disappear. All the discussions were about how to get back to skating. Many discussions became heated and my mother would frequently lash out again. You have to understand that skating had become my mother's life, maybe even more so than mine. As much as I missed it she missed it a hundred times more. As much as I was in pain from the injury, she was in more pain from not seeing me skate. I was the one who couldn't skate but she was still capable of going to the rink. For her not to have the schedule of bringing me to the rink and back, preparing me for skating, and the excitement of the whole journey, brought great frustration to her. While I enjoyed the freedom she missed not having a purpose. I had been her purpose and for me to take this away from her made me feel incredibly guilty and her feel helpless.

Every day was tortuously long and filled with despair. I felt incapable of making the situation better. The only way I knew of helping everyone except me to get over this was to get back on the ice. My spins would heal them. From the time of the injury to the first time I went back on the ice was six months, but it felt much longer. That was the longest that I had not been on the ice. I went back on the ice for my mother and my father as I saw the longing in their tearful eyes. My mother said she and my father and the whole world were missing my spins.

Guilt set in and I started back slowly. I made a promise to myself that I would do this for my parents and if something else happened to my spine and I was paralyzed it would prove that I had done everything I possibly could have to thank them for the devotion and utmost love to me. I was willing to take that risk for them as they had taken risks for me. It was a dangerous promise but I felt to skate was the least I could do for them. I owed it to them to bring them the fruit of their labor. I have to admit I was very scared about my body and I prayed that my angels would stay with me.

It seems amazing that I started training again, carefully and cautiously. I did not know what I was training for but just left the goal in the hands of God. How quickly my life had changed. Just one year ago I had basked in the spotlight excited about more great skating to come and now I was back to square one. A year ago finally Switzerland had wanted to give me many opportunities including ones in television, commercials, magazines and endless endorsements and now I to become just an invalid was hard to digest. When your whole career is based on your body and you lose that one thing, you feel you have lost your whole life.

One day in the spring of 2000 we received a phone call from a skating agent who was in America. He wanted to represent me and he wanted me to turn professional. He told my mother my opportunities would be endless and that jumps would not be required of me. He could get me any show I wanted and my spinning would be my forte. He emphasized his point by bringing up the fact that no one was doing them like me and I had the big chance to be the "special one" and become famous. He reeled us in with grandiose words of persuasion. He said he could arrange right away to have me skate in Sun Valley, Idaho for the entire summer doing a show once a week. I could then decide how I would want to proceed. The shows in Sun Valley during the summer were very famous in the skating world and although we had heard of them, we had no real idea of the situation there.

My mother, always loving any new adventure to do with skating, thought it was wonderful. We talked it over a little and since we were "yes" people we sprang at any opening. We never thought things through or weighed options. My parents and I were so accustomed to having a knee jerk reaction while having to make decisions very quickly. We were always on the go from one continent to another, and we never had had the chance to sit down and think things out or wait for other chances. Whatever first came up, due to pressure or the circumstance we were in, we always felt we had to take. The mentality with the Ruhs was "It's better to have a sparrow in your hand than a pigeon on the roof that you could not catch at any moment. But what if you waited and baited that pigeon in? But waiting was not a word we used. We took the proposal. We did not want to commit to anything more quite yet but wanted to give it a chance to open my horizons.

My back pain was subsiding a little, perhaps because of my mental strength and having once more a goal I needed to attain with no excuses. Mind over matter might work after all, but there had been no magic yet and my bone in my spine was still protruding. I mostly just did stroking exercises and footwork as I tried to get my feet back under me. I did not dare jump. As for my spins, I just succumbed to doing the basic ones. Spinning was so engrained in my blood that I knew when the time came for the world to see them, I would just bite my lip and do them. It was a natural habitat for me and this habitat needed not much grooming. Doing spins for over fifteen years resulted in a great deal of confidence.

However, I was not confident about how my spine would react with the protruding bone in the exact spot where I needed to bend my back all the way down in the laybacks, and the same spot where I twisted sideways in my spin creations, and exactly the location of all the stress in the Biellmann spins. I would have to manage somehow. I left for England to have some new programs done by a famous British choreographer. We were scheduled to do just one new program but since I learned it so fast we had spare time and did another. Another, another, another. That had been my life. More, more, more, and when done more would be done. It was never enough. Nothing was.

I was set with two new show programs and I would be skating at the Sun Valley ice shows once a week for three months. The roller coaster ride would never stop. I was literally spinning my way from one continent to another, into one situation to another, into one disaster to another. I would go on my own since we wanted me to grow my own wings and Sun Valley would be the beginning of a new life—hopefully a wonderful new life.

The trip to Sun Valley was a long one, as if life did not want to take me there, and making all the stopovers a chance for me to turn back. But I would not. At long last I arrived at what would be my new home for the next three months. I was excited to be on my own and I didn't feel scared or lost just because my map had no route and no destination. I was actually quite excited to be in the spotlight once more and not have the pressure of judges. It was a world I knew and I could now express all my raw emotions on the ice. I liked my new programs and liked that I did not have to skate by the rules.

The shows were fun and different than I had experienced before. It was enchanting to skate outdoors under the moonlight and spotlight, confusing as to which was which, amusingly similar to how life or I looked upon me as well. To have the spectators on their candle-lit dinner tables watching us made us feel prestigious, yet hungry. Hungry for more in life. Hungry for a real life and not one of caged imprisonment. You could feel that you were part of the history of old Hollywood and old skating stars alike. You were walking in their footsteps.

The first few weeks with all the excitement and hype around me were enticing, but I was getting very lonely and the shows became very repetitive. I called my mother and father a couple times a day and cried on the phone. It reminded me of when I went to skating camp in Japan, on the phone crying for help with my only lifeline. I was still in pain and not happy. Other skaters were coming in and out for the shows, and the dance and pair-teams had each other, but I was the only one who stayed for the three months and had absolutely no family in all of America, and no friends, and I was lonely.

No matter how much admiration I received on the ice from my skating, no matter how many fans came just to see me skate, no matter how much fan mail I received, nothing could give me comfort like a hug from my mother or father. I felt my agent did not really care about me either, and I felt I had been transplanted from one zoo to another and this one made me pace back and forth. It felt like he had just plopped me there expecting me to just adjust and figure everything out. I was at a complete loss for words and movement.

My agent did not visit me and my parents could not come till later in August. Every day I went to the post office and there was a care package from my mother from Dubai. Every single day. It was incredible! I would walk to the post office with a frown and emerge with a smile. There were cards and gifts filled with a piece of my mother's heart. I missed her terribly and my mother missed me too. That is the only thing that made me smile each day. Going to the post office to open the surprise package all the way from half way around the world was the excitement of my day. I read and reread all the cards over and over again. I placed them all around my apartment. I was turning twenty-one that summer and I had still not broken away from my mother and father. I had still not gone through that separation. It was much later in life than when most girls go through it. In the life we had led we were completely dependent on each other, so much that when separated we felt the other part of ourselves had been lost. We did not know how to survive without each other. I had nowhere to turn.

I was also dealing with my recurrent stomach infection. Since leaving China when I had first contracted it, I had been on many bouts of antibiotics for it, each doctor finding and treating another infection and perhaps another virus or bacteria in my stomach. Luckily as time passed the extreme pain and symptoms I had had from China healed, but now my symptoms seemed to be stemming from elsewhere and just manifested into feeling a constant nonstop mild nausea with severe headaches. I was dizzy all the time. My ears felt blocked all day and I had flu symptoms that wouldn't get worse or any better. I was in pain from my knee and back injury. My neck hurt. My shoulder injury had started to flare up again. In this state how could I enjoy skating, let alone everyday life? Where was this all coming from?

The one-hour time that I was on the ice for the show was great, but during the rest of the week being alone was worse than knowing how good the show was. The strange contrast between performing in front of an audience of hundreds that are sitting in darkness while you are under a spotlight and all alone in the light unable to see anything, was extreme. I went to the juice bar in town and told my friend I needed the help of his psychic friend. I was desperate. I was troubled about a few things and they were total polar opposites of each other. I had to basically decide if I wanted to stay amateur (meaning compete at the Grand Prix, the World Figure Skating Championships, and the Olympics) or turn professional and do shows, tours around the world, and at that time there were quite a few professional competitions too.

It was the hardest decision of my life so far. It felt like being eight years old all over again when I had to decide between ballet and skating. I was torn. I was torn because of my injuries and physical health and I was torn because I still had not had the Olympic experience. If I turned professional that dream would be dead and dormant once and for all. In my heart I truly wanted to remain an amateur. I wanted to compete and have that tight relationship with my mother and coach and have that excitement of preparing for a competition. It was the only life I knew.

Yet I knew I couldn't do my jumps because of the pain I was in. I also did not like the show life and I had always said I never wanted to be a show pony. Yet I thought I owed it to my parents to use my spinning to do something with what I had. My agent laid more guilt on me by saying I owed it to my parents and could pay them back one day with all the money they had spent on me like a flowing river if I turned professional. Nice dream! To add to the problem, if I wanted to stay amateur and compete I wanted to do so only if I could train with my Chinese coach. He had left China and for whatever reason, was now in Tokyo. We had moved nonstop for skating and we really felt, coming to our senses, that to then move back to Japan to train with him with all my injuries and illness was just not worth it. Could we really just go on and on like an energizer bunny, not only spending all our money but also really wanting to fight once more only to find myself in dire situations? What was this worth? I had my spins. Why not use them? I did not need any more medals to perform with the rest of the world and Olympic champions. I was lucky.

My agent could not understand my confusion with it all. He pushed and pushed and I felt cornered. For me it was so hard to give up the Olympic dream, and then on the other side of the spectrum even today I can't forgive myself for spinning for money. I just felt so dirty. I felt that receiving money for something that was so sacred to me ruined everything. It would ruin my spins, my soul, and my life. I felt this deep inside of me. I felt I was selling my body and I felt I was doing something terrible. Spins were to be done at times like a prayer, not to be done over and over again like a machine on autopilot! I did not seem to see however how the spins were making everyone else so happy.

I had also wanted to model. When I was younger in Japan I did some modeling at the young age of about nine and I had loved it so much. I loved dressing up. But then skating took over and there was no time for my other interests. As I grew up I also knew my mother detested modeling and for her only skating was to be honored. I was scared to bring up anything unrelated to skating in case my mother would erupt at me. I knew she did not want me to have any distraction that would disrupt my skating career. Now that I was alone I thought I had the chance to explore modeling and entered a modeling contest that I saw in one of the fashion magazines. I snail mailed my application.

My mother arrived in Sun Valley in late August as the shows were ending and decisions were to be made. As my luck would have it, the answer from the modeling competition came in the mail while my mother was there. She opened the mail and saw that I had been accepted to quite a big modeling agency and she became furious. She hit me a lot that day. I cried and cried, not so much because of the hitting but because I tried so hard to understand my mother and I couldn't. I never seemed to be able to make my mother proud of me unless I was spinning. Spinning my own web of confinement. If it breaks, start over and spin another web.

The summer shows ended and we decided to go to where my agent was living in Hackensack, New Jersey for a while. We needed more time to decide on my future and my mother saw how devastated I was with everything. We decided not to make a final decision then and there and just to see how the months progressed. We thought perhaps I could do shows while still leaving the amateur ranks open for me. What we did decide was that for me to return to Japan was out of the question. It was too insane an idea for nothing tangible. We would stay in the States. We were in the dark concerning not only my future but also even the present. Something would reveal itself soon enough. My life seemed to be out of my hands. I was powerless and so was my mother. We decided to run with the tide. We had no more wishes, no more goals, no more wants. We were more than exhausted. It was the end of any certainty.

12

Broken Wing

(HACKENSACK, TOURING THE WORLD, DUBAI)

Humans need to suffer to become angels.

Just as I started to have my wings grow they would be clipped. I believe everything happens for a reason and I do believe that every situation, every person in your life, is a lesson in disguise. There is never a moment that is not a lesson. I too believe that blessings can come in many shapes and forms. They can be concealed, and in life one ought not to make a judgment on anything or anybody since you never know what lies beneath that disguise. You might miss out on a chance and sometimes what you are looking for is not what you ultimately want, but what you finally get, if you let the universe do its work, is actually what you wanted all along. Those that can learn from life every second have truly mastered the notion of living in the "now." We are all too busy always pondering what happened in the past and working for what "will" we truly always miss what is happening in the present.

Months passed by, and as I was training in Hackensack, New Jersey and still debating my decision, I was also traveling all around the world for amateur skating shows. With my traveling and my name growing in fame, I had many suitors here and there, but I was not interested. I was really not in that space for a relationship. I had so many life-changing and challenging events happening to me simultaneously that I was not available and not open to love. I also was again going through serious bouts of what appeared to be the stomach virus or bacterial infection and I was in and out of hospital emergency rooms every week. It was getting very serious and rounds of antibiotics were doing more harm than good. But at last a stroke of good luck would come.

A big opportunity arose from invitation to me to attend the World Professional Championships held in Washington, D.C. in 2000. It was definitely an honor to receive such an invitation and my agent cautioned us not to turn this down. It would, however, turn me professional and training for the Olympics would then become just a distant memory. This invitation was the turning point and the deciding factor. Only five ladies were invited to this competition each year and usually only those of Olympic or world gold medal status. For me to be wanted there, was pretty huge. I felt a rush of excitement and I felt this was a sign from up above. I did not want to pass this one by, and so it was decided for me to turn professional upon accepting this invitation.

It turned out to be a stupendous decision. It opened doors for me like never before, but with my health problems I could not accept most of them. Many doors would be closed due to my failing health. I would, however, always have a chip on my shoulder about never having been given even the chance of becoming an Olympian. I had done everything I could have in the world of skating, but to realize that I would never be able to say I was an Olympian would always make me sad.

I skated incredibly well at the 2000 World Professional Figure Skating Championships. I was in my element. I needed to do only a few jumps and I could spin and be as artistic as I wanted. I had standing ovations and performing in front of thousands of people was incredible. I loved it, and while I had never received the perfect score of 6.0 in amateur figure skating competitions, I now received at the professional level many perfect scores of 10! I was the Hallmark video of the day. I got many offers, but once again not really intended for me to accept since at that time I was not American and they were obliged to first use their American champions. I was at the bottom of the totem pole concerning endorsements. We did however have many different agents come up to us who wanted to represent me. But what truly are agents other than people wanting some of your money? I wished to have open doors leading to glorious opportunities, not agents hunting us down and closing the doors behind us!

The best part of this competition other than coming back with a bronze medal was that my parents and I were invited to the White House for lunch. The speechwriter at that time to President George W. Bush had been at the competition and was so enthralled with me and my skating that he personally invited me to come. I was elated. I had met him and his colleagues at the after-party and they were ecstatic over me. I felt like my spins had brought happiness and I could not have been more happy. More than for me, I could not wait to give the gift to my mother and father of a visit to the most important house in America. What an honor it was. We gladly and gratefully accepted. We visited the White House in December 2000 for a private tour and a wonderful lunch. We could not have been more thankful for such an amazing and memorable experience hosted by such gracious people of the government.

At the time I turned professional the world of ice skating was not too distressing. Of course it not as wonderful as when it hit an all-time media frenzy in the 1990s but it was definitely much better than it is now. There were tons of tours and shows all around the world available to us, which is different from now. I was invited to do some skating shows over Christmas and New Years' in the Caribbean islands that were produced by a famous male French champion. I had never been away from my family on Christmas day and was not too sure how I would handle it all, but I felt it was time for me to take the opportunities to grow stronger mentally and in my skating experiences as well. The young skaters that grow up in America have many chances to do shows, perform showcases, and have the chance to skate under spotlights, but where I had grown up in Asia there were no such opportunities. I also wanted to get used to traveling back and forth, living out of suitcases and being able to perform my best even in a second's notice.

So off I was to the islands. It was an experience to journal. It was incredibly scorching hot on these islands. After all it was the Caribbean. I am not at all much of a beach person. Mountains and snow please my senses far more than the sticky sun and sand, and even more so during holiday time, so I stayed in my hotel room for the most part and read a lot.

Also, touring is not what you might expect it to be. The skaters that are pair or dance teams stick to themselves since they have each other. Skaters of the same country stick to each other while speaking their native language and they tour so much together that there isn't much space to give freely to a newcomer. I did not belong to any nation so I was different and separate. I also am totally to blame for some of this isolation. I had become very insecure and apologetic in my life and with myself. I'd rather hide in the corner avoiding conflict and liked to sit behind everyone so I had a clear view of what was going on and have no fear of someone behind me stabbing me in the back. I also did not really know how to socialize. So they saw me as the spoiled one instead of seeing my shortcomings. It stems from the constant fear I grew up with that everyone was against me and having been always an outcast. Having been treated always so differently I ceased to expect anything else.

With my stomach never feeling right and my never feeling in my optimal health, I was scared I would catch even something more serious when in the Caribbean. I was very careful with the water and fruits and ate only grilled food or fruit I could peel myself. I was living in constant fear of my health. I was not feeling well at all and would never wake up feeling refreshed. I was lonely on this tour since my family was celebrating Christmas day all together and I was alone in my room most of the time with no Christmas tree to peer upon and let me escape into my fairy tale world. Again I felt my agent did not understand me. But who ultimately did? Not even I understood myself.

The show itself was unique. These were islands, so figure skating was the last thing the natives thought about, let alone had even heard about. Ice to them was definitely foreign other than having ice cubes in their drinks. I think they thought these were strange people who had arrived bringing frozen ice with people skating on it to their island of paradise! I don't know if it was the smartest idea, but for sure it was something that had never been done before and would never be done again! When we arrived the team was setting up the ice.

They had put water down with a refrigeration system and were waiting for it to freeze. There was a meek attempt at having a tent-like cover over the ice surface so that the sun's heat would not beat on the ice directly and reduce it to a puddle of water! When the show started the cover would be lifted. We had to wait two days until the ice was ready for us to skate on. It was hilarious when just after a few minutes of our skating and jumping on the very thin ice surface, the holes we created, both big and small, caused the pipes to explode. They were exploding everywhere. The ice surface was incredibly small already and now we had mini fountain springs all over the place. It became dangerous and we tried skating in and out to avoid them.

The team tried to fix them, but soon as one was fixed another pipe would break somewhere else. It was complete disorder. The shows were starting that evening and there was no way there was enough time in the heat to freeze a new sheet of ice and also no way the shows could be canceled. Also as the night darkened, we would not be able to see where these little water springs were when we were skating and we could get seriously injured.

So the team decided to put potted plants on the ice on top of each and every broken pipe! It felt like I was skating in a garden! It was funny as well as frustrating because these potted plants were not lit and we had only an approximate calculation of where they were. I was worried that when under the spotlight I would skate right into them and fall on my face! As far as the spectators I was not so worried, because for them if you just did a single jump or an easy spin it was Olympic material to them. So I smiled and put on a show face and on I skated. Luckily no one was seriously hurt. For every show we had for those few days more and more potted plants were placed on the ice! By the end there were more green areas than white. We were hopping over the pots. I was relieved when the shows were over and it was time to go home. I was melancholy because I had missed a family Christmas for this tour. I didn't know if it was worth it.

Show life was very different from what I had been used to and how I had been trained from the age of four. There was no structure. No regimen. No support, no goals. No real training. It was just trying to keep at the level you were since there was no time for improving. It was sleeping in one hotel to the next, from one city to another, skating under one spotlight to another. It felt like a circus on the road, but more prestigious, with more money invested in the production. And our wishes were to be granted to a certain extent. I was lucky, however, because in some skating tours the skaters are treated terribly. I was on the best and most honored tours in the world so I couldn't complain. I was treated like a star. I was a star. Some productions were incredibly produced with top-rated lighting and fans worldwide followed the entertainment. To see them so happy made it all worthwhile.

Even some travels to the shows were stupendous as well. After I did a show in the early evening in New York City I was taken by limousine to the helicopter pad and taken by helicopter to the next show where I performed later that evening. We were almost waited on hand and foot. After all, the success of each show was a direct result of how happy the skaters were with the production and whether we would want to skate on that specific tour again, and so our happiness was the producers first concern. And, oh my, did some skaters take great advantage of it! Later on, one of the tours I was part of was conducted the whole time by a private jet. Yes, I was living the life, but was I really? For me to be content in life I need to be stimulated mentally and spiritually as well, and that part of my soul was hungry. Very hungry.

As I kept on touring, all these troubles and my unhappiness mounted and I was stuck in a rut. My back hurt non-stop. I dealt with it by taking painkillers every day. My stomach pains were terrible and I was eating less and less. I was so limited as to what I could eat that my diet remained very imbalanced. Basically I was eating only fruit when I was on the road since most of the food served was not to my liking. I also wanted to stay thin so I just ate certain food groups. I was very strict and disciplined with myself as I had been all my life. I never ever gave in to myself and punished myself for every mistake I made. I was still tearing out my eyes lashes and eyebrows out and picking my skin until I bled, but hid it all too well. I was not calm and not in my element.

One of my next tours was in France. I never went on the practice ice, not even once for the two week tour. I couldn't. I was too weak, tired, and unwell. I stayed in the tour bus's bed all day until a half hour before the show started. Then I would drag myself to the rink and into my costumes, paint my make-up on as well as my smile, and push myself through the show. I almost fainted each time I finished my solo performance. I trudged on. The other skaters were not my friends. The tour's organization was a mess as well. It was France after all! The show never started on time, not ever. The bus driver sometimes would even drive intoxicated. We hit so many lampposts on the way it was ridiculous. I am not sure the bus driver was even qualified to drive but in France anything goes!

A new experience for me as well was that skaters were drinking and smoking a lot on the tour. I had always been in such a "clean" and "good girl" environment with my mother that this felt all too uncomfortable and too real for me. I liked my dream world better. Starting relationships with others while on tour was also very new for me to understand. I was single and I had too many other issues at hand that were far beyond the dating world. I thought it rude and inappropriate for skaters to hook up randomly with others in the bus, but I closed my eyes and ears and just tried to rest so I would be well enough to survive another day. My issue was survival, not if someone liked me or not.

Also, having been so sheltered my whole life, I had never been exposed to such behavior. I did not belong there. I did not fit in their world. I had expected that skaters like me, having worked so hard all our lives, would be so appreciative of the new life of being a star. Instead, their mentality was that they needed to take it all with them as long as it lasted and they would step over anyone if needed. Their greed mounted; they took advantage of the situation and of people and were rude and pushy. I did not feel it was my place to say anything so I just watched, observed, and stayed quiet. They might have thought I was the dumb and weak one but I'd rather they looked at me that way than enter their world. Maybe I was crazy and they were sane but I had always preferred being my crazy to their normal. It was such a pity I never could enjoy my own skating.

The German tour was next. I did not want to give up. Germany was another three weeks of shows. I seriously did not know if I would be able to pull through when I was so sick. It was the same tour that I had performed with right after the 1999 World Championships in Helsinki and where I had so much success. I loved the producers and tour manager of this tour and was excited to see them again. To my dismay the tour did not feel the same and it was not the producers but the skaters who had changed. It was not the same group and once again I was alone. I talked only to the producer and the tour manager and otherwise just stuck to myself. I was becoming even more unwell. I was nauseous every single day for twenty-four hours. I was very, very skinny, but I still thought I wasn't skinny enough, and I hardly ate anything.

The producer called my mother asking her if I was all right and if I had an eating disorder. I did not. There were some skaters on the tour who did, though, and my roommate for the tour was one of them. She had stacks of candy, chips, and chocolate hidden under the beds in each hotel room. She would not eat anything in front of other people, but then would binge on all the snacks she had hidden and then she would throw everything up. I was so sick I couldn't eat. That made me skinny enough. Maybe unconsciously it had become my psychological weapon as well.

On this tour I was more in hospitals and doctors' offices than on the ice. The tour manager was an incredibly wonderful man and he accompanied me to all the hospitals holding my hand. I was scared and he was my support. We were in the eastern part of Germany and my sickness was getting so awful that they arranged for me to get an upper endoscopy to see if I had an ulcer or something worse. I was hesitant to go to just any doctor but I trusted the producer. We entered the hospital. It looked like a building that had just barely survived the war. I am glad it was still standing when we exited. The inside was barren. Nobody and nothing was around. It was completely quiet and desolate. The atmosphere was as if a bomb siren had just gone off and everyone was hiding underground.

One nurse directed us to an empty room where I was instructed to lie down. I was shaking and fearful of what was to come as the manager held my hand. The doctor entered and without saying anything took this long, very thick black tube and was about to jab it down my throat. I yelped and said I needed a minute to breathe first. The doctor waited a minute and the manager tried to calm me down. I wasn't given any sedative nor was my throat numbed. I realized he was going to put it all the way down my throat! I panicked but did not know any better and just thought I needed to be brave. I figured it was always done like this.

When the doctor slid the tube down my throat and all the way to my stomach it was so painful and I felt like I wasn't able to breathe. My manager could barely watch as he squeezed my hand. The doctor had been looking at the images the camera at the end of the tube was taking. He told us he did not see anything abnormal and walked out. That was it.

I have been often misdiagnosed by medical doctors. I don't know quite why, but I am sure it helped to make me a very strong person. I barely finished the tour. I had to save just enough energy all day to survive my solos and be able to pull through to endure it all. I just made it to the finish line. But not one other skater knew of my dilemma nor did the audience. I covered it all so well. When done I was so depleted I could barely utter a word. My body just collapsed. I decided I would go to my parents to be in Dubai until I became well. I could not wait to fall into the arms of my parents and keep my skates at bay.

My parents, understanding my pain and hearing how sick I was, had tried to persuade me to stop the tour and come back earlier. But I wouldn't have been able to live with myself if I had given up, no matter the consequence. I would have rather died skating then stopping to heal myself. For me it would be more honorable to go that way than to have said I needed to rest to get well. I see now that my psychology then sounds so totally upside down, but at that time I did not know any better. Skating was my life and the actual skating I loved and even though I was too sick to skate I felt I would be even more sick without it. At least that is what I felt like, and so it could be classified as an addiction. Withdrawing from anything that is done repeatedly to make you feel good in a disillusioned way may be more painful at first, but will always be worth it in the long run by curing you from the inside out.

But I did not know any of this then. The way I was continuing to live my life, by just digging my own hole of illness deeper and deeper, I ended up denying myself my own happiness. For any wound to be cured you must admit to having it first. I was nowhere near realizing my dangerous fascination with spinning to escape my pain from life. That realization would be a long time coming. What would it take to wake me up? I am lucky I did not die in the process.

13

Deadly Frozen

(DUBAI, TOKYO, HACKENSACK)

To be or not to be. Dying is simple compared to creating and being something that will live forever.

I never wore watches. As a young child, curiously enough, I had never wanted to. I never wanted to know what time it was. Maybe it was because my whole life was running and rushing by and against it, never with or within it. Everything was calculated by what time it was and what time I needed to be where, as if time made me suddenly visible. I could never be too early or too late. I had to always be on time. Everything was measured by that round object with little hands moving in a clockwise direction going around and around. I saw it to be pointless, but much more importantly I did not want to imprint the time in my body. I did not want the time to rule me and therefore become a slave to it. Why should I be a slave to something that was only relevant to the little place where you lived? You moved a little east, west, north or south and it would be a different time. To me it is irrelevant and petty in the whole world scheme of things.

To me time is insignificant. It does not exist. No one can tell you what time it really is at the moment because the minute they say it, it is already in the past and there is a new time. It is like never living in the now. I don't want something in my life that is not real to be my dictator. I have given up time.

When I used to spin, time stopped. It had no significance. It did not matter what time it was. Time stood still. That is how I want to live my life. Don't you realize when you are having the time of your life you do not care what time it is? You only look at your watch when you feel it's time to stop whatever you were doing to do something else.

Feeling unwell, I arrived in Dubai. It would be my first time there. It was the early summer of 2001. My parents had lived there for about one year. The airport was inviting and there was a sense of newness, excitement in the air, and it flooded people's veins. Upon arrival everyone seemed to have the urgency to explore the land beyond the airport as quickly as they could. They all seemed in the biggest rush to get out of there. I did not rush. I explored the airport first. Airports to me, having travelled so much, have always given me the first glimpse and first insight into the land beyond the building walls. It mirrors the whole culture of the people in this one space, in the food, in the mannerisms of the people, in the smells, in the attitudes of security check point personnel, and in what you observe in the luggage claim area. You can size up a whole country just by their airports. They are fascinating to me and I love them. I took my time and visited the restroom. I was so elated to see they had one stall like there was in Japan with the hole in the ground. I excitedly chose that one. I felt a slice of Japan in the most intimate settings. I smiled.

To my surprise the place where my parents lived and still live to this day, has a rooftop pool on the thirty-first floor and an ice rink on the first floor. The same molecules in liquid and in frozen form are each on different spectrums of the earth. How ironic. The liquid to the heavens and the frozen deeply rooted in the earth. The pool was to my delight, but the ice rink was to my dismay. Every time I passed it I would feel guilty not to be on it practicing. I had to force myself to not go on the ice and really let my body heal and relax.

I did, however, succumb to my spinning addiction. Once again it truly felt like I was a show for people to watch. Since I felt uncomfortable skating and spinning in all my positions in public in such tight unitards that denied people any illusions about body movement, I covered myself up and spun in sweatshirts and baggy pants. I was incredibly skinny and pale and ghostly compared to all the beautifully tanned foreigners who had been basking in the sun's rays. I truly looked like I had been in a refrigerator for a while, and I had. A frozen container with all the delights, good and evil, at people's fingertips to become addicted to, was truly a depiction of an ice rink!

Needless to say, I was not well. I could not eat much and I was weak. I was continually having flu-like symptoms that were getting worse. I feel ridiculous about listing all my ailments, but let me put it this way. It would be much easier to say what part of my body was well. Maybe my little toe. Actually no, since I had broken one as well, and it was actually still swollen. I was contemplating stopping skating once more. I did not enjoy, to say it nicely, the tours. I did not enjoy the traveling and living out of suitcases. I knew so many people and so many people knew of me, yet I did not have even one friend I could turn to. My mother and father were all I had. Please understand that I am not complaining, but it caused a lot of my problems that there was no one outside my circle who could clearly judge my situation. I had totally lost my joy for skating. Skating had become torture for me when I was so sick. I could not enjoy the moments on the ice. It was survival and not skating. Something needed to be done.

My parents suspected that a lot of my illness was again mind over matter and were confident that if I were happy my illness and all my physical torment would go away. But how would they be able to make me happy if I could not do that for myself, and the one thing that was making me unhappy I would not let go of? It is clear now but then, oh boy, was it confusing.

After a month or so I mentioned how I really wanted to go to Japan to see my Chinese teacher. I thought that maybe he would be able to rekindle the fire within me to skate again and as always I thought skating would cure me. I realize now I should have stayed in one spot longer to get myself grounded but my family and I were so used to packing up and leaving and trying to fix things by "doing" instead of "letting go" that I was off to Japan not long after I arrived in Dubai. We were always up and running, feeling guilty and lazy the minute we sat down. Our minds would always be running hundreds of miles an hour. Sitting down rarely done in our family and if we were to sit I would have to exercise my brain. Not one minute was to be wasted.

But if time did not exist how were we wasting it? Being in Dubai for a little holiday I felt very lazy and felt unproductive. Producing is the key word here as producing was always what I measured myself by. Little did I know that by not doing anything, I could have given my body the chance to do something. I was twenty-two and had still not gone through puberty and I was still growing. If I had let my body rest and rejuvenate what was to come would never have happened. But then I refused to see this and I carried on like a Good Samaritan.

I missed Japan a lot and we felt to leave for Tokyo on my own for a little more than a month to enjoy being "home" would do me good. I would stay at my coach's home where he lived with his wife and son and I could train with him until I felt confident again and well. I was excited but very tired and over-exerted. It felt like I had been running for twenty years nonstop. I had been feeling like my body could no longer move. This was not in my imagination either. It was real. My body felt extraordinarily heavy and it seemed nearly paralyzed. I would have to lie down and just rest. But again we all refused to see what was happening and went to the outside world to help me feel better. My mother always told me to just put a smile on my face and be happy. That made everyone else think I was happy, but it would not heal anything I was going through since the happiness did not stem from within me. I had to change and I did not know how.

At the last minute I started to panic about leaving again. I did not want to go anywhere but I felt it was my duty to heal myself and do everything possible to skate again. The one thing I was striving for was the one thing that was killing me. When the flight was boarding I made a last call to my mother and father to say good-bye from the pay phone. Situations felt like they were on automatic mode and were being played over and over again for me. I felt like the days at skating camp and like the days in Sun Valley where I would cry on the phone to my mother and father not wanting to ever hang up. I was calling once again in desperation for them to stop me and pull me back. I was alone and frightened. When you don't feel well and don't know why, it is the scariest thing in the world. I feel it is scarier then when you know why you are in pain or sick because then you can actually do something about it. With no doctor's diagnosis, there is no solution. When there is no possible solution it feels like you could die in any minute.

Everyone had boarded except me. They were motioning me to hurry up. I had to hang up. I forced myself to go on the trail leading to the plane. I was crying hysterically. I did not want to go but felt I had to go. I did not have the courage to turn back now. I would be a failure to myself and to my family. If I were to turn back I would just be in Dubai feeling guilty about resting so it was a catch twenty-two.

The feeling was terrible. I could hardly walk. My body froze and I had to hold my legs and pull them one in front of the other to make myself move. I felt frozen in time as if a huge concrete wall was in front of me that I could not pass through and I could not see the other side. I do not know how I got on that plane. Even now, re-writing this time brings me to tears. I was in such denial of the whole situation. I was trying to please my parents so much and they were trying to please me so much that in the end nobody was pleasing anybody. I plopped in my seat and sobbed. I looked out of the window as tears rolled down my cheeks. I must have cried the whole first three hours of the trip before I fell asleep. I did not know if I was to survive. I was so terrified and lonely. I had never felt like this.

The whole journey was a blur. God must have been holding me in his hands. I took a taxi to my coach's home. It was small and in Japanese style, not like the massive homes we had as expats, but I liked it since it was authentically Japanese and I felt at home. His home was near an ice rink, one that I had skated on many times for competitions and tests while I lived in Tokyo. It held many memories. There was a bridge over a highway connecting where he lived to where the ice rink was. It was all within walking distance.

I put the experience of the plane trip in the back of my mind. I tucked it away safely with all my other experiences where light was not to be shed upon. I settled in and decided to get on the ice with my coach to see if my moods would get better. I really did not want to skate anymore when the pain overrode the joy but I was willing to try. After all that is why I had come all the way back to Tokyo. I managed to get on the ice every day for the first week and seeing familiar faces brought back the old times. I explored Tokyo on my own, visiting my old school and my teachers. I spent a lot of time with my old math teacher and his wife whom I had loved so much. It always felt wonderful to be around him since he was like my uncle.

After the first week of skating I started to despise it even more. He wanted to train me for the Olympics and I tried to explain to him that the Olympic dream was now dead. It was all too painful and I saw absolutely no reason to skate anymore. To top it off, since I was not feeling well I felt too weak to train.

One night I awoke around 11:00 p.m. not feeling well. My body felt very heavy and I felt dizzy and faint. As I went to get out of the bed to go to the restroom my legs gave way and I fell to the floor. When I got up to open my door, my coach and his son who were talking in the living room asked me if I was all right, saying they had heard a big thud. I said I had fallen, they laughed, and I went into the bathroom. I came out feeling worse and collapsed in the arms of my coach. The next thing I knew I was back in my bed and they had called the ambulance. The paramedics couldn't find my blood pressure, the same as the time I fainted in California and my body was shaking. I was freezing. They rushed me to the hospital where once again I was treated for exhaustion and malnutrition. My coach and I left the hospital in the wee hours of the morning. The fainting for the second time had me really scared. I was scared to fall asleep or to wander too far from his home in case it happened again. I was frightened of my own body. It was thought that I was fainting due to exhaustion and although that was a huge factor there were many more serious factors to be unveiled in the next few years.

This trip's purpose had been to cure all my ailments, but it ended up exacerbating them. After my first week in Tokyo, gradually my emotions took an even deeper downward spiral. The first week I had gotten myself to the rink and had been able to skate a bit at a time. The second week I got myself to the rink but I was not able to lace my skates and get on the ice. After a few days of not skating I found myself unable to even get my body to the ice rink. I just could not walk over the bridge. The feeling that I had boarding the plane in Dubai was with me again. Oddly enough I could walk everywhere else, to town, to go shopping, or wherever else I wanted to go. But to go to the ice rink or do anything having to do with ice skating, I could not do.

Even when trying with all my physical and mental strength to get myself over the bridge to that big white building that enclosed the frozen water like a prison, I could not move. I would look at the building, collapse to the ground, and sob for hours. Looking back I can't believe how every single day I did this. Sometimes twice a day! I would try and try again to get to the rink with my skates in my hands. Again I would not reach the building. I know now that even just the simple feeling of actually wanting to go somewhere has a lot to do with your actually physically getting there.

One day as I was trying to get myself to the ice rink, I hit an ultimate low. I paused at the bridge to look below at the cars whizzing by. I felt so sad and was in so much pain that I felt like jumping off into the freeway below. I wanted my suffering to end so badly as I looked down intently with fear. As I stood looking at the cars below, I suddenly felt a strong hand pull me back and a loud voice telling me, "NO, you cannot do this. There is a bigger reason and purpose for your existence on this earth than skating and you must live to tell it. I promise you this." Whether it was my own inner voice, the voice of God or a higher power, or my parents' voices, I will never know.

But it made me step back and fall down onto the bench and I sobbed. I never cried that much. I don't know if anyone saw me but in a moment like this you don't see or feel anything around you. Nothing else exists. Instead of taking the plunge, I had stepped back from the edge. My will to live was still much stronger than the will to die. I knew that killing myself would not solve anything. I wanted the situation around me to die and so I had contemplated ending it in this way. But in the end I could not fathom to be so selfish as to take my own life. To take the biggest gift you receive away from yourself would be pure cowardliness. Also, with the fear of the pain it would cause my parents in ways impossible to describe, I could never, ever do this. That would be too much of a sin. After what seemed to be hours, and the day had turned into night, I got up and solemnly walked back home. I would never skate at that rink again.

At that time I did not tell my parents any details but just mentioned that I was not getting any better. Being so far away from them and not having them right next to me, made it impossible to say some things. I was embarrassed as well, and situations like these are not made for a conversation over a wire that is stretched for miles and miles. I also did not want them to worry. I thought I should be able to take care of myself. A mother is always a mother however, and she could feel from the beginning of my arrival in Japan that something was severely wrong. My mother confesses to me now she was terrified for my life during this time and had sleepless nights. As for my coach, I just told him that I was just too tired to skate with him. I was a great actress after all and hid everything pretty well.

A few days passed and as not skating was making me feel like there was a huge hole in my life, I did tell my mother, father and coach that the only way I would be able to skate again is if I were to be invited to the most prestigious tour in the world, Smucker's Stars on Ice in America. Then and only then would I get back on the ice. I felt I had done everything else, and never liking repetition, I needed something new. The shows were starting to be all the same to me. I was already the best spinner in the world, leaving my mark in history and I could not do more than I had pushed my body to do. Stars on Ice was the only thing left I wanted to be part of. They understood but unfortunately it was not in their hands to make this happen.

To add to all this upheaval, my coach and his family were not happy in Japan. They felt like outcasts (welcome to my world) and they wanted a chance in America. I absolutely love doing things for other people. I always have and always will. I love to strive to make other people happy even if I end up sacrificing a part of myself. I told my coach that I would take care of his whole family's visas and that I would make it possible for him to work in the States. After all, I was not skating and maybe this is why I had come to Japan. This, however, was a huge task to take on for a twenty-two year old. A whole Chinese family's destiny was in my hands.

No matter what had happened in the past, I felt this was my way of giving my grateful thank-you back to my coach for giving me the wonderful skating time I had in China. It was my way of repaying him, and I knew that no amount of money could ever be equal to it. He made it possible for me to land all the triples and had made me feel like I had accomplished all there was to accomplish on the ice. After suffering with my jumps for so many years that feeling of finally succeeding is indescribable. I was confident I could do this for them, and mostly for him. Loving to make things happen, I was willing to make all the phone calls and do all the paperwork necessary.

I called the necessary people that needed to be a part of this to make it a success and got to work. Because it was almost a twenty-four- hour a day job it took my mind off all my pain and hospital visits. It was a lot of pressure since it would be a one-time chance to accomplish this. You can't keep revisiting the embassy for a visa. If they deny you for any reason, then you have to wait before you can try again. I had only a few weeks to do all of this. I was determined.

My parents were very astonished that I was undertaking this task and were afraid I was taking a risk as well. If it succeeded we would feel and be responsible for many things to come for the whole family. I am not sure they wanted me to do it, but I was very stubborn, thinking I would help the whole family just like he had when he helped me with my jumps. None of them had ever lived in the United States, nor had his wife or son ever even stepped foot on U.S. soil. They did not speak very much English, either. It might have looked like a disaster waiting to happen but to see my coach so miserable in Japan, I could not just do nothing.

Through endless phone calls with lawyers and ice rink managers, translating nonstop, embassy visits, and emails, I worked and worked, sometimes staying up all night because of the time difference. It was a big job, lots of sweat and tears, but it was all worthwhile when I truly succeeded. By the time I had to leave Tokyo a month later, I had given the whole family a chance at a new life. My coach and his family would have a new home and it would be in the best city in the world, New York City! I managed to give my coach a teaching job at a famous ice rink facility in the city, and for him and his wife a visa to live in the U.S.! All in one month! The son would have to wait a few more months until his parents settled in the U.S. and then they would be able to bring him over but even he would also have a job waiting for him, all arranged.

I handed it to them on a silver plate. When I got word that their visas were accepted and informed my coach we had a celebratory dinner. They had tears in their eyes as we stood in line to go to the U.S. Embassy to get their visas and they could not have looked prouder. The American dream was now alive to them and I had been a part of it. There was joy and excitement in the household. My parents, and even I, were incredibly proud of me.

When I set my mind to something, I push everything and everyone including me aside, and so I decided for their sake that I would not return to Dubai, but would go directly back to Hackensack, New Jersey where I still had my apartment. My mother would meet me there as well to help me. I would have to arrange everything for the family's arrival in the U.S. I would need to find an apartment and furnish it for them and make sure they would be comfortable right upon arrival. It was all on my shoulders and my responsibility as I had been the one who had made it possible. I did not want to ruin it with any ridiculous mistakes. They were scheduled to arrive in New York City in the beginning of August of 2001. What was awaiting us would shock not only us but also the whole world. We could never have fathomed or imagined this one.

Confusion. What is it? How do you define it? I must say confusion was the motivation for a search for knowledge in my life. Everything around me seemed so complex and confusing in my mind from a young age. I used to repeat to my mother over and over again from when I was four years old, "I am all mix, I am all mix." Life and circumstances confused me. Nothing seemed right. Nothing seemed as it should. People were voicing things that they did not believe. People's actions did not follow what they believed. Everything looked like a lie. I had always wished everyone was just truthful and lived a life of honor. What you don't or can't understand is always more intriguing then what you can and that is always what fascinated me. To be confused is to pay attention, and I would pay close attention. The whole world has so much information yet very few people have real knowledge. Real knowledge is what I would search for.

14

Terror

(HACKENSACK, NEW YORK CITY)

To mourn or to celebrate?

I feel that death is such a complex matter, not so much for the person who has passed on but for the people left behind because they have to keep living with the fact that their loved one has passed. But maybe, just maybe, that soul who has crossed over is smiling up above or maybe already back on this earth in a new body and living right beside you once more. Each and every soul has a purpose and a journey and when that journey is complete in the vehicle that it resides in, it must continue to evolve and leave for a short while, change costumes, and come back down. I believe anything is possible. So, are they to be mourned or is their life to be celebrated? What are we actually mourning? It is our loss more than anything else.

Perhaps we should not mourn for them. They have chosen their path in one way or another. That is what I believe. You will never know the last conversations the soul has in those last few minutes on earth. You will only know the conversation your soul will have. When the time comes I truly hope and believe that in the heart and minds of those who pass on their last moments are filled with peace. No matter how we go I pray and keep my faith that every single person can be blessed in their few last minutes on this earth.

I believe that the soul lives on and never dies. It cannot die because it does not have an end or a beginning. It has and always will be alive. A soul is not tangible. Therefore it can never be destroyed. I believe that when people are born, they cry and the world rejoices, and I hope that every single human can live such a life that when they cross over, the world will cry from missing that soul's magical presence, but they will also rejoice. We must not hang on to the fact of death but rather to the fact of how he lived his life. In the end that is all the soul will take with him.

I arrived back in Hackensack, and my mother met me there. The month of July would be action packed. A lot would have to be done before the arrival of my Chinese coach and his wife. This was an exciting time of new adventures. I only wanted to continue skating if I could be in Stars on Ice and my wish was granted. I was thrilled and elated and couldn't believe my ears. It was a great birthday gift. Now I could get back on ice and have a purpose once more. My Chinese coach had always said in essence that I should never give up loving what I could not do anymore, and always find a way of loving what I could do. Waking up in the morning, eating breakfast, breathing, anything, really. Always to love what you do and find the love in whatever you do. I was not a warrior yet in my mind but having this opportunity brought back my love for skating.

It was time to find my coach a new home. Since they had never lived in America before and had no financial credit, I thought to make it easier on them I would get an apartment under my name and one that we could all share in the beginning. Then once they were used to the city, they could venture off in their own direction. I would have to be their tour guide so I wanted to be close to them so they could rely on me for the all the new experiences they would have to live through upon arrival.

My mother and I, knowing he would teach in the city, were looking for an apartment close to the ice rink. I would be skating there as well so it would all work out well. We found a wonderful apartment in Tribeca, right on the waterfront. From the apartment the view was beautiful on the peaceful Hudson and the other side you could see a glimpse of the Wall Street buildings standing tall and strong, and of course the stoic Twin Towers rising above the rest. It was perfect. My coach was still in Japan and through phone calls and visual interpretations of the apartment he agreed to it and the lease was signed. My apartment in Hackensack was up as well so the timing was perfect. We would move into the apartment at the end of July and they would arrive a few weeks later in August.

My mother and I decorated the apartment. It was two bedrooms and two bathrooms so that my mother and I could have one half and they the other. We would share the kitchen. We made sure they would feel comfortable by adding an Asian flare to it as well. We knew that moving to a different country and continent together with a foreign language would have its challenges and we were sensitive to all the little nuances. We had done it so many times before that we knew what was needed.

August arrived and I was enthusiastic about their arrival. My mother drove to the airport. I had driven in Sun Valley but I was not comfortable driving in big cities. The cars rushing by scared me and brought back memories of driving the highways in California. Something about the speed absolutely terrified me. I felt like all the high speed was generating too much energy around me, like life was passing by way too fast. I did not feel in control of my life; therefore, I did not feel in control behind a wheel.

At the airport we waited for them, looking intensely at the passengers lugging their suitcases coming out of the doors that opened and closed and opened and closed. Every time the doors opened we would feel a rush of adrenaline and when it turned out not to be them, we'd feel a wave of disappointment. Up and down our emotions went. Were they even on the plane? Did they freak out in the last minute? Our minds were going fast but to our delight they finally exited. They looked totally lost but grateful to see our faces and they rushed over and hugged us. It was to be the start of an incredibly mournful journey.

They loved the apartment and were grateful for our all that we had done for them. The next few weeks we let them settle in and my coach started work right away in the city. We skated together and he taught me on the ice, but more importantly taught lessons on life, and helped me get back on my feet in preparation for the tour. For them everything was very new and different. New York City takes a while to adjust for some since it "never sleeps" and wherever you look there is a lot of live flesh and a lot of dead concrete. You could feel suffocated and engulfed and so alone and alienated, and I was hoping they would not give in to it. You could tell from their bewildered eyes they would need some time to adjust.

My coach and I got bicycles so that we could bike up and down the Hudson River to the ice rink. He looked the most comfortable on these rides, loving the freedom of the bike and his expression with the wind blowing in his face made him look like a little kid loving his very first ride. I loved that about my coach. He put meaning in everything he did and said, throwing nothing away into the universe. Everything and every moment were sacred and beautifully orchestrated.

My mother and his wife sometimes stayed home. They would cook together, and my mother took her around the area to show her places such as Chinatown and taught her how to use a washing machine and dishwasher. She had never seen appliances like ours and to her they must have seemed as foreign as space objects in their shining silver metal. It was like placing a woman from the 1800s into the world of present day. She was overwhelmed and had a lot to learn. My mother and she went for evening walks after dinner and they became friends with no speech. I was very close to my coach and we would skate together, do off-ice together, and play tennis together. We were a great student-teacher team. It was a special and memorable time of two totally different cultures living together under the same roof, understanding each other, helping each other out, and devouring each other's foods and culture. On top of all this I was also elated that my father had scheduled to come visit us in New York on the thirteenth of September. I couldn't wait.

During the duration of that short one month everything was going very smoothly. No trouble, no fighting. His work and my skating were good and they both liked the city. On September 10th in the early evening I felt like going to the World Trade Center shopping area to look around a little. I had been to the shopping area numerous times and loved the hustle and bustle of it and the atmosphere. It felt so grand and powerful to be in the presence of people that were such a huge part of the whole world's economy. To me it seemed like history was being written on every desk that was deeply rooted in the ground yet way up above on every floor that rose to the sky. I went to the shops and bought a few things and walked back home.

The next morning was September 11, 2001. My coach went to the rink earlier than I since he had lessons to teach. My mother and I left home around eight a.m. My coach's wife stayed home. My mother en route to the ice rink mentioned she had forgotten her phone at home. We were going to go back to retrieve it, but there was already so much traffic that morning and we thought we would be back home soon enough so we continued our way to the rink. As usual I got on the ice around 8:20 a.m. The ice rink was at Chelsea Piers and there were many televisions in the dining area adjoining the two ice rinks. The morning news was always on. The ice rink was sparse with only a few skaters and a few coaches. Students had already left for school.

I was having a lesson with my coach when suddenly the rink manager came into the rink and told the parents of the skaters to come take a look at what was happening on the television. I and some other skaters and the coaches continued with our practice. The parents came back into the rink and sat back down and continued to watch us. Not longer than five minutes later the manager came back in and said that we should all get off the ice since something serious was happening. His voice had urgency to it and without questioning him we took our belongings and got off. As we got off the ice we could see in the distance smoke rising into the sky. It looked frightful. Not knowing what had happened, we all with our skates on huddled in front of the television screen. The first tower had been hit and when the parents had first seen it, the event had not seemed so bad but by now the situation had escalated. We were all speechless looking at the television monitor.

Then we became motionless as the second tower was hit. Still with our skates on, we watched. People in the rink were running back and forth and chaos started. We skaters just sat there with big eyes not comprehending the situation. My coach called his wife and they briefly spoke. My coach sighed with relief that she was all right. He told her to stay put and not go anywhere. We called my father and told him we were at the ice rink and were okay. We couldn't believe our eyes and ears. The journalists were still trying to figure out what was happening.

We all stayed glued to the television. I was still at the ice rink with my skates on long after both towers fell down. We did not move, not knowing what to do or where to go. By now hundreds of people were running uptown and it felt like they were all rushing to where we were. I felt like we needed to run uptown too. We all started to panic. My mother, coach, and I would not be able to get back to our home. Our home was in zone one and everyone had been evacuated. My coach became more frantic as he tried and tried again to call his wife. By now all cell phones were not working and there was no way he would be able to reach her. His face turned white. It was arranged for us to stay at another skating coach's apartment for one night. We thankfully accepted her invitation and that evening was terrifying.

This is what war had to feel like in the olden days where everyone was hiding in their homes, not daring to step out, and just huddled together watching the news. It felt like the sounds from the radios and televisions were echoing throughout Manhattan. For a city that never sleeps the city felt dead since there was no soul in the streets. There was the smell of death and burning metals that layered the city from the fire downtown and it would stay for weeks. You could smell it all the way uptown.

That evening my coach could still not reach his wife and he looked so devastated. He looked like he was about to collapse. My mother said that maybe she had been evacuated to New Jersey or to Brooklyn and we were sure she was being taken care of. My mother and I felt so responsible and we hid our fear. We could only stay one night there before we would have to find another home to stay at. It was arranged through another skating friend that we could stay a week at a beautiful friend's home on the Upper West Side by Central Park. We felt like balls being juggled left and right.

The next morning before we left to go to the next home, we all went to the ice rink so I could practice. Like I have said before, even if the sky were to fall above us you would have found me at the ice rink lacing up my skates. They had wanted to use the ice rink as a morgue but all the bodies that were found in the rubble had disintegrated so much that the ice rink was not needed. It was available for us skaters. I tried to skate but could not. I just burst into tears. Skating seemed so pointless after what had happened, so irrelevant, so useless at that point. I did not want to practice. I got off the ice.

My coach continually tried to reach his wife and at long last after my practice he was able to reach her. His face lit up like I had never seen it before! She said was going to bike up to meet us there. My mother, coach, and I waited for her. As we saw her approaching he ran towards her like welcoming home a war veteran. It was beautiful to see such love and admiration and care for each other. They tearfully hugged for a while and my mother and I smiled from our hearts. As we understood, this is what happened to her. Since my coach had told her to stay put, and since she did not understand a word of English, she just stayed in the apartment. The building was evacuated but she followed her husband's orders. She only once quickly ventured out to the rooftop to see the fire but had to quickly get back in since the smoke was suffocating her. Once back in the apartment she could not see anything as the black smoke engulfed the whole building. She lit candles since there was no electricity.

Earlier in the evening she had taken her bicycle, and following a policeman she rode all the way to Chelsea Piers but could not find us, so she rode back down to the apartment. How she rode back and was let through I have no idea but luck was on her side and she slept that night in the apartment! It was quite a story to tell and she was a remarkable lady. She even said she was not scared. Her survival instincts had kicked in and she just did what she thought needed to be done. All back together again we went to the new home where we would be staying for a week or so. We felt homeless but we felt cared for and grateful that we had a roof over our heads. On the other hand, half way around the world my father was stuck in Switzerland. He was supposed to arrive the next day but all the flights had been cancelled. He said he would wait there until the first flight took off again to New York City.

Every day my coach and I would go to the ice rink to practice. I had many shows coming up and rehearsals for Stars on Ice would commence soon and I could not be off the ice. I forced myself to go through the motions. The atmosphere was heavy and it was hard to even try to work on the ice. My heart went out to those who were suffering so much through this ordeal. On the Hudson River, Pier 40 had transformed into a meeting point for those who needed to retrieve their pets and for those who needed to go back to their homes to retrieve belongings that were down in zone one. My mother, while we practiced, would walk to Pier 40 to see if they would let her go down to our apartment to get our passports and all the necessary belongings and paperwork we needed. The authorities said we probably would not be able to return to live in our home for a month or more so it was urgent that we go there to retrieve some valuables. They would however not let anyone go down there yet. It was too soon.

My mother walked to this pier every day. She recalls these walks as being like those she had walked in war stricken Tehran twenty two years ago. Sometimes I went with her after skating and sometimes she went alone. My coach told us that if and when we were allowed to go to retrieve our belongings he wanted me also to bring back one of their suitcases for them. They explained to me which one they wanted but since I had never intruded into their bedroom, I had only a visual image of their description. They were old-school and since hiding money under the mattress was a normal occurrence to them, this suitcase probably had all their savings in it! It was very important to them that I take this suitcase. I promised I would.

We were not allowed to go to our home until about one week after 9/11. We were first in line and my mother and I were granted permission. My coach and his wife wanted to go down with us but they had no identification that they lived there, so they were not allowed to go. Two policemen escorted us to our apartment in Tribeca. It was a long walk from Pier 40 and there were hundreds and hundreds of people lining the streets of the West Side Highway cheering with their flags and applauding all the ambulances, fire trucks, and policemen that were driving up and down the highway with their sirens echoing in the air. It was an eerie experience to be walking down this highway with two armed policemen, one in front of us and one behind us. It felt like we were part of the military and on a mission to save lives.

At long last we reached our home. Our apartment was on the 20th floor and since all the electricity had been cut, the elevators were not working. The building was quiet with not a soul anywhere. It was spooky and the disaster area was just a short walk away. It gave me the shivers. All four of us walked up the twenty flights of stairs. By the time we reached our apartment my mother was so nervous that she fumbled with the house key. The policemen had a look on their faces indicating they thought that we might not even live there, but I took the key from my mother and calmly opened the door. The policemen said we had only five minutes to pack up and go. They would look at their watches and time us.

My mother and I ran into the apartment and as quickly as we could we filled two suitcases and I grabbed the suitcase my coach had described to me. "Time's up," the policemen shouted and out we had to go. We were nervous, and panicky. We closed the door and locked it with the key. Down we went twenty floors with our suitcases in tow. We tripped a lot but the policemen did not help us with our load. We had one policeman in front of us and one behind us. Walking down in silence we heard only our footsteps and the occasional bump of the suitcase on the walls that made the staircase so narrow.

As soon as we were out we parted ways with the policemen who said they had to go to help other residents like us who were waiting for their escort into their apartment.

My mother and I were left on our own to walk back up the highway to Pier 40. The side streets were so packed with people behind the barricades and policemen holding them in that we were told to walk up the highway in the right car lane where it was empty. We were the only ones walking up this highway. We heavily put one foot in front of the other lugging our heavy suitcases, exhausted physically, and mostly mentally, and as we passed the people they started clapping and cheering us on. They must have seen our despair on our faces, or they might have thought we had been rescued, but whatever the cause, we were cheered on like heroes. It was wonderful and at the same time embarrassing since we had just gone to retrieve our belongings and felt unworthy of such cheering. It did help us tremendously, however, to give us the strength for us to be able to walk all the way back up.

My coach and his wife told us they would be waiting for us at Pier 40. We trudged on. Finally we saw them from a distance and as ambulances and police and FBI cars were continuously whizzing by us we were able to manage a smile when we saw their faces in the crowd. We reached them, and the police let my coach and his wife out of the barricaded area to greet us. But as soon as we hugged them his wife started to scream at me—really screaming and shouting at me. I realized I had brought the wrong suitcase and she was fuming. I started to cry, feeling they had not been appreciative and had not even voiced a thank-you before complaining. As she was screaming at me in Chinese and I was crying, my coach tried to pull her back and police surrounding us tried to calm us down. Even psychologists that were on hand appeared to ask if we needed help. She quieted down and we left the area distraught and took a taxi to the place we where we were going to stay.

We were all hurt in one way or another by all that had happened and the tension rose among the four of us. My mother and I would go to eat Japanese food for dinner and they would go to eat Chinese food. We became separated and it felt like they were mad at us for making them go through all of this. But it hadn't been our fault that 9/11 had happened. Although we felt sorry for them that this had to be their experience of America just one month after arriving, we were doing the best we could as well. While my mother and I stayed a little longer in the apartment, my coach and his wife must not have felt comfortable, and they left to stay in Brooklyn with another Chinese skater's family he taught. We lost communication for a few weeks thereafter. It always feels like you are intruding in someone's space when you stay too long and it began to feel like that in the apartment. Although everyone in New York City stuck together during this time, it can't be overlooked that the people were tense and scared and it did not help the situation. It seemed to work perfectly that I had to go to the International Skating Center of Connecticut in Simsbury, Connecticut for a skating show the third week of September and then continue to stay there to start rehearsals with Stars on Ice. I departed the city with a big skating fan of mine and went by limo up to Connecticut leaving my mother behind. With my father arriving on the first flight available to New York City shortly after I left for Simsbury my mother would wait for him. Together they stayed at yet another friend's apartment for a short while before they joined me. It felt a relief to be able to escape from the city. I felt like I could breathe again and step back away from all the chaos. In many ways it made me feel guilty that I had not stayed in the city and suffered together with the New Yorkers but I had work to do and promises to keep. I felt that it was a time that people needed to see joy as well as sorrow and I hoped to contribute in that way the best I could. Because I had no costumes with me and had not been able to retrieve them when we went back to the apartment, I did the show with practice clothes. It did not matter. Nothing seemed to matter anymore. Glitz became irrelevant. Truth and life became virtues.

I dedicated each skating performance to those who had been taken away and those who were left behind suffering. The motive and magnitude of what was behind this tragedy was incomprehensible to me. I dealt with it the only way I knew and could. I stuffed it away within me and skated. On the ice I just skated from my heart the pain I was feeling for others. I felt that was the least, and at the same time, the most I could do. My experience had only been a small fraction of those much more affected and there was no excuse for me not to keep the faith, hope, and beauty going by skating. I wanted to keep the spotlight shining so that all those that watched might, just might, catch a glimpse of beauty and magic that would make them feel a little more hopeful then when they arrived, even if it only lasted a second. I strived to do that for everyone I passed and every time I stepped on to the ice that year. I strived to love what I did for the sake of those who paid heavily. I would do my best to spread the magic on the ice.

15

Glitz Within the Terror

(NEW YORK CITY, 72 CITY TOUR, NEW YORK CITY)

"We, the unwilling, led by the unknowing, are doing the impossible for the ungrateful. We have done so much, for so long, with so little, we are now qualified to do anything with nothing."
Mother Teresa

Devotion is one of life's grandest and most powerful attributions. I was raised to have devotion—devotion to my parents, to coaches, to skating, to working, to being the best I could be in everything and for everybody who came my way, but I was never taught to be devoted to myself. Without the sake of devotion to others I would not have survived, and I also would not have spun my way into oblivion. Unremitting devotion is unselfish. It is almost the giving of the soul if it is taken to the extreme. It persuades you to forget about yourself and live for others in the best way possible. It releases your ego and you find yourself reluctantly bowing your head to the people and things that you think are most important to you. You cannot lose your soul without devotion to your goal. It lets you erase all else so that only your goal is visible.

Devotion is captivating, enthralling, and it brainwashes you in such a way that you will push anything aside to stand by your reasoning based on such immense feelings. Devotion is a way of life. You can understand the astronomical value and affect such a trait can have on a being. Yes, devoted I was. Devoted to the ones I loved and to my skating. I wish now that I had as much respect for myself as I had for others so that I could have been also devoted to myself, in heart and soul. Then just maybe I would not have ruined my own creation. Perhaps I would have had enough understanding and love for myself to protect myself from my own wrongdoing. Then perhaps I would have been awake enough to realize the world around me and within me. I had given my soul away through my devotion and maybe at that time it was a blessing in disguise. I had been unworthy of carrying it and it was better off in someone else's possession. Until I could be who I was meant to be I would not be given back my devotion. Now, in the present, since I am worthy once more of the soul I was born with, I carry it ever so gently in the palm of my hands and in the depths of my heart.

Stars on Ice rehearsals commenced and I was in great joy to be a part of such an elite and prestigious family of skaters, choreographers, and agents, along with media galore, privileges, and wonderful productions. I was disappointed, however, about being cast as the show queen of the show, undermining my skating abilities and spinning technique. I was not even given a real solo. Yet, I thought to myself that this would be easier on me and I should just enjoy the journey. The ego conflicts of many skaters in such an elite group would prove detrimental to becoming a cohesive group. Through our rehearsals our bonds grew tighter and we looked out for each other and enjoyed each other's company, but we would not become close friends. We were all still in our own bubbles as figure skaters.

Skaters are brought up as individuals who never compete with a team. We all want to win with our other individual competitors doing their best as well, but we also would rather they make mistakes so that our win is easier. It is not in our nature to want to be negative towards anybody. It is just the nature of a sport that is judged on individual performance. We are all brought up being separate. How else could we think? How else would we survive in such a pack of animals all waiting for the same bait? We do not learn team skills. At least I did not and my skating training did nothing for a team mentality.

There were twelve top skaters, "la crème de la crème," the tip of iceberg of the skating world, and even though we all are on the ice together, we could sense and feel the bubble around each of us. We would not dare burst someone's bubble. It is their survival mechanism. However, I was most friendly with the top male skater who I adored and looked up to, and I was also friendly with the jolly and enriching crew and tour director. They were my friends to lean on and they were my friends that put a smile on my face. That seemed to me like their most important job of all.

At the end of November after our month long rehearsals, during Thanksgiving was the opening night of Stars on Ice. It was held in Lake

Placid, and we would have one show and then a break before touring sixty cities in America and twelve more in Canada, starting right after Christmas. The opening night was glorious. My dream had come true and after completing this tour I would feel that I truly had done everything I could have in the skating world, despite my feelings about the Olympics.

Thanksgiving was special as well since it is not a holiday my family ever celebrated and my mother and I enjoyed it thoroughly. My father had stayed for the special event. It felt like we were part of a very elite group and had become part of a family— a special family it was and always would be.

I had almost forgotten a special incident on the day of the opening night. At this time of my life my hair was my natural brown and short. The evening before the opening night after the dress rehearsal the producer came up to me and told me that the production team all wanted me to go back to blond, if I agreed to it. It wasn't really a question. It was more of an order. They said they felt it fit better with the character I was playing as the show queen threaded throughout the whole show. I agreed since to me it did not really matter. Sometimes I wanted to change my hair color every week!

So the next day they arranged for me to go to a hair salon in the area that would color me back to blond. It took around eight hours of my sitting in the chair! My hair went through a rainbow of colors, each more shocking then the last. Red, orange, yellow, green, anything but blond until the very last hour! I liked the result although my scalp was burning and itching like crazy. So I had awakened in the morning as a brunette and ended the night as a blond in sparkly costumes and head dresses! What a life!

After the opening night, it was incredibly odd to be back in Tribeca and so close to where the Twin Towers had been. It was even stranger not to be able to see them anymore in the New York City skyline. It was still disorderly downtown where we lived. It was very dirty with soot covering the ground like a blanket covering the deceased, and the stench was still looming over the area. My mother said when she returned to the apartment the floor was covered in soot as well. The windows had been closed but as the fire engulfed our building smoke entered the apartment and covered it in black ashes. It gave me the shivers to think what it really consisted of. My sadness returned as I stepped back into my home.

A few days after my returning home, my Chinese coach had become incredibly sick. The stress of 9/11 had caused tremendous anxiety to my usually calm, meditative, and collected coach. The incident had been too much for him to handle. My coach literally glowed orange. His eyes turned that same color as well and it was terrifying. He was rushed to the hospital and had to undergo surgery right away. He had a liver infection. I felt it had been my entire fault and I felt so guilty. I had brought him and his wife to America. I had made it possible and now within the first few months, 9/11 happened and now he was sick. I could not understand what I had done wrong. Maybe I should have never intervened. Maybe it hadn't been my place. I had tried so hard to give them a new life and yet all I had done was bring more chaos to the whole family. I couldn't catch a break.

Sometimes when you try to make someone else happy it could do more harm than good when you yourself are not in the position to make a situation better. I now know it is important to always see and check on yourself first. Are you happy? Are you in a good space? If you are, helping others will be a good thing, but if not, then fix your own life first. It will cause much less havoc to everyone involved in the end. My coach would end up being fine, but the tension between the four of us grew and we would grow apart little by little over the next few years as they dealt with their struggles and I with my own.

Since we were living in zone one, the building management gave all the tenants the opportunity to cancel their lease and move out. My coach and his wife wanted to move out and be on their own, so we canceled the lease and my mother and I moved into a smaller apartment in the same building. We had no time to look for another building in another area. I would not be there much. I was in and out of Manhattan for the next year since I had so many shows, photo shoots for the upcoming tour, and other obligations and competitions to attend. In the end, for the four of us, it was to be "to each his own." We parted ways leaving a bit of our heavy hearts in each one of us. We left unfinished business. In this way we knew our paths would cross once more.

I went to the World Professional Championships once more and placed third with the bronze medal as I did the year before. The critics said I should have been placed second, but being judged and dwelling over other people's judgment is truly a waste of time in my opinion and I was just happy to be alive and skating. Shows were exciting that year. Foxwoods, Mohegan Sun, and Atlantic City were to be rated the best. The casino show settings were beautiful and serene as the audience was only on one side and the spectators were all at dinner tables with candle lights burning.

After 9/11 at each show I dedicated the performance to those who had passed on. That year each show felt to me as if they were watching from above and we were skating for them, too. It felt like it was our responsibility as performers to bring back joy to the world in our own little way. Each performance was, however, a little eerie. With many people still traumatized from the event they did not want to leave the comfort of their homes. We would skate to half empty arenas throughout the next two years. It was depressing, but the show must go on, and go on we did.

The holidays ended as quickly as they had come that year. It was sad to be in the city with the memories of 9/11 lingering and I was eager to be off on the tour. The whole tour including Canada ended in June of 2002. It would be a long six months of living out of suitcases and in and out of hotels and performing incredibly shows! We were treated like royalty, staying at the best hotels in all the best cities. Even our luggage was taken care of. I did not need to lift a finger but just to skate well. It might have been the last year of such luxury from the sponsors for the skaters on this tour, since the skating business would crash soon after.

But the best part was traveling by private jet. That was truly awesome. There is no better word for it. My mother and father and even my sister would come to visit me on tour and giving them the gift of flying on a private jet made me proud. I felt I had achieved what we had all worked for, for so long in my life. I took every day of the tour with stride and care and I soaked it all in with every sense I had. I became more and more comfortable as the tour went on and I made a couple of great friends on the way. There was no bigger honor in skating professionally then to be on this tour. However, and this is a big however, there were lots of consequences of those experiences that hampered the ability for me to be truly in my element and enjoy the skating.

I only speak the truth, not to offend anyone but to protect my promise that this book is the whole truth. The first was that I did not like the role I was given or the costumes I had to wear. I, from the time of being very young, had never wanted to be a show pony and this role made me feel like a Vegas showgirl. Many things are not what they seem to be, and although I might have looked grand and rich I felt cheapened and discarded. Everything I had to do was exactly the opposite of what I wanted to embody and represent, which was elegance, magic, and refinement. Please do not misunderstand me. The costumes were well and thoughtfully made but were just completely out of my element. They had surely good and wonderful intentions but I was so uncomfortable. I had many changes of costumes throughout the night as well, but not one seemed to be me at all. I had to wear headdresses and all sorts of things that totally hampered my spins.

In the beginning I was supposed to open the show with fireworks of spins in all different areas of the ice with the spotlight going on only when I was in the spin so that the audience would be in suspense as to what would happen and where I would spin next. But egos always get in the way on such occasions and someone had that part removed. Maybe it was too good, maybe it was bad, but it was not to the liking of some other people involved who all had a higher rank than I, and so it had to be taken out. So it ended up that neither the costumes nor the role were to my liking but I did not speak out and was too afraid to tell my agent in case they would then not have me tour. I did not know how to stand up for my rights and beliefs and no one else did it for me either. Plus I felt just so honored to be part of this incredible family that I would rather do what they envisioned. I was so excited to be on this tour.

Second, it was an Olympic year and sometimes for this reason it was very hard for me to skate. I was the second youngest on this tour and the only one younger than I was an Olympic champion. So I felt robbed of my youth and felt I should still be on an amateur circuit competing at the Olympics, being an Olympian. Since we were on tour during the Games everyone watched it on television but I could not. I turned away and read a book. I wonder what the other skaters thought of me on that tour. I often sat alone, was very quiet, and was in my own world. I never spoke much nor did I party with them. I never saw the use of sharing chit-chat and gossip. I could not bear to hear it either. It was all gibberish to me. My mind was wondering about the creation of man and the world. I was a loner. They might have seen it as arrogance.

I recall my agent and some producers telling me that they remember me as always being alone in a corner. Not because I was timid or shy. No, not at all, rather the opposite. But discussions in intimate settings were not my thing. I had so much to say, but I knew that saying what I wanted would only get me in huge trouble. So I just locked all my words away and I turned to the act of observing. I was lost, too within my own world.

Thirdly, I was not well. I was in constant pain from my back and living on painkillers. My hips were starting to hurt a lot as well and they were popping out of their sockets frequently. My health was deteriorating. I was still in a constant flu-like condition with my nose running, my ears blocked and ringing, now more than ever, and had constant migraines and sinus headaches. I had a serious deep cough that wasn't improving. I was dizzy and weak and my legs felt swollen. Mind you, I was feeling all this together every single day and no one knew. I always prayed at night before I went to sleep that I would wake up the next morning with all my ailments healed and find it all was just a nightmare. But it never happened and every day I was more exhausted then the day before. My immune system was in such a low state.

I was now twenty-two and would be turning twenty-three, still without having gone through puberty. One of the skaters came up to me once and said, "You know, why are you always sick? You're the only one here that is always sick every day. What's wrong with you?" There was a tone to the voice that was condescending and mocking. I did not say anything and just smiled and walked away. What was I to say? How was I to explain? Sit down and go through my whole life? I thought my experiences were so different from theirs and so complicated that in no way was it possible for the skaters to comprehend me. They had no idea and I was too tired to explain. My stomach was in constant pain. I could only eat white boiled rice and grapes. Then here and there I added fat-free brownies. I would eat only things that were fat free since I got sick from any oil. Those were the only things I ate for six months! My mother had given me a rice cooker to travel with and bags of rice and I made my own every day. It was the cutest rice cooker, a *Hello Kitty*. I enjoyed the little and simple things. I wasn't into the grandiose materialistic world. I wanted a simple life of truth and peace.

So I was struggling with myself through the duration of the show. However the actual performing and spinning was wonderful. I so wished I was feeling healthy so that I could enjoy every minute. I wanted that so badly. I liked the tour manager and the one male skater and we became great friends. They were both such goodhearted and goodhumored men with gentle souls and they were the ones I turned to if I needed help. Our friendship would last forever.

What I thought of as my recurring "flu" got worse at a certain point in the middle of the tour. I was used to it by then, but I was so sick with a bout of the serious influenza type of illness that as I would spin the fluids would flow from my tear ducts and I wouldn't be able to see clearly for the rest of the time I was on the ice.

It was one disaster after another. I was a human just surviving. I did and do believe that through sickness the soul is rejuvenated and there is a reason for illness. My body, the vehicle, was failing, but at the same time I knew and felt my soul was starting to heal and come alive. Just how long would I have to be sick? I told myself, "Well I had made myself sick from the age of nine and that was now so many years ago? So it might take a few years to recuperate." If I did not have that belief so engrained in me I don't know what I would have done.

Believing is power and that belief kept me alive. It was like I knew and felt things would soon be incredibly good. I just did not know when. Patience would be my lesson. It did not feel like I was climbing a never ever-ending mountain. It felt like I was in the deepest hole and just kept dropping further and further into the darkness, and until I would drop so deep into the earth that I would come out of it on the other side, I needed to search deeper into my mind, heart, and soul. Deeper into the meaning of life and its purpose. Deeper into my destiny. No richer does health seem to someone than when they become sick.

Most of the other skaters on tour seemed so balanced—balanced in life, in their demeanor, and their eating habits. They seemed so normal. I was not normal for sure, and so physically off-balance that it astonished me I could keep my balance so well on the ice and in my spins. But I was clumsy off-ice, bumping into things and dropping stuff all the time. Maybe the spinning was catching up to my health and me. My male skating friend mentioned to me that in order not to be dizzy I must spin in the other direction off-ice to unwind my body. I never did, but now looking back perhaps I should have. Perhaps it might have saved me from a lot of trouble. The spinning was winding me up like a doll, and my brain was in such a twirl that I was feeling like I was spinning off-ice as well. My brain felt like it never stopped spinning.

Sometimes on off-days individual skaters were called to do press releases in the cities coming up. On one such occasion when I was called I had to fly to Texas from California for a one day television and radio media press junket. I was excited since I loved appearing before the media but I was exhausted. I arrived in Texas in the evening and went to sleep. The next morning I woke up and at the breakfast table I fainted. This time I was revived quickly and I did not need to go to the hospital, but once again memories surfaced and all day I was in fear. That evening I flew back to California and the tour continued. I am sure someone in the team must have heard of what happened but no one said anything and I felt they did not care. As the tour progressed my fainting spells often recurred. Strangely, they repeatedly happened around 2:00 a.m. I would fall asleep after a show and then awake about two hours later, white as a sheet, sick to my stomach, and the room would be spinning. I would drift in and out of consciousness and they would call the hotel doctor.

It was frightening and I felt I had no one to turn to or to take care of me. My parents were back in Dubai and I had no family in the U.S. It happened so often that it would change my life forever. I had no idea how significant these occasions were. The fact that no one helped me terrified me as well. I remember one specific time the doctor asked if someone from the group could sleep in my room with me in case of another emergency and to check on me when I was so ill. Although I was embarrassed to say I was unwell and ask for help, I called several people from the team but no one wanted to lend a hand. The feeling of being all alone and sick was alarming. The fear started to live in me, in my veins and in my heart. These fainting spells were scarier than you can imagine, and that they were real and not a part of my imagination was paralyzing to me. My life was turned into a kind of explosive despair.

In June my touring was over for the time being. No matter what was good or bad during the tour, the members of the skating tour would become my family for a lifetime, and for that I am extremely grateful. It made me a part of a fabulous entity of people that in one way or another would always support me and be a part of my soul. It decorated my life with the celebration of a way of life and I can only be thankful for that time. The adrenaline had kept me going, and now that the tour was finished I collapsed in a big heap on returning to my home in New York. My mother had come back from Dubai to wait for my arrival. I needed her. I was in such a dire state I needed my mother desperately. By now I was scared to death to fall asleep alone. My mother would have to hold my hand and sleep next to me. I was so afraid of falling asleep and then never awaking or waking up and fainting. I cannot tell you how scared I was. I was more scared then when my mother hit me and more frightened than when I competed in front of millions. I had never been this scared but it was only when it was time to fall asleep. Not yet did this fear overtake me at any other time of the day.

I needed a break from skating and took a few weeks of just roaming the city and enjoying all the life and culture it had to offer. I walked and walked for hours at a time. Although it felt as if the atmosphere in New York had changed dramatically since 9/11 it still was bountiful with energy and sophistication, hustle and bustle, and a feast for the shopping eye. I had fun during the day, but in the evenings the fear would creep over me. It was a terrible time, only to get worse.

During this time I finally underwent many tests for my ailments but doctors could not find anything significant other than total exhaustion, not realizing that this was a very significant diagnosis. Yet they were baffled by my poor health. The more the doctors were baffled the more I became absolutely terrified throughout the day about fainting. I felt so weak that I felt like I could faint at any minute. Both the brain and the body were working together against me, or actually they were trying to tell me something but I had shut down so much I did not want to hear it. Which came first? The body or the mind? I think in my case it was a mixture of both from years and years ago. Maybe one of my injuries had caused pain, which caused fear, which caused more injury and illness. Or maybe the fear and emotional pain was first and they caused injury and more pain and illness.

It hindered me so much that by the end of the summer I could not go anywhere without holding my mother's hand. Otherwise I would burst into tears, my body would freeze and I would just collapse. Miraculously I continued with skating. This was the wrong thing to do when skating conflicts were the basic cause of my misery, but not wanting to give up the one thing in my life I still had, I had to continue. It's not like it was giving me more joy but it was making me feel like I was accomplishing something. I felt there would be no life if I stopped, yet ironically I had no life continuing with skating, either.

The next season of 2002 to 2003 I toured the world with shows and performances. National Geographic interviewed me for a whole hour show about my spins. They had professors and scientists from all the top New York City universities who came to the rink as I did my spins to try to explain the phenomenon of my talent. It was a very interesting television documentary, but with no interesting outcome or explanation of my spinning ability. Maybe my spinning was meant to be a magical secret from the heavens after all! It felt more sacred that way and I was glad that my spins were not explained in terms that withheld magic.

Up and down my emotions went and my ailments remained. During some shows I was too tired to want to go and I would cry in desperation. But once on the ice my smile went on, my spins were faster than ever, and I had standing ovations. I was an actress in my own movie and a good one. No one knew what I was living through and it was kept that way to keep the fascination of my role alive. As long as I skated, that would be my role. Everyone wanted me to spin.

The most wonderful show was the 9/11 memorial at Madison Square Garden in New York City. I had attended numerous performances at this stadium yet each time destiny brought me there it felt very special. The reason for the show was so beautiful and the New York Rangers joined the skaters. Times like these were memorable. My fear would not be with me while performing, because most of the time when on the ice I felt like I left my body anyway, and it was not really me skating. The fear, however, would be with me before I got on the ice and right back after I got off the ice. I would eventually have problems with performing, but for this time I had a slice of peace while skating. I could push the fear aside with my focus on what I had to do.

Since my mother understood that, she thought it was best for me to keep on skating so I could just push my fear to the side. But what we did not realize was that it was still there and one day it would inch its way back to the center to erupt like a volcano. My mother had to come with me everywhere. I refused to go anywhere without her. The money I received from all my touring and skating would never amount to what my parents had spent on me. Either because I never had anyone standing up for me or I was not an Olympic gold medalist my salary was not one to brag about. The amount compared to the stardom I was getting was actually usually quite hurtful because I did not feel appreciated. Compared to what others got I can only imagine the difference. The money we were spending for my mother to accompany me everywhere, even on the German tour I participated in for the third time, hardly made the money I earned from my work seem worthwhile. But I was not in it for money. I actually despised getting money for selling my spins. It felt cheap.

The state of my stomach was terrible and I was still on rounds of antibiotics, but now I had also visited a doctor in New York City who had treated the Pope! I thought this man of such stature could definitely cure me. Many more antibiotics and medicine was administrated to me but I feel the real cause was not being administered and I don't know if I felt any better. The state of my back was terrible and I was in so much pain. I could barely walk at this point and I cried before and after each show just bearing the pain. I could not practice. My mother and I decided we needed to finally get, after all this time, a second opinion on my back and my hips.

We then visited a famous orthopedic surgeon in New York City where we finally received a true diagnosis of my spinal condition. I had to take MRIs and numerous X-rays. When the results came in and he sat us down. He told us seriously and sternly that I would need urgent surgery. He said he could tell I had previously had a huge spinal fracture. And now, because I had continued to skate, I had two discs and three bones that were all crushed together, and there could be even more serious damage to my back. I had big bone tears in both hips as well. In fact, he said, he did not see how I could walk. On hearing this, I fainted. I was in shock, especially since I had skated all this time with such a serious injury and that worse things could have happened to me. I felt so thick-headed to have continued skating when in such great pain, but that had never stopped me before so why would it have stopped me then?

The doctor then looked at the old pictures I had with me from Switzerland and said sadly I had been wrongly diagnosed. I should have been treated properly and not allowed to be back on the ice until the original fracture from my fall had fully healed. My mother and I had no words, or tears. We were dried up.

I can't believe now, however, that I still continued to skate after his devastating diagnosis. For some reason this wasn't a big enough wake up call for me. After several talks my mother and I decided against surgery. Now we wanted more opinions. Whenever the news was bad we did not believe it, and when it was good we did. That was the way we went through life.

Everyone in the skating world knows my mother. They know her to be the sweetest and most honorable skating-mother ever. Just recently I bumped into an old ABC director who has known me since I was little and she told me she loves my mother. She said she was the best skating-mother she had ever known. My mother was loved in the skating world for her generosity and kindness and blunt truthfulness. Truth is written all over her. She would hug other skaters and even compliment them in front of me. I only wanted her compliments for me but I respected her honesty. Others saw our strong bond and envied it. But now the situation was different. My mother was now with me not just for support but because I could not be alone for one second. The fear was that powerful, that engulfing, that enraging. It is one hundred percent paralyzing to the body, brain, heart, and soul. To top it off I was still fainting.

Once you have lived with a fear of this magnitude that stops you from being able to do most things in your daily life you never want to talk about it. You feel other people will not understand and you do not want to be belittled. Skaters started to tease me and mock me being now twenty-two years old and still attached at the hip with my mother. And so I lived with the mockery and gossip and no one knew the truth except my mother and it was a secret so heavy to carry it would break me into pieces.

April 3, 2003, would mark a big day for me and I would be given a label for all the hard work I had endured, but as it did not bring magic to my spins it did however bring me a sense of pride and great accomplishment. It was the day I had my name printed in the Guinness Book of World Records. That day I made the first attempt to win a record for spinning on NBC's Today Show. The previous record that I would have to beat for spinning duration was sixty rotations on one foot continuously without changing feet or starting over. I had been on many morning shows throughout my skating career and it did not faze me that millions would be watching. I loved it and I did not feel any pressure since I was confident in my talent. What did scare me a little, however, was the ice condition and the fast wind that was blowing that morning. It was freezing and the ice was very uneven and choppy.

The wind was blowing me in all directions but I became world-famous as the world's longest spinner with one hundred and five rotations to only later that day at Chelsea Piers NY, beat my own record and bumped it up to one hundred and fifteen continuous rotations on one foot! It was a great success and gave me great happiness of doing something considered the best in the world. It was documented and would be a part of history forever. I wanted also do the fastest spin per second since I have been clocked at six rotations a second, but I was told at that time there was no category for this feat. I know my parents were and are very proud of me but for me nothing was ever good enough and the minute I achieved that I was on the hunt for the next thing to accomplish. It was a never ending trail to self-destruction because I would never be perfect and perfection is what I was striving for.

During that summer of 2003 I turned twenty-four years old and the clock was ticking. I had not evolved into my own person. I actually had become less independent, more dependent on my mother, back to being a child who could not fend for herself. I was panic-stricken and sick. Once again, the only way I knew how to deal with everything was to leave. 9/11 had also in many ways traumatized me and I could not bear living in the forsaken area of New York any longer. I wanted to go far, far away. In my heart I wanted to go to Mongolia and sit on top of a mountain and just do nothing. I wanted to live in my own world of meditation and just breathe and be reborn once again. But after all my parents and I had been through, for me to escape that far away sounded ridiculous. However, a tangible place like Los Angeles seemed okay to consider.

I was not afraid of fainting and dying. I was afraid of living. I was afraid to be who I was. I was not afraid of being mediocre, I was afraid of having power beyond measure. I was afraid I would erupt and destroy everything around me with my strength. I was so used to living a life of feeling powerless that I did not know what would happen if I did wake up my powers. The disgust I had for myself for not being who I truly was made me feel so angry that it scared me. I was afraid to live my own truth and I was afraid of my own body.

16

Stars In or Out of Line?

(LOS ANGELES, HAWAII, DUBAI)

If you continually hesitate with your next move you will stand on one leg forever.

In my life everything was always out of the ordinary. I was always out of my comfort zone so the only person or situation that was constant was the presence of my mother, and she knew it. She knew she had to be there or I would collapse. When would we each get our own wings and learn to fly? Somehow I had always felt so very sorry for my mother. She never was able to be the mother she really wanted to be to me after I turned nine years old. She had to become my best friend, my father, my teacher, my therapist, my everything, and ultimately the person she wanted to embody most of all she could not. By the end of the day there was no more time to be the mother. She had to fill all my expectations and fill all the big gaps. The burden of this on her shoulders must have been immense. It was almost like she had to raise me as a single mother and help me become an adult very quickly. There was no time for child's play. Elders who were my teachers and formed my life on and off ice endlessly engulfed me.

We moved to Los Angeles, then had a short stay in Hawaii, then ended up back in Dubai with my family, all in the next few years. It is all quite a blur accompanied by gallons and gallons of tears. No matter what we did nothing seemed to alleviate my physical pain. I was loved wherever I went for my skating but tensions were rising in other areas of my life. I was visiting doctors and hospitals nonstop trying to figure out my problems. We moved from one place to the next trying to cure me. We would try one doctor's treatment for a few months and when nothing was helping we would try to find another specialist. One doctor took great advantage of my situation and his treatment bordered on sexual abuse, but I kept quiet about it. He said what he did was his technique to cure my back. I just wanted to heal, and to be at mercy of doctors is a dangerous situation to be in. I was going to so many specialists it was driving me insane. I had one for my stomach, one for my ears, one for my nose, one for my head, one for my eyes (as they were now in so much pain and very swollen), and I had doctors for various other problems.

My back was still in great pain and we continued to get more opinions. Four out of five surgeons suggested surgery but since one did not suggest it, we went along with him. This seemed easier since we did not want my life more complicated. I decided to live with the pain. That was easier than going through surgery and not knowing the outcome. I already knew the outcome of just being in pain so I was comfortable with that.

I was diagnosed with either everything under the sun or nothing at all! I was anemic, I had thyroid issues. I was hormonally imbalanced. I had chronic fatigue syndrome, fibromyalgia, Lyme disease, osteoporosis, and arthritis. You name it, I had it. But then there were some doctors who said I had nothing at all, that it was all in my head. The cure to it all? Nothing, or every pill under the sun. A few doctors then and a few years later also wanted to give me medication for depression. Now, I knew in my heart I was not clinically depressed and I totally refused to take any sort of medication for it. I just believed I wasn't depressed. I knew I was sad, disappointed, exhausted, and exasperated about all that was happening to me but I knew that medication would not help me enough. I was more afraid of the side effects than the help it would give me. I wanted to cure myself the way I thought was the proper way, by feeling every emotion and every pain, because if I had gotten myself into this mess I could get myself out of it too. Regarding this, I stood up for myself completely.

Still in Los Angeles and already very skinny, I then lost another fifteen pounds. All my clothes were hanging off of me. Many days I just lay in bed and did not move. Due to my physical problems I could not go anywhere without my mother and I never drove. I was too dizzy and felt too weak and did not want to get into an accident. I felt drowsy all day, every day. I missed so much the freedom of driving that I had experienced before. When I had an audition or a party or an event, my mother would force me to go and had to wait for me in the car.

What an incredible mother! The fact that we never gave up this way of living astonishes me even more. Looking back I can't believe how we never stopped! How my mother or I never woke up one day and said, "Look, it is ridiculous to keep on pushing and struggling this way. Let's try to change this ..." will always be baffling to me. It was more like we were driving a broken car through all the red lights in life. We never, ever stopped. That is just not what a Ruh would do. We were trying to fix the vehicle while driving in it a hundred miles an hour. We did not want to stop in fear that everything would collapse even more and even though life was scary and painful, if we stopped it all, life as we knew it would cease to exist. A new life was far scarier and so we ploughed ahead the only way we knew how.

Somehow during this time I kept on skating and doing shows here and there but by now I wanted to stop skating badly. I started for the first time in my life to really voice to my mother my inner feelings and my wish to stop skating entirely. As I expected, and what I had been afraid about for so long in my life, was exactly what happened. My mother erupted more than ever. She fought with me nonstop. Well, not really with me since I never fought back, but at me. My mother could not contain her anger and the hitting got worse again. I would sometimes run out onto the street and drop to my knees and cry and cry and just pray to God to bring peace to us. It was terrifying and my mother lashed out continually. It was a "dammed if I do and dammed if I don't" decision. If I had not told her my feelings, I thought I would be sick forever and eventually kill myself. And if I told her, I felt like I would be killing her. I did not know what to do and it was traumatizing for both of us.

I somehow managed, while being half awake, to skate through the shows I had obligated myself to do. I don't remember much of them, probably because at that time my life was so painful that I shut down even more. I felt I no longer had an escape route. In 2005 I was part of a big skating competition and show on Japanese television and I toured the world once more in all the prestigious shows. I should have been the happiest girl in the world. Art on Ice in Switzerland was the biggest show in Europe with more than ten thousand spectators at each show for five nights. It was an incredible production with great performers including both singers and skaters. I had done this show in 2000 and had gone back there every year since then. My former Swiss coach was the producer and he always wanted me there. I was the star.

This time I could barely practice for the shows because of my condition that no one ever knew about. For the minutes I had to be on the ice I took whatever I had left in me and skated it all out. His Art on Ice show in 2005 would be my last performance. I am grateful I did not know it at that time that it would be my last. Therefore it was not a tearful one. It was just another performance.

What my mother did not realize was that her lashing out had really had an effect on me. It wasn't the only cause of my illnesses and distress but it had greatly contributed to it. I could not master enough courage to tell my mother that she had been wrong and had hurt me badly with her actions, as I was more afraid to hurt her. I had hoped someone else could tell her or she would come to the realization on her own from all the things that happened to us, but she never did. It was a very delicate situation. I could not get out of the situation. She did not see that she had anything to do with my severe state emotionally and that I was just in a survival mode.

She also did not see she was hurting herself in the process as well. She only saw how she had given and tried everything for me. And it was true that my mother had given up her whole life for me and had always had the right intentions. It would be some more time before this was resolved. For now I would still be hit because of my mother's frustration about life.

I was feeling so sick that I didn't think I would ever be able to describe the magnitude of how bad I felt. I am truly amazed I survived to tell my story. I am more amazed that I kept on going! My blood pressure was so low that I yawned all day and was barely able to move. Everything seemed to be moving in slow motion. I was now very close to giving up skating completely. I felt finally that I now had enough reason to do it. It is not to say that I hated skating, of course. I hated though what it had done to my body and most importantly to my family. I knew I could not survive it any longer.

All I wanted was for my mother and father to yank back the reins, insist that I stay with the family in order to let me heal, and to comfort me, day in and day out. I wanted us to be a family again, but in the meantime they were so busy doing everything they thought was good for me, that they ceased to really be paying attention to me. Out of pure fear, I could not be the one to say I just wanted to be with them and do nothing. Reacting from past experiences I thought that they would be just so upset that I was giving up everything for which they had worked for so hard.

I wanted them to say, "You need to rest and heal" and say "NO" to me. "NO, don't skate, NO, don't exercise, NO, you can't go there, NO, you cannot work. NO, do not spin." When they had heard about my fractured back I thought, "That's it." Now they will never let me skate again. But that did not happen.

Since I was so fearful of my mother's reactions, I had no voice and so I wanted them to run after me and take me back home. Whichever city I was in did not add or take away anything from me. My life was not a struggle because I was in a specific place. Had I gone to Africa or Alaska my situation would have been the same because the reasons for my troubles were never addressed.

My parents always believed in me and always will. They never in my life doubted my ability to succeed. They never made me feel like I could not be the best. Therefore my story is not a story of someone told that she couldn't do what she wanted to achieve. My story is one where everyone supported me, said I could do it, believed in me, and when I failed didn't understand what they and I had done wrong. There is much more pressure and higher expectations when other people know and believe so powerfully that the person is capable of anything. There is much more disappointment as well when then the person does not succeed. It felt like everyone was waiting to watch me do the impossible.

It is a very interesting dynamic and has rung true throughout my life. I felt I was trying to succeed for others while loving to spin and my parents were trying to succeed for me so that I would be successful in life. In the end I did not know what my parents wanted or what I wanted. But the good thing is that I will forever be humbled by the great confidence they had in their daughter. I do not know how I made them feel so sure of their daughter's potential. I know somehow I made them believe in me and their belief has made me a stronger person and made me always strive for the best. For this I will forever be grateful. I could not be where I am today without their belief in me.

No one around me or in the skating world seemed to know anything about what I had gone through. Knowing absolutely nothing about me, they were all questioning me about whether I was still performing. It totally baffled me since it was so impossible and improbable for me to be able to skate ever again, yet I realized all these people were clueless about what I had gone through. I knew that one day I wanted to recount my story for people to see the truth about me and understand my life. I wanted them to learn from me and felt it would be a disservice to myself and my fans not to express my experiences, not because of how great I am or how good my story is, but because knowing about my life could mean something to others. I want to awaken the destiny and truth in another and hopefully inspire them to understand themselves in order to succeed. I love the uniqueness in everybody and in everything. My talent and my story are unique and I want my telling of it to help others.

Almost every day I was flooded with emails and phone calls from people wanting me to skate in their shows. It was so painful for me to turn them all down and even more difficult, I think, for my mother. I was young and I had a life ahead of me. My mother was much older and I felt so guilty not being able to skate for her, just that one last time. Always that one last time. It was like when my skating coach used to say, "Do it just one more, one last time." But that one more time was never just one more time. It was again and again and again. I felt my mother still believed so strongly that I would recover and skate again.

However, I knew inside of me that, this would never happen. I knew that the time had come when I needed to start having a life with friends, maybe a man I would love. I needed to grow my wings. I needed to become a woman. I still was a little girl in many ways. I knew if I kept on clutching tightly to my skating boots, I would miss my chance to ever learn how to walk in my own shoes, let alone learn to fly. I had always said to myself that I never wanted to skate until I was thirty. I had always seen my skating career as a short one and a launching pad for something bigger in my life that would serve me better. Skating was a lesson for me. It was a big, big lesson, one of huge proportions.

At this stage nothing was really working and all I truly wanted was to be with my mother and father and the only way that was to happen was for me to return to Dubai. There I continued with new doctors and treatments. I was feeling like a pincushion, poked and manipulated and given so much medicine. But no one was covering up the holes that were already there and it felt like now I had new ones to deal with as well. But one positive thing began that winter of 2005 in Dubai with a holistic doctor. I finally started puberty!! It was like a miracle. We couldn't believe it. It was the very first time a treatment had actually worked and it was a sign that my body was waking up. I was twenty-six years old when it first happened and it was not until I was twenty-nine that my menstruation became regular. But at least my body had started the process.

It might surprise people that I am so open about this part of my life, but If I can help someone else I would do anything for them because I know how my parents and I had longed for this help while I was growing up. I am not ashamed about anything because I have led my life with the best of my ability. I am truthful about all else so why not talk about this part? It is only human to go through puberty and having it happen much later in my life affected me in more ways than you can imagine. I do hope that women reading my story will not feel the need to stop the natural process because of another goal, whatever that may be. Your health, body, and mind needs to come first, because I promise you I know that without them nothing else is possible in life. Please do not disregard those like I did. I did it all for my skating—to stay thin, to do the unattainable, and to be the special and invincible one. My ego had gotten the better of me and I paid the price.

Going through puberty is tough enough when you are a young teenager but to have to go through it in your mid-twenties is even tougher. Hormones take much longer to stabilize when your body starts to change later than the normal age for puberty. It was especially troubling when you have been brought up to believe that image is so important. I felt incredibly uncomfortable about my body and its changes, and it took me a while to fall in love with myself again. At that time I did not know how to deal with it all, and was afraid as a person in the public eye that people would now view me differently and perhaps not like me as much. Although I was so happy to have my body finally wake up, I had a fear of my body, which now felt new and foreign. It was like I had a whole new vehicle to drive.

Once more the promise my parents and I had made to each other that I would NOT move from Dubai until I was one hundred percent well would not be kept. I had the beginnings of going through puberty but my mother and I were antsy that I needed more medical care and even more antsy about our delusional perception that I was not doing anything. I was resting, reading, relaxing and healing and my mother and I were not used to it. I had never done that in my life!

Since I wasn't being treated for everything else that I was going through we thought I needed the more specialized care of a doctor in America. I had pushed my body into being dormant for twenty-five years without giving it a minute to breathe so I knew in addition to specialized care I also needed to give it more time and space. But we were as usual more interested in doing more and more and more. We were on a ball going downhill so fast we could not stop it.

When an opportunity for me to teach in a new ice rink in Wayne New Jersey came up my mother sprang at the opportunity. I did not. I cried inside. At that time, the very last thing I wanted to do was teach and especially did not want to move away just for that reason. I wanted to stay with my family, and not go back to America. I did not see the point in moving once more to a place because of an ice rink. Why did this opportunity come up? Was it a test to see if we had the strength and courage to dismiss it and let my body heal without being on the ice? If so, we failed miserably. My mother insisted I needed to make a living. She said that after all the money my parents had spent on me why was I so selfish to say no to making money in the sport I knew best? That would be outrageous.

I could not win with my mother and did not have enough energy to fight back. I got more distraught seeing her so upset. I could not understand her wanting me to teach and even still wanting me to perform when I was so unwell. This decision to move to Wayne, New Jersey was my mother's. If we were moving back to the States, in order to go to a hospital for my needs where I could be treated, I would have agreed, but not an ice rink. Once more all the things in life that I was now trying to leave completely behind so that I could heal would once more be continued and again I would fall back and be frozen in time.

I remember the evening before our flight to New Jersey. It will be etched in the painting of my life forever. My mother knew I did not want to go and she could not contain her frustration with me. Why was I always making it so difficult for her? She lashed out at me and had one of her serious fits of hitting me, screaming, and utterly going crazy.

In the commotion of it all I called my holistic doctor to see if she could calm my mother down. She was not able to do this, but told me sternly that my mother and I should not go since she felt we were not ready to embark on a new adventure. We did not listen. I don't know what use it was having other people trying to help us since my mother never listened when it came to herself. She was the puppeteer, the captain of the ship. I looked at her and for a moment everything went in slow motion and all was silent. I just watched her body and lips move, and all I could see was sadness, desperation, anger, fear, love, and despair inside of this beautiful, majestic, and strong woman who had absolutely no more hope, dreams, or will left in her in life. It was the dance of terror.

It rang true to me when my mother would say, "I am going to die soon anyway." Those words hurt me more than my mother will ever know. To feel that I was the cause of all her despair was something I could not live with. Even my father could not stop her behavior. My heart sank and bled. I did not care if it bled to death. I wanted to die for my mother. I did not know what else to do. I have no idea how we boarded the flight, but we did, and once more went on the way to times of more terror awaiting us. We had all lost our minds, heart, and soul, and for what? I, Lucinda, had become invisible.

17

Doctors Galore

(WAYNE, LOS ANGELES)

*Doctors are men who prescribe medicines of which they know little,
to cure diseases of which they know less,
in human beings of whom they know nothing.*
Voltaire

Living within a lie while knowing the truth, yet having no way to live the truth, is the most painful and destructive situation that can be given to you or that you can take upon yourself. The one thing I loved most could kill me. The one thing I lived, breathed, and had strived for every single day of my life, day in and day out, had been my spins. Now I felt God had given me a gift but in return had taken everything else from me. How could I truly comprehend anything anymore unless I was Lucinda with and without the gift? There had been always so much more to me than my spinning but I had never been allowed to show it.

Emotions are not deadly things and yet I feared them. Emotions are merely part of your body and mind telling you what your heart and soul is feeling. But since I had to live so long being emotionless, especially when being a part of the Japanese culture, I did not know anything about my feelings. Sometimes I think the surroundings of a person's childhood can be even more influential than their own DNA and I feel I had morphed into some of the characteristics of a Japanese person on the inside rather than being who I truly was. I needed to understand my emotions. What I came to understand is that letting go of and releasing emotions can help one's sadness and one's own suffering, but if you turn your emotions back on yourself they can become the source of madness. I had learned to stuff all my emotions deep within me and therefore I had become mad. There was no way around it. I had created my own suffering.

Wayne would be filled with days of teaching at skating rink and days of doctors' visits and treatments and I already dreaded the days to come. I could feel we were there for no reason and no fruition. I felt it was only a required bus stop en route to my destiny. I thought I was definitely not on the fast track of life. I was on the bus that stopped on every corner to refuel. Maybe this way I was to see life more clearly then have it whizz by me. Maybe this way I was meant to experience every single wobble on the earth's surface and every single rut and pebble under my feet. I was meant to feel that pea under the mattress. I was meant to suffer for greater things to come.

For each doctor I had so many symptoms that they did not know where to start, where to end, what to look at first. They were trying to look at the whole picture but if you don't lift off each stone in the right order to get to the source, a way to heal me would not be found. I was having so many therapies that I was busy around the clock watching the time in order to take what medicine from which doctor at what specific hour. To top it off I was getting frequent IVs because I was so weak. The IVs lasted for almost three hours and lying next to cancer patients and people with many other illnesses, was incredibly depressing. I was always the youngest in the doctors' offices. It was incredibly sad for my mother to watch me lying down with needles stuck in me with a solution dripping into my veins. She sometimes watched me cry and I know it tore her apart. It had come to this again, and for what? To kill myself in order to do something in the world that no one else did?

I was composed when in public but at home I started getting crazy. The illness was making me absolutely nuts. To be feeling sick every single day for seven years was just too much for me to handle anymore. It felt like my skin was crawling and I desperately wanted to shed it. I wanted a whole new body. I tried so hard to contain myself but I could no longer. I was now starting to have mini-seizures as well. My body would shake and become paralyzed and I could not move my lips or fingers or arms or legs. It was terrifying and my mother rushed me to the hospital many times. I felt so sorry for her. It was understandable that my mother once again broke into her fits many more times. We were all trying so hard and yet I never woke up feeling any better. I was actually feeling worse than ever before.

We stayed one year in Wayne, New Jersey until near the end of 2006 and were unable to find any doctors who improved me with their treatments. I wanted to go back to Los Angeles where someone had recommended a reputable and famous doctor who specialized in all my symptoms. One thing my mother and I did was to never give up hope. We had so much of it somehow. It seemed unimaginable to have that much in times like this but God was giving us strength. My father far away gave us all the support he could and kept up his hopes, too. My mother and I really had no one else to turn to.

Once back in Los Angeles my mother and I were happy to start treatment with a new doctor. The little bit of energy we both had left we gave to our hopes and trust in the new doctor. I would go through five different major doctors' treatments during my next two years of living in Los Angeles, four treatments for all my different ailments and one specifically for my back pain. All the while, my mother drove me to all the ice rinks around the city. Every day for two years consisted of driving to the rink to teach and train while still holding on to the hope I might skate again, and then driving to doctors for treatments, then driving home to sleep, and then beginning this all over again the next morning.

When in the past I ate, slept, skated and studied, now I was to eat not much, sleep not well, teach in tears, and be treated at doctors' offices. I was a dead-alive person. Really, there was no other way of putting it. I felt truly dead emotionally, physically, mentally, yet alive because I was still breathing. When would my luck change? I could not believe how long my mother and I endured this hardship. This was our second time to try having a good life in this city and we hoped for better results.

From 1999 until this time I had thought that I had hit rock bottom so many times that I would be able to see the light at the end of the tunnel fairly soon. But I had never hit as far down as I did in those two years in Los Angeles. The only way I could think was, "Let me hit so far down that I will create such a big bounce when I come back up, that I will reach high, high up into the stars." That was my only hope and without it I just wanted to die. I made myself believe it. What else could I do? It took about one hour for my mother to drive me to my first doctor in L.A. and I slept each way. I underwent tests like never before, such as being x-rayed by having my body filled with all kinds of liquid solutions so my body would light up under the machines. I even had a sleep apnea test that I was so scared to go to that my mother had to sleep next to me in the bed. I was hooked up to so many wires I looked like a robot.

I never met so many doctors and underwent so many tests as then. Every single day I was being tested and tried, bruised and banged up. I was exhausted, terrified and sad beyond expression and belief. They analyzed me once again for everything they could think of, all reaching one conclusion of chronic fatigue syndrome. I could not believe and did not want to believe I had that. I just did not feel it in my bones.

But I went through the endless treatments. I had to take so many pills I was hardly eating anything. I could not stomach anything else. I had my IV treatments twice a week. My arms were black and blue from all the needle punctures. I was on every diet imaginable. I had gone through being a vegetarian, eating only raw food, or only protein, or only wild grains, or a type O blood type diet, or having only juices, or just fasting and cleanses. I mean my body had gone through so much it felt like it was starting to reject every single thing I put in it.

Every day I read self-improvement books and health and diet books. Anything in the bookstore sold to help the self was in my library. I read and read and although I had become such a health fanatic I was getting more and more sick. What was I doing wrong? One of the doctors referred me to a hormone specialist in Beverly Hills as well, since all my hormones were completely off-balance. They said I had adrenal fatigue, thyroid problems, and again everything you can name. In addition to all my pills from the first doctor this second doctor had me rubbing and swallowing hormones at all times of the day.

Sometimes I was completely confused about what to take when and what reaction to expect from each. My hormones were completely out of sorts to start with, but they just went off the charts once I started the hormonal treatment. I went from growing mustaches to losing hair, from having my breasts grow and to then having them disappear completely, from having a period once a month to having a period lasting for a month, from crying every day to giggling every day. I became a walking health dictionary and an emotional wreck! I knew everything about everything but knew nothing about what I had. The problem was I had so many problems.

For my back pain I went to another spine and nerve specialist since I was in knife-like pain everywhere in my spine and hips and the pain was going down my legs. More MRIs and X-rays were done and they wanted to give me another medication for the pain and nerve damage but since I was already on so much medicine I refused to take that one. By now I had seen three doctors and almost a year had passed. I had everything you can imagine to try to heal me. I had healing bracelets, healing beds, healing mattresses, healing towels, healing cushions, healing rings, healing massages and Reiki sessions.

All these doctors cost my parents an arm and a leg and a heart and a brain! Many of the treatments and medications, especially all the alternative ones, were not covered by our health insurance in Switzerland. I was burning a hole through my parents' bank accounts once more. I felt so incredibly guilty and I could not really do anything more than I already was.

The first doctor had prescribed Adderall for me because I was more than exhausted, to the point where some days I could barely utter a word. My arms were so tired that I could barely pick up the phone. My legs were so tired I could not walk up and down the few stairs we had in our new home. I was on the sofa bed all day too tired to read or to watch television. I just lay there looking at the ceiling waiting for the hours to go by, hoping to sleep at night. I was more tired than ever, yet inside my nerves were so shaken that I felt like I trembled nonstop. I was totally physically and mentally broken down. Consequently the doctor had me on pills to wake up and pills to go to sleep!

Then the first doctor prescribed for me to inject myself twice a day with Heparin. They said my blood was clotting and not circulating so I needed to thin out my blood. I had bags and bags of needles and solutions. My home looked like a walk-in pharmacy! Medicine was everywhere. My whole stomach and legs looked like chicken pox from needle holes. I felt like a very sick person when injecting myself twice a day, but I would have done anything to be well.

I would not have minded doing all the routines the doctors prescribed if I had felt better but nothing improved. I stayed with those first three doctors for almost one year. It was an absolutely crazy life. It wasn't a life. It was hanging on to the last thread of life. I can't explain it any other way.

We decided it was time to find another doctor and start another treatment plan. The fourth was an alternative doctor. He supplemented his treatments with a lot of herbal medicine, claiming he had treated and cured many celebrities. We were up for anything so we agreed to his regimen. For another six to eight months we allowed my body to be treated by him since prior to him each and every doctor had seemed helpless. They were so baffled by my situation and did not know how to help.

This new alternative medicine doctor complained about my being on so much medication. He told me to throw it all out. I don't know what he was complaining about when he just replaced them all with his herbal medications. One day I counted the pills he had me take and they amounted to almost seventy pills that I had to swallow a day!

Again I did anything I was told. I made sure I did not skip one pill and I did not eat one thing I shouldn't. It was a full time job trying to get healthy! I believed in each and every doctor and treatment fully since I knew believing was powerful, but nothing changed. I just became more and more sick, more nauseous, and more tired. I was rushed to the hospital by ambulance many more times within the next eight months for mini-seizures and fainting spells.

At this time I had no social or work life—no friends, no boyfriend, and no acquaintances. I mean how could I even go somewhere or meet a friend when I was so tired and unsociable and had to have my mother by me all the time? As much as my mother was trying to push me to enjoy my young life, it was impossible.

Suddenly, toward the end of the summer in 2008 something drastically changed. I made a decision, basically because I just had no more strength, to give up fighting the flow of life. I completely altered my mentality. I did not mind anymore if I did not wake up the next morning. I knew in my heart I had tried everything. I thought if I did not wake up, I would then be at long last free of my pain. It was a little scary to not care at all but also quite freeing. I gave up my fight to push what maybe was not my destiny.

Every night before falling asleep I spoke to God and said, "If you really do not need me on this earth and it is my time to go to you, please take me now, because it is too painful for me to be here. But God, I promise you, if you let me live and become healthy once more I will do everything possible in my life to be an inspiration to help to heal others. I will serve you. I will try to protect those who need protection as I needed it while growing up. I promise to heal the world in my way." I would cry myself to sleep as I tirelessly repeated this conversation with God over and over again. Every morning I awoke to the sun shining, and therefore I knew God needed me more on earth than in the heavens. But, I continued to just let go of everything, to not think, to not want, to not try. I could not fight anymore. I had been told all my life to fight and I had no more power to do it.

Surprisingly just as I was giving up and not caring truly if I lived or died, and not wanting to learn one more thing about what or why my body was going through all of this, someone we knew referred us to a well-recommended doctor, He actually recommended that I see him for my back pain. It was truly destiny that would bring me to the new doctor.

My mother and I, smiling as usual and with our heads held high, visited the doctor. My mother and I told each other that this was it. After this, if the treatment did not work, we would just go home to Switzerland. This time we did not expect much and maybe the less you expect the more you get. I mean how could we expect anything when we had been let down time and time again? How could we expect good results after nine years of continual struggle with my health? Since all doctors were different in their methods, we said nothing as he did his battery of tests. Once more I was prodded and poked and my blood was wanted.

He called us back about a week later for his findings and diagnosis. Since we thought we had heard it all, we were more interested in his recommendation of treatment than the diagnosis, hoping always that he might help with whatever on earth my body was going through. He sat us down. He was a man with a wise demeanor and calmness.

He began to talk. And the more he talked the more light bulbs started to flick on in our heads, and the more the events and situations in my life started to make sense. This doctor was saying things that none of the other doctors had mentioned. Yes, he said, I was certainly traumatized, overexerted, and mentally and physically broken down. At that time my head, ears, nose, and eyes were still all swollen from pressure and flu-like symptoms and my body was tingling from weak blood flow, my stomach was upset all the time but no one had been able to explain to us why I experienced this.

This doctor then got to the point and made his surprising diagnosis. He said he concluded that I was suffering from post-concussion syndrome and a related post-traumatic stress disorder. He believed that I had suffered many concussions as I spun with the force, speed, and power of my spins. He said I had been spinning so fast for so long and for so many hours a day that I had caused mini-concussions of my brain every single day that I did my spins. My quick and powerful entrance to the spins, then the fast acceleration of rotations themselves, followed by the quick or slow exit from my spins, had caused so much brain and head damage that it had affected my whole nervous system and therefore my immune system as well.

He also interestingly mentioned that when you suffer a concussion the pituitary gland is also injured and since this gland regulates hormones, my hormones were not in balance. He explained that the concussions caused my inner ear to be damaged, had blurred my vision, and was the reason I had vertigo, felt sick to my stomach, and had constant exhaustion. It was all linked to the brain and the fluid that the brain was floating in.

His diagnosis clearly made perfect sense to me. It was that I was feeling the effects of an ongoing concussion every day. I had been spinning much more and much faster than any other skaters I knew. I had been spinning at least two to three consecutive hours a day, and many more hours on some days, every day from the age of four. Just spinning and spinning in one direction.

The doctor ordered that my body would need much time to rest before it could even begin to heal. He said I would not be allowed to spin at all, and if ever again. We never had imagined or realized this. We had all along thought the spins were too beautiful, magical, and elegant to cause any trouble to my health. Although it wasn't easy to hear this, to say the least, we were thrilled that finally we had found a doctor who made sense. It was even more emotionally anguishing than what we had heard previously but it was a great relief to finally have an explanation for why my body was reacting the way it was.

Of course, I still wanted to spin. I had come to the point where I was addicted to the feeling of spinning, and it was my fame, my treasure, and my product of twenty years of work. And so I would miss it terribly and I would miss the feeling it always had given me. I had always been very determined to follow doctors' orders but this would certainly be the hardest order yet.

How could I permanently stop something I loved and was starved for every day? How could I stop the only thing that I thought had kept me alive all these years? Stopping spinning would come with great consequences just as stopping any repetitive and compulsive action does.

The doctor started to treat me with chiropractic work, acupuncture, and also some homeopathic medicine for my symptoms but firmly stated it would help only a little, but the most important factor was rest and not to do any physical activity. I would have to let my body heal itself. Surprisingly, within a few months I was really starting to feel better. I actually started to feel like I had a little more energy, maybe also because now I knew where all my suffering was stemming from. It was a huge relief filling in the last piece of the puzzle. My mind was able to relax a little more and, even though none of my symptoms had truly disappeared yet, I felt some energy to at least start waking up from my fog and dream state.

The more time that passed without spinning on the ice, the less dizzy I was and the more within my balance I became. The less I spun the less my ears were ringing, the less nauseous I felt from gastrointestinal illnesses, and the fewer headaches I experienced. The less I spun the less I was having more concussions, but of course I still needed to heal from all the damage I had already done to my body. It would take time, patience and prayers. Still today I am recovering, and I feel that only now does my life once more begin.

The main lesson that was presented to me here and now of course for my reader as well is not to learn that concussions caused my illnesses. They did cause me to become very sick, but that is not what is to be taken from this lesson. Rather I hope from the bottom of my heart that this lesson relates to all people of all walks of life. The lesson is that anything in moderation is quite fine but when taken to extremes like I did, no matter how wonderful and beautiful and luscious it may seem at that time, it will bring much more harm than goodness. This is true for any obsession about anything that is not in balance with the world and its people. This is one lesson I learned and I promised to God it would not be repeated in any other way in my life.

18

I Know

(NEW YORK CITY)

The longer I live the less I understand and the more I know.

At that time I came to see in myself, and find this even truer today, that the older in age on earth I became, the younger I evolved in spirit. Like Pablo Picasso said, "It takes a long time to become young." A child does not really understand anything, yet he or she knows everything, sees everything, and can feel everything. Children are innocent yet knowing. The older I became the less I understood about life and the more I was in the knowing of life. I did not need to understand to know. It was an incredibly fortunate aspect of my life then and now, because everything was simplified. It unexpectedly brought all I needed to know to the surface.

As oil rises above water so does the truth in life, and the more I eliminated obstacles around me the more I saw clearly. All the nonsense started disappearing and all the clouds started lifting. I always felt I needed to prepare for my chance that would one day come to me, and now I felt my whole life had been preparation for my life to come. I wanted to put all my genius into the way I was living my life and my talents and hard work into the work I was to do.

Not many doors had easily opened in my life and many doors had shut, but now the roof seemed to open to the sky for my health. I feel the more you let yourself mourn a loss, the greater the possibility you'll have for the old to be released and for a door to open for new blessings to enter.

I had to stop spinning but I also had to cure all the other traumas I had incurred emotionally from my life. I let myself mourn more and more and whenever I felt like it. Previously I had never allowed myself to feel emotions as I had always been expected to smile and be happy 24/7. If I was upset or sad at something my mother felt guilty that she was unable to make me smile and would in return be mad at me. Since I did not want to see my mother upset I had refrained from expressing my feelings at all. To allow myself to be emotional was scary at first but freeing at last.

I was still living with all my ailments but I now knew what I needed to do. I just let myself cry from exhaustion. I stopped swallowing every single medication, vitamin, and pill with whatever was in it. I threw them all in the garbage. I threw away all the books I had tirelessly read on health and self-improvement. I threw away all the health drinks and steamed food. I had not eaten real food with flavor in ten years!

Where others in life needed a coach, or a teacher, or someone to guide them, one of the most important lessons I learned was that I now needed no one to tell me what to do. I had been desperately searching for a teacher, not realizing the teacher within me. You have to understand, that all my life I had people telling me what and how to do every single thing in my life. I could not walk or even eat without someone telling me I was doing it wrong. I was criticized all day every day in hopes of my becoming that perfect person. In my life when given two sweaters as a gift and having chosen which one to wear that day, I would be criticized for not having worn the other! I never could win and it was not a matter of wining but a matter of feeling like I could do something good. Now for me to cure myself I knew I had to follow no one, no treatment, and no plan whatsoever in any aspect of my life. I had to make my own decisions about life and I had to decide everything for myself. I had to have silence and only hear my voice.

When I was younger I remember thinking my head was going to explode because it was filled with monsters coming to get me that were all talking to me at once. In other words, I had to silence all other voices so I could hear my own, rely only on myself, let my wings spread, and let no one disturb their growth. I had to become the butterfly I was meant to be. I had to relearn how to take a shower, how to dress, how to eat like I wanted to. I had lost the meaning of life and now I had to find it again for myself. I was twenty-nine years old, and I hoped that I would never have to suffer like I had, ever again. I prayed that my body had gone through all the illnesses needed in this lifetime and that only health and happiness was to await me in the rest of my life.

I had deprived myself of almost everything considered self-indulgent and enjoyable in the last twenty years. So now that the world was my oyster you would think I wanted everything but rather, to the contrary, I did not want anything. You might think it was easy for me to decide to do what I wanted but it was extremely hard. I had no idea what I wanted or who I was. I was at a loss for everything

I had not enjoyed food since I had left Japan due to dieting, illness, and image. I decided I would start there. I would start eating real food of substance and flavor. I had to start not feeling guilty about eating. I had to forgive myself to really eat. It was very hard but I was motivated not to fall back into the state I had been in. It had been so long a period of such pain and despair that I would do anything not to fall back. It would take time and great forgiveness of myself, but I felt confident I would be able to do it.

Next, because I was so used to exercising nonstop, it was hard for my body and brain not to just automatically push myself to exercise, no matter what condition I was in. When I had exercised I did it until I shook and bled. I had no boundaries and did not know when to stop. I needed to now decrease exercising to the point of not doing any at all. Exercise had become detrimental to my life and it was incredibly hard to force myself to rest. I had to learn how.

So many people in this world lecture and teach others about how important exercise is, yet almost no one ever talks about how detrimental it can be as well. No one was out there to help people like me and I am sure there are many others who go through this. Think of it this way. I exercised about ten hours a day every single day nonstop for about twenty-five years from a young age when the body is trying to grow and mature. I was over-exercised to say the least. I had never recovered from the very first practice session that I had done on the ice at the tender age of four. I had never recovered from my spins.

As I did all of this healing, after a few months I was finally awakening. My senses slowly were starting to come back to me. I am not saying it happened right away. It was a painful experience but it was the way I wanted to go through it. I wanted to feel every emotion and pain in my body to fully be able to heal it. I was in a tremendous emotional recovery of life. I did not want to miss even one emotion and did not want to mask any of my past and how I had felt about it. If I did, I knew it would come back to haunt me later. I was meticulous about every single detail. I was missing my spinning incredibly but I had to put my health first. There had been years and years of torment to my mind and body so it would not heal in one day. It would take time to unravel it all. There was a beautiful park right below my apartment building and I took long slow walks along the river praying, meditating in my own way, and figuring out about life and myself. Here I did the most healing.

I knew I also had to forgive myself. If I did not forgive myself I truly could not forgive anyone or any situation. Forgiving myself was the hardest thing to do because I was the angriest at myself. I was angry and disappointed that I had said or communicated very little, that I had never stood up for myself, that I had nearly ruined my whole family, and that I had almost killed myself by not resting. Now I had to forgive everything that I had done to myself and to others. I knew as soon as I could forgive myself and therefore trust myself, I would be able to live again.

After forgiveness I needed to love myself. Once I did those two things I could forgive and love everything and everyone else. You can only do onto others what you have done for yourself. You can only expect from others what you expect from yourself. How can you have someone love you when you don't even love yourself? How can you demand respect from someone when you don't even respect yourself? I know this because I have lived it. I had been swimming up tide for years and I finally made a u-turn and swam with the tide. I let life take me once more to who I was when I was so young in Paris.

As I was healing, it was decided by the heavens above that my life would take me back to New York City. I had no agenda. For once I had absolutely no clue as to what I was to do in the city but I knew I had to be there. I did not understand why or where I was to go but I knew I had to be there to start afresh. In the eleven years from leaving Japan in 1997 to in 2008 I had moved fifteen times! It was an incredible journey, an education and enrichment, and I know I received lessons that I can live by forever and that I would never have learned otherwise. I felt I was an old soul and I felt lucky I had survived my ordeal, but even luckier that I had gone through this, because only now could I help another person in many more ways than my spins could ever have. I was now my only master, my only teacher and ready to be the inspiration to others.

I had so much to learn about life in the areas where I was still a child, such as communication, being social, enjoying life, not being worried that I was always being judged, and letting go and allowing myself to really enjoy life. I had always been in the mode of performance and competition. I was so used to being on stage that my whole life had become my stage. I was so used to representing someone on the ice that my whole life had become representing that someone. I never had the time or the space to be me and figure out and create me. The skating world was not truly a good mirror image of who I had been as a child.

If it hadn't been for my sister's skating I probably would never have wanted to skate at all. I have her to thank and to also forgive since her path had forced me into mine without my true consent. As a child I had been happy to play with the birds and animals and insects as in a true nature-filled wondrous fairy tale. But then life might not have taken me to where I am today and not have showed me the world and given me its lessons. And for that I am truly grateful because I could not be happier than I am today. I am finally living again.

It so happened that it seemed the reason I had come back to New York City and the true reason of regaining my sanity and sanctity for love and life was to know the love between a man and a woman. I had begun to love myself and now having let the past go, I was ready for love.

On October 11, 2008, I met a dashing man and on October 16, 2010, we married at our dream church of St. Patrick's Cathedral in New York. How lucky I was to be able to step a foot in his path that was not reserved for someone with a past like mine, nor was mine for a past like his. Or maybe our paths had been so similar in so many ways that we had run parallel to each other and now that we both had taken a turn in life we were destined to cross. He is a man of exuberance, intelligence, sophistication, and a subdued but magnetic presence with a hidden wildness to him. He is a world mixed with finance, justice, and law, and professor-like notions in the Einstein world of mathematics. I knew him right away. I did not need to understand, I just knew him. But, when I met him, he was a slate of charm and love. He represented a slate of vitality and truth. He carries me into his world and life, a life that had been as unique and misunderstood as mine. Full of passion stemming from the core of the earth right through his heart into the palm of my hand and onto my forehead was a kiss he would plant.

He introduced himself as Anthony, but I accidently called him Antonio. As he would ground me, I immediately give him the value that I accepted him for who he truly was beginning with his childhood, since unknown to me his birth name was Antonio. He is my root of laughter despite withholding that tear in his eye. We both are old fashioned romantics and I told him that "I love living and being in a man's world, but just let me be a real woman within it." And he does. He had given me strength by loving me and gives me the gift of courage the more I loved him.

Our love is one no words can describe. We stand strong yet delicately on a powerful foundation of trust. He makes me produce that perfect tear. Lucky is the man who is the first love of a woman but luckier is the woman who is the last love of a man. Love is to never want anything else in return and we love for who we each become in the presence of the other. Love can only make you wiser, make you know more about love, which ultimately is all that life is about.

I have been truly lucky to have been so loved all my life—to have been introduced to eternal love from my parents, to have admiration and love from my fans, to find my own love of self, and now to have the love between a man and a woman. Much more love is to be experienced and I am preparing for all the love life has to offer me in every which way …

19

Finale and Opening the World for Me

(AT HOME, WHEREVER I AM)

Life gives answers in three ways, it says yes and gives you what you want,
it says no and gives you something better,
and it says wait and gives you the best.

I waited and therefore the best had come to me. I have won the game. I feel in many ways that it is my destiny to share my experience and expose my vulnerability. I wish to keep on inspiring people with my story. As my spins inspired my fans, I do hope my insight about my life will do this as well. Now, I live life, love myself, and I live in the truth. I have found my peace. My soul can once again reside within me. It was an excruciating as well as glorious thirty years and I hold immense gratitude to those that have changed my life in the process. I have to come to realize that anything difficult one goes through is fine as long as you can recover from it, and therefore my life is victorious. What is most important is not what has happened to you but what you do as a result of it, and I plan to do honorable actions in my life. I would never want to relive what I did, but the lessons I learned are priceless. Skating taught me powerful determination, concentration, hard work, a will to achieve anything I want, and an ability to adapt to any situation no matter where in the world.

Although I led a life of privilege in so many ways, I have also led a life of real hardship. I have conquered obstacles in ways I never imagined I ever could have, overcoming extraordinary adversity to achieve unique recognition and worldwide admiration. I know I have overcome enormous mental, emotional, and physical abuse at the hands of ego-ridden trainers and emotionally exasperated family members in order to achieve my spiritual strength and personal resolve but I know it was worth it. I hope to think that I was a brave little girl who took on the world—only to find myself desperately searching for the innocent little girl I had left behind and only to ultimately ask of myself, *Why am I here and what greater purpose might I serve?* I feel my story has been, above all, a story of recognizing love—love for self, love for others, and love for the sacredness of life, even in the darkest and loneliest battlefields of overwhelming inhibitions and impossible probabilities. I now know that *truth, courage,* and *love* remain the greatest medals of all. In essence, in telling my story *I humbly hope to awaken the extraordinary in others* and I hope to encourage others to find their own balance and to find within themselves the inspiration to become their own champion in life no matter what the obstacles are and no matter who they are or what they do.

In no way do I think I needed to tell my story because my life has been more grand, more painful, more joyous, more heroic, or filled with more tragedy or success than other persons. My experiences may be nothing to tell compared to other painful injustices inflicted on mankind or the heroic moments that have changed the world. I only express truthful words of the life that I have led in hopes of helping someone in the best way that I pray I can.

My mother always said that in life you can watch, or you can teach, or you can do, and she encouraged me to always do. I feel that to be a spectator in life is to avoid and escape reality and suffering and so in my life, I do, and I teach from the experiences I have lived through. As I guide new prodigies on the ice, I don't view my role as teaching them only skating skills to make them gold medalists. Rather, I feel I am there for them as a mentor to teach them how to be the best they can be, and that there is more to life than achieving a double axel. I am to them as I wished a coach had been to me at their age. Sometimes as an athlete, the one jump or that one spin can become your sole obsession, and it can feel that nothing is more important than achieving that one goal. I feel a responsibility to guide them in how to become a champion in life by respecting themselves in ways they might never have imagined.

It's not only on the ice but off the ice as well that I hope to continue to inspire children by speaking to them at schools and at charities. As I do on the ice, I guide them to find the courage, respect, and confidence within themselves to achieve their goals. I love the feeling of being able to give back by encouraging people of all ages and walks of life to learn from my mistakes and for them to see their full potential.

This book is ultimately for my parents. I love them to the depths of the universe and to the length of eternity. They hold my gratitude, my respect, and my profound thankfulness. They are to me my wonderful and perfect parents. They might not be perfect in other people's eyes but in my life they presented to me what I needed to learn and for that they are perfect and I could not be more grateful.

My mother had absolutely treated me like a princess when I was little and when the pressures of the skating world were not yet present. I had been truly spoiled in a good sense in more ways than one. She would write cards almost every day, either wishing me good luck, or congratulating me for a great day, or even thanking me for my love, elaborating each and every one with stickers and little drawings of smiley faces, angels, and fairies. She raised me with meticulous care and love and attention to every single detail. I am eternally grateful for the art, love, and beauty she presented to me, as it prepared me for my life for how I now take care of others. The toughness of the skating life then covered her true self and I missed my true mother. I truly never regret that path of life, but I so regret the fact that we could not enjoy each other and the wonderful and prestigious life I had on and off the ice because of our pursuit to achieve that unattainable perfection.

Readers may ask where my father was all this time. He was ever-present in spirit but due to circumstances that could not be changed, he missed a lot of my growing up and his presence was greatly missed. He unfortunately did not have the chance or the occasion to know or understand the magnitude of my struggles with skating, my mother, and later with my unrelenting health problems. My mother and I had always tried to show my father only the best side and the good results. I missed my father terribly during those years. Last Christmas he shed a tear of remorse for not having been able to protect me more but I know that my father did everything possible and to this day I know I will be his little girl forever.

You may ask where my sister was all this time as well. Here, too, I wish she could have played the role to me of being a helpful older sibling, but in this life so far, circumstances have blocked her. I only hope as we encounter each other and ourselves over and over again in many disguises, she will one day be granted this kind of role to play for others or for me, as I will be a good sibling for her.

I have truly only wanted to be good to my parents. My parents have lived all their lives for my sister and me and they gave their hearts to us. The love that my parents and I have has always been so strong that I knew nothing would break it. Nothing had truly broken it, but we became quite fragmented, and from that experience we now have more love and respect for each other. As I had to heal, my parents, my mother especially, had to heal as well, and I pray that our journey together has awakened the light within her. I pray that in the end I truly gave her more than I took, since I will give without remembering but I will never forget what I've taken.

    I have spun and created positions, with speeds and lengths on the ice that even today no skater can imitate. I have been a creator; I have made sculptures on ice. I have been coached, trained, and had my programs choreographed by the most famous leaders in the skating world. I have skated at eight world championships, six national championships, and two world professional championships and have been a guest at the White House. I toured and skated professionally with the best tours in the business and have skated live with dozens of incredible world famous artists on stage. I have done what others may only dream of. Yet I am the most proud, not of the medals and accolades, but of my overcoming so many obstacles and hindrances to achieve what I have and surviving an array of hurdles with my strong perseverance. This is what I hope is to be your inspiration. It is remarkable as well that now that I have stepped away from my performing, I finally seem to be able to feel and understand the magnitude of the effect I had on people with my spins. Strangely enough, more than ever I now do feel appreciated for what I have given to the sport. Maybe I had to remove myself from my own skating to see how much I had accomplished. I am now truly grateful when I hear from fans or fellow skaters how I made an impact on them with my art. This brings that perfect tear to my eye. After all, I can be proud of myself in the most humble way.

    I will have to live the rest of my life with injuries that will never be completely healed from the fatigue, dizziness and other ailments resulting from spinning, concussions, and over-training. I will never be all healed but I am better for it. I am the new Lucinda with markings unique to me. I have become wiser and stronger. I am truly thankful for each and every day as I have gotten a second chance in life and I will never take life for granted again. This time instead of grabbing my chance ferociously with two hands and pulling the reins myself, I let them gently fall into place and allow the universe to take me on my true journey meant for me.

    I hope that you can be your own master in life, knowing that no matter what lies in front of you, you will always be able to overcome it, as long you believe in and love yourself first, and as much as you believe in or love someone else. Sometimes I feel we tend to believe in others more than ourselves. At least that is what I had done. I had given all my power and all my beliefs away. Just remember that no goal is ever grand enough to sacrifice the loss of yourself, your self worth or your self respect in the process. Trusting yourself first and standing up for what you believe in is what makes you who you are, and what makes you wonderful! Being who you are and loving yourself is the first step to your own greatness

Mother and father, I thank you that you showed me the whole world in its purity and true essence. Thank you profoundly for loving me and for caring so much about my dreams. I thank you for giving me all I could want, all I did not even know I wanted, and more. Without skating I would not be who I am today. I thank you from the bottom of my heart for opening up the whole world and endless opportunities to me.

My mother, father, and sister, I love you more than words can say or dance could ever express. I love you more than ever. Now I, and hopefully you, will carry flowers in both your hands to give and to receive the beauty of ourselves and life to eternity!

The most important relationship that you will ever have in life is the one with yourself, and once that is conquered, everything else in your life will fall into place.

Afterword

BEING THE MOTHER OF LUCINDA

I feel that being a mother is the most incredibly difficult yet rewarding job on this earth, and to say that I did everything right all the time is not possible. I just did my best with all that I knew. The one thing I know I have always done, however, is to love my daughter selflessly and with immeasurable depths. I lived for her and maybe through her, and my husband and I without question, gave all that we could, with no limits either emotionally or to the expenses in all forms.

When Lucinda first stepped on the ice, at barely four years old, she looked confident and seemed to be so familiar with the ice. One reason, of course, was that from the time she was only a couple of weeks old she had been around ice rinks every day because her sister, who was nine years older, skated tirelessly. Without her sister, Lucinda probably would never have become a skater. In one way, this would have been a waste of her great talent; in another way, she could have been saved from injuries and a broken heart.

As her mother, I found that skating became addictive. It was just mesmerizing and amazing to watch her progress. She had great feeling for the ice, she had enormous charisma, and she learned with such great speed. It felt like nothing could stop this little girl from achieving everything in her path. In the beginning there was so much joy on the ice every single day. It was then, that her skating became the joy of my life as well. She became a shining star. This start gave us a lot of strength and without it the rest would have not been possible. Lucinda continued to win all the important competitions, which is what gave me the confidence that it was the right thing to pursue.

On top of the demanding skating regimen, Lucinda excelled in whatever she did, whether it was school, ballet, jazz dance, piano, cello, or even learning her fourth language, Japanese. The schedule was incredibly tough and soon I found out that all this was too demanding, even for my tough German style view of work, work, and more work. I decided she had to focus on only one art form and, of course, school. School would always come first. It tore my heart apart as a mother to have to give up anything for my daughter especially when Lucinda was excellent in all that she did. Lucinda chose skating at the age of eight and sometimes I think I should have given her more time in life to decide what she truly wanted to do. If she had taken more time she might have chosen something she really loved even more than skating, but, alas, hindsight is always 20/20!

Skating was then our main focus, and very quickly became my obsession, too, since skating is not something a child can go to and do alone. You have to bring your child to the rink and stay there in case of injuries, and the lessons last only twenty minutes. An ice rink is not a day care center and no one is really looking out for your child. The rest is practice, practice, and practice, and you cannot expect an eight-year-old to do it all alone. They need support at that age and all I wanted was to be there for her. Therefore, skating then becomes not only the child's dream, but evolves into a dream for the child and the parents together. However, since the parent is the adult, the dream tends to lean more into the parents' hands and direction.

I became more and more involved, and it was as if there was an immense force I couldn't stop. Lucinda listened to everything I said and I was making all the decisions. However, it was somehow not the Olympic dream and the Olympic champion that I was chasing after. It was more a dedication to the practices every day of our lives as we aimed for perfection that consumed me. Lucinda became gloriously magnificent, and so I thought my way was perfect for her. The better she became the more I wanted her to reach perfection in every aspect of skating.

But while Lucinda was still young, the skating life and our addiction to it overtook everything, and I no longer allowed her to be a child. I felt like I wasn't allowed to be just her mother and unfortunately, knowingly or perhaps unknowingly, I made the fatal decision that skating was more important than anything else and that it would teach my daughter more than anything else. Now I truly feel like it was a disaster of a decision and I do regret it with great sorrow. As I let myself fall into the spell, there was more and more pressure from coaches and the nonstop competitions as well as the pressures of school. The school became more demanding and the work on and off the ice became tougher. We both had enormous discipline and whatever I said she should do, Lucinda did twice as much. Soon I wanted three times as much and she wanted four times as much, in a never-ending practice. Lucinda tried so hard to please me all the time as I was trying to please her, resulting in much sacrifice on both ends.

As time progressed, there was not enough sleep and way too many ongoing injuries, concussions, fractures, and broken bones, but for some reason I didn't listen to her or her body. Maybe I felt the power of what she could do on the ice would exceed all else, and since she never complained I somehow believed she was invincible. It was a big mistake on my side as I continued to push and push. As beautiful and easy as the skaters make this sport look, it is a hundred times harder in reality. I entered a vicious circle when surrounded by a society of such devotion and discipline and I caved into their ways. I should have guided her more moderately, giving her time with friends, or perhaps some days off. But I did not, as I felt every day or every minute playing would make Lucinda less perfect, and she was so good on the ice that why in the world would I take that away from her? I saw this as a beautiful chance for her and I felt it was my duty to nourish it in any way I could.

Looking back I would never again encourage my child to do a national sport while not being in our own country, due to the lack of real support from the national team surrounding the child who is a foreigner. That is also why I felt like I could not be a real mother, and so I struggled with myself in many ways. I felt no moral support since my husband was away a lot and I had no one to confide in, and I regretfully say I followed what the other mothers did. It is shameful to say, but what they did, I did as well. I thought it was the way to make my child a better skater and so I followed suit. I followed them instead of putting my values first. I followed others instead of looking out for the best interest of my child and her life. I followed others and put skating, and most importantly the coach's words, above everything. I however do take full responsibility for it.

Now I know I should not have listened to the coaches, but at that time I trusted them and only them before I trusted Lucinda or myself. You go blindly into everything new in life and I did not know any better, and unfortunately both my child and I suffered. I never intended to hurt Lucinda. I reacted to her coach's complaints and so I disciplined Lucinda. I never thought it a bad thing then, but now I do. At that time it was just a reaction to please the authority. My husband and I even allowed the family to be torn apart when Lucinda was just fifteen and we decided to not join Lucinda's father when he was called back to Switzerland for his job. I always put skating first, which now I see was not right. But then it seemed right or otherwise we would not have done it. There was extreme loneliness as it was just us the two of us struggling against the tide. Yet sometimes when we did hit a huge successful wave just right, all the pain would be forgotten, and that is what kept us going and going.

Somehow the success continued to offset the pain and we kept trudging on. Lucinda continued to become the most extraordinary and beautiful skater, a phenomenon in her own right, as she did something nobody had ever done. So, in many ways the path we were on was right and I am very thankful and feel so lucky when Lucinda says in this book over and over again that she has only gratitude for me. We had something no one could ever truly understand unless they lived through it.

If there is one thing I learned, it is that if I had known the negative results of our dedication to skating from all the injuries and the illnesses and our two broken hearts, I would not repeat our journey. But looking back is always easy. Since in many ways Lucinda was a prodigy, perhaps I would do it again after all, just in moderation, giving her myself as her mother only and letting her be a child. This way she might have even been better on the ice, but in my eyes Lucinda was and is perfect and I am thankful to her for having given me this one of a kind journey of memories. Lucinda, I am from the bottom of my heart sorry and thank you for being my angel who fell from the sky. I know, Lucinda, that you understand me and the love we have for each other is therefore only stronger because of this.

About the Author

Lucinda Ruh is one of the most admired and creative skaters in the world. She is well-known for being the fastest spinner on ice, having clocked in at a remarkable six rotations per second. Her official skating record is impressive: two-time National Champion, two-time World Professional figure skating Bronze Medalist, and Guinness World Records Holder for the longest spin on ice. Always a trendsetter, she pushed the limits—from making the unitard a fashion statement to changing the rules for spinning by her record-breaking unique positions. Lucinda always told her fans a story the minute she stepped on the ice. Dubbed the "Queen of Spin," Lucinda made her mark on figure skating history forever by creating over twenty different spin positions over the course of her career. It's no wonder that she was twice listed among the "25 Most Influential Names in Figure Skating" by *International Figure Skating Magazine*. Lucinda Ruh has competed at eight World Championships and has performed with the most prestigious tours such as Stars on Ice, Champions on Ice, and Art on Ice. Her majestic style has given her opportunities to skate live around the globe.